Completing
the Task

Completing *the* Task

Reaching *the* World for Christ

Edgar J. Elliston & Stephen E. Burris, Editors

 COLLEGE PRESS
PUBLISHING COMPANY
Joplin, Missouri

Library of Congress Cataloging-in-Publication Data

Completing the task: reaching the world for Christ /
  Edgar J. Elliston and Stephen E. Burris.
      p.   cm.
    Includes bibliographic references and index.
    ISBN 0-89900-729-5 (hc)
    1. Missions. 2. Missions—Theory. 3. Evangelistic
work.   I. Elliston, Edgar J., 1943-   . II. Burris,
Stephen E.
BV2061.C645 1995
266—dc 20   95-13769
                                                CIP

Table of Contents

9/535

Preface

The purpose of this book is to provide an overview of the World Christian Movement. To assist in fulfilling this purpose, the book is organized around four foundational themes about which every mission minded Christian should be informed.

This book aims to serve students, people who are interested in serving in a mission setting, missions pastors and missions leaders in local churches. Many will find it a helpful companion to the "Perspectives on the World Christian Movement" course as the book's basic structure mirrors the 1995 edition of that popular course.

Biblical Themes

The first theme, chapters 1, 2, and 3, concerns biblical and theological foundations. Robert Kurka and Paul McAlister set the table for all that follows by highlighting the central fact—from beginning to end God is a missionary God and He expects His people to be partners with Him in carrying out His central purpose.

Historical Themes

The second theme is the historical development of the Christian movement. As we examine the expansion of the world Christian movement we see how the church enjoyed spectacular victories and also suffered devastating setbacks. Stephen Burris in chapters 4 and 5 gives a basic overview of the expansion of Christianity from Pentecost to the present. Chapter 4 covers the first 1800 years. Chapter 5 begins at approximately 1800 and concentrates on that portion of history known as the modern missionary period.

To understand the task remaining we must keep a clear view on where we have come from, beginning with Genesis up to and including this very day. Therefore, chapter 6 is an appropriate bridge between the biblical and historical themes and the strategic and cultural themes.

Strategic Themes

Chapters 7 through 10 focus on strategic themes. Chapter 7 proposes a strategic approach to completing the task of world evangelization. It is not intended to be comprehensive, but, rather, to give some insight as to how the church might complete this very achievable task. Rondal Smith proposes a perspective rather than providing specific strategies. A number of contextual factors will determine a specific strategy. Doug Priest Jr. suggests strategies for reaching the unreached in chapter 8. Building on what has preceded this chapter Priest moves toward a particular application targeting the remaining unreached peoples. Edgar Elliston highlights the priority of church planting and evangelism in Chapter 9. Chapter 10 introduces some of the difficult issues of Christian community development. As we consider the task remaining, what place or priority do these matters occupy?

Cultural Themes

The final five chapters explore cultural themes. Chapter 11 focuses on the relationship of culture and mission. How should the missionary view culture? In what ways does an understanding of culture aid or hinder the missionary? Robert Douglas, building on the groundbreaking work of Thomas and Elizabeth Brewster, indicates ways that the missionary can not only work within a culture, but can use cultural factors to benefit the gospel in Chapter 12. How can the missionary communicate the gospel to those who view the world differently?

Doug Priest tackles the difficult task of communication in Chapter 13. What place does a people's worldview play in the meaning they place on the message presented? What communication keys can the missionary use to unlock a "resistant" people, turning them to a "receptive" people? Chapter 14 follows with an examination of how to communicate the gospel to different societies.

Chapter 15 clearly appeals for Christians to cooperate in completing the task. McAlister appeals to again consider the slogan, "we are not the only Christians, but Christians only." As we are able to recover this spirit of cooperation and unity within the church, we can complete the task. This cooperation will require a unity built on a proposition that those who view issues differently remain fellow believers. The resurrection of another old slogan may help. "In matters of faith, unity. In matters of opinion, liberty. In all things, love."

One obvious concern is that a book such as this will promise more than it can deliver. We have chosen to broadly address foundational themes rather than to go into great depth on any one issue. You will find a wealth of help in the additional resource section toward the end of the book. These resources focus on various components introduced in this present volume. To understand these themes adequately requires a lifetime of serious study. Our intention is to introduce you to this exciting, dynamic field of missiological inquiry. If this is the result then we will have fulfilled our purpose.

Edgar J. Elliston

Stephen E. Burris

Pasadena, California

March, 1995

Introduction

Why should we compile another book about missions? Do we not have many excellent books that treat the wide range of missions topics? Do we not have access to historical, theological, anthropological, biographical and strategic books and articles? Obviously, the answer is yes in all of these categories. However, current books that serve to introduce missions broadly are still lacking. As we have sought to introduce missiological perspectives to college students and local church leaders, we discovered a satisfactory introductory text is needed.

Several key theological and practical issues emerge in the following pages. We, as authors, hope that the thoughtful church leader including the minister, elder and the one interested in future ministry will be encouraged to see the mission of the church as the mission of God. We do not see "missions" as an optional "add-on program." Mission is central to the life and purpose of the church. God's mission to deliver humankind into his full blessing did not begin with Jesus. Rather, it began in the garden of Eden as will be seen later in this text. God's desire for his people to join in delivering the good news of salvation neither began nor ended with the "Great Commission." We hope that church leaders will be encouraged to serve more effectively and thoughtfully as they know God's consistent purpose as revealed in Scripture and demonstrated in history.

Knowing the biblical foundations for God's mission to the world provides the basis to revolutionize the ministry of a local church. Church leaders may be further encouraged to serve by seeing God's faithfulness through history. As you read through this text, you will see that the biblical patterns for God's faithfulness have continued through history even up to the present. Different historical periods have seen his working in somewhat different structures to accomplish his consistent purpose. Now that the world and the church are becoming much more urban, new structures and means for working with an urbanized world are emerging.

Many Christian renewal moments including the Pietists, the Methodist movement, the Restoration Movement, and younger movements like the "classical" Pentecostal movements of this century tend to drift from the early missional vision toward a routinized apathy. The lack of commitment for mission reflects an inward change of focus. Every new generation then is called to reflect on the mission of God as revealed in Scripture and demonstrated in history. This generation is no different. The aim of this book is to encourage the ongoing process of renewal for mission.

While cultural sensitivity has accompanied Christian witnesses since the Day of Pentecost, cultural issues today have taken a strange turn in the U.S.A. "Multiculturalism" has become a "politically correct" perspective. This perspective affirms the individualistic freedom to do what is right in one's own eyes; that perspective heaps criticism on the person who would advocate religious conversion. Such a person is openly ridiculed as a narrow-minded, provincial bigot. This text then seeks to clarify a Christian view of culture which while affirming cultures and their diversity also holds a high view of the biblical mandates to make disciples of all nations and to love one's neighbor.

While an introductory text is limited in the breadth and depth of strategic perspectives that can be described, we do seek to introduce the idea of strategic planning in mission methods. Long before William Carey made the term, "mean," popular, Christian leaders were thinking and acting strategically to fulfill God's mandates. Whether looking at specific methods, the possibility of working through social structures or at the remaining task, strategic thinking clearly remains an essential part of an effective mission effort.

Whether one is in a church in Indianapolis, Cincinnati, or Calcutta, the "co-mission" is to communicate. We are called to work with the Holy Spirit in his mission to bring all of humankind to know and accept Jesus as the Christ who will become their Lord and Savior. Often the context of that attempted communication is cross-cultural. The same communication principles which serve the North American missionary in east Africa to gain an understanding will help another person in Chicago to communicate cross-generationally or across a cultural barrier based on ethnicity. With the ethnic mix growing increasingly complex in virtually every city worldwide, understanding the basics of cross-cultural communication is essential.

The importance of understanding before seeking to be understood is a basic theological, communicational and missional truth. The authors of this text weave this theme from a range of perspectives. Whether thinking about local church leadership or the planning for evangelism and church planting across cultural boundaries this principle continues to apply through the following chapters.

While the task remaining may threaten the fainthearted, the mission and the task are the Lord's! He works in and through the church. He empowers his witnesses. He convicts the hearers of sin, righteousness and judgment. His wisdom directs to result in his own glory. While we are expected to faithfully and competently do our best, ideal techniques or technologies will not finish the task. Our best methods will not overcome the complexities of cross-cultural evangelism and church planting. Only as God's people fully commit themselves to the task remaining under his guidance will his power be released.

Completing the task is the driving motive behind this text. As the apostle Paul, we seek to encourage every Christian witness to "become all things to all men so that by all means . . . [he/she] might save some" (1 Cor. 9:19-23, esp. 22).

As a reader and presumably a leader in a local congregation, we invite you to think with us about the biblical, historical, cultural, and strategic bases for mission. They are integral to the life of a local congregation. We believe if you seriously consider any one of these arenas, it will transform your perspective and your ministry. If you consider more than one, they will transform the congregation where you serve.

1
God's Purpose and Plan
The Bible—A Missionary Revelation

Robert Kurka

> The supreme arguments for missions are not found in
> any specific words. It is in the being and character of
> God that the deepest ground of the missionary enter-
> prise is to be found. We cannot think of God except in
> terms which necessitate the missionary task.[1]

With these words Robert Speer, the great early
twentieth-century missiologist, implicitly expressed a
fundamental biblical truth. Scripture is, at its very
core, a *missionary revelation*, rather than a book which
only incidently records a mission mandate (Matt.
28:18-20) and several missionary narratives (Acts,
3 John). Speer further contends that the very deity
who is revealed on every page of the Bible—the triune
God—is one whose very nature and work are best
understood within a missionary paradigm. This
hermeneutic, however, is strangely absent in the writings of most theologians, as well as in the thought and
practice of the general Christian populace.

---

1. Speer, Robert E., *Christianity and the Nations* (New York:
Revell, 1910). These words are all the more remarkable given that
they are penned shortly after what Kenneth Scott Latourette
termed as the "Great Century" of missions—a period that was by-
and-large motivated by the Matthew 28 commission and marked
by the absence of a serious mission theology (Braaten, *The Flaming
Center: A Theology of the Christian Mission*. Philadelphia:Fortress
Press, 1977). In an era of great missionary activity, Speer's theological reflection is especially noteworthy.

Missions Myopia

Several reasons exist for this current "missions myopia" regarding the biblical text. First, the history of Protestant theology. The years between the Reformation and William Carey's 1792 *Enquiry* saw very little mission activity generated from the noble camp of *sola scriptura*. The finished work of Christ was cherished, the authority of the Bible was championed, and the priesthood of believers was celebrated, but the Christian's obligation to tell his global neighbor the Good News was some how omitted. In their zeal to do responsible historical/grammatical exegesis, the Reformers and their heirs took the missionary words of the risen Christ and restricted their intent and focus to the first-century apostles and the world of their day. This lack of understanding resulted in effectively "shutting down" world evangelism in both the psyche and practice of Protestants for over two hundred years.[2]

---

2. David Filbeck, *Yes, God of the Gentiles, Too* (Wheaton, IL: Billy Graham Center, 1994), p. 28.

Dr. Filbeck contends that this conspicuous lack of Protestant missions can be traced in part, to a "missions-myopic" interpretation of the Bible. He notes four characteristics of the Reformation hermeneutic, which in turn inhibited world evangelism:

(1) Biblical studies were not oriented towards discovering what the Scriptures had to say about missions but rather focused upon buttressing key Reformed theological positions: i.e., priesthood of all believers, the Lord's Supper, salvation by faith, the all-sufficiency of the Scriptures.

(2) Many applied an overly-rigid historical-grammatical exegesis to the Great Commission, concluding that it was given to the Apostles, alone in their time period. Furthermore, some Protestants even went so far as to conclude that "additional" missionary movements to unreached peoples actually represented a denial of God's sovereignty.

(3) Many Reformers believed that the second coming of Christ was imminent; there was simply not enough time for missionaries

Resurrection of Missions

The "resurrection" of missions spurred on by such stalwarts as Carey and Hudson Taylor as well as the vigorous student movement recovered the "Great Commission" as a continuous call to every generation of believers. This most positive contribution, however, generally failed to build a broad missions theology.[3] While the words "Go, disciple" have proven to be an inspiration to thousands since 1792, the overall effect of such a single-text interpretative method has been to promote a reading of the Bible. This reading, in effect, largely sees missions as a "jog" in the road instead of, as Speer would intimate, the road, itself.

Reading the Bible . . . with Jesus and Paul

The physician Luke penned two helpful passages of Scripture. These passages provide us with an explicitly missiological grid by which we may read the Bible. These passages help us see the mission perspective of both Jesus and Paul.

In the concluding chapter of the third Gospel, the soon-to-be ascended Jesus gives one of the most specific, most easily to be comprehended hermeneutic lessons ever written:

> He said to them, "This is what I told you while I was still with you: Everything must be fulfilled that is written about me in the Law of Moses, the Prophets and the Psalms. Then he opened their minds so they

---

to reach recently discovered lands.

(4) Protestants, who had come to the conclusion that the Commission had been given to the Apostles, alone, openly opposed and sometimes persecuted others who believed that Jesus' mandate was still operative in the contemporary church.

3. Carl Braaten, *The Flaming Center*; David Filbeck, *Yes, God of the Gentiles, Too.*

could understand the Scriptures. He told them, "This is what is written: The Christ will suffer and rise from the dead on the third day, and *repentance and forgiveness of sins will be preached in his name to all nations, beginning at Jerusalem* (Luke 24:44-48, *emphasis added*).

In essence, our Lord has reduced the multiplicity of Scriptural themes to a core of two: (1) The Bible (Old Testament, specifically) is oriented around the suffering, death, and resurrection of Christ—on behalf of humankind (the "gospel message"); and (2) This redemptive message has always had a global focus, *especially* in the Old Testament.[4] Jesus does not see His ministry and message in conflict with the Jewish Bible, but rather as its very fulfillment (cf. Matt. 5:17-20). Thus, world evangelization is not a first-time idea of the resurrected Christ to His church, but rather is an essential thread which unites Genesis to Malachi.

Biblical Missions Mandate

The mandate to "disciple the nations" is in actuality, an *echo* of a missiological summons given to Old Testament Israel. Consequently, we are left with the conclusion that when Jesus read His Bible (OT), He saw the cross and *cross-cultural witness* permeating its pages. This insight might help us better understand the true nature of the intense conflict that existed

---

4. This is an interesting premise given the fact that the bulk of the Old Testament scholarship has dismissed the idea that a canonical center can be located (cf. Kaiser, *Toward an Old Testament Theology*, pp. 23-24). Apparently, Jesus and Paul do not have any real difficulty in "reducing" the many Old Testament theological threads to these two integrating themes. Kaiser would also contend that the finished work of Christ and world evangelization (identified under the broader categories of "seed" and "heritage") are properly summarized by the term, "promise" (*epangelia*), used by the New Testament writers in some forty passages which reflect upon the essence of the Old Testament (Ibid., p. 33).

between Jesus and the Jewish religious establishment. The latter could search their Scriptures with legalistic intensity. They not only failed to see their very redeemer (John 5:39), but also missed His inclusive ministry. The authors of Scripture had always shown God's inclusive demands of those who had received His grace. The religion exhibited by Jesus' Jewish contemporaries had little to do with essential Old Testament faith and was more a demonstration of their protective response to intertestamental Hellenism.[5] Genuine Old Testament religion, on the other hand, would have embraced both the Christ and an "other peoples" ministry.

Pauline Messiah Missions Hermeneutic

This "Messiah-Missions" hermeneutic was also the approach taken by the Apostle Paul. In Acts 26, Paul both shares his own "spiritual pilgrimage" and defends his mission to the Gentiles before King Agrippa. Paul's detractors had continually plagued him with the charge that he was preaching a message in violation of the OT Law (Acts 25:8). They expected the Scripturally-literate Agrippa (at least in the eyes of the Empire) to be able to validate or discuss this accusation. As Paul explains that his preaching to both Jew *and Gentile* was in obedience to his heavenly vision (26:19,20), he candidly declares:

---

5. This is not to insinuate that the people of Israel practiced their prescribed faith, consistently in the Old Testament—obviously, they often did not. A fundamental tenet which was true of OT religion, however, such as that revealed to Abraham (Gen. 12) or Moses (Ex. 19) was clearly Gentile embracing. The Judaism of the Diaspora (post-exilic) was highly missionary (although co-opted by Hellenism), whereas its Palestinian counterpart (practiced by the Pharisees or Essenes, for example) tended to be more rigid, legalistic, and less concerned about evangelism. Cf. Roger Hedlund, *The Mission of the Church in the World* (Grand Rapids, Baker, 1991). See especially pp. 141-48.

I am saying nothing beyond what the prophets and Moses said would happen—that the Christ would suffer and, as the first to rise from the dead, would proclaim light to his own people and to the Gentiles (Acts 26:22,23).

The apostle is marking in no uncertain terms, an indissoluble continuity between his message and that of the Old Testament. Paul's gospel is nothing other than the message delivered by Moses.[6] (This statement, like Jesus', seems to further support my conviction that first-century Judaism provides a poor reflection of genuine Old Testament faith.) Furthermore, Paul sees the gist of Scripture distilled in these two previously-noted themes: 1) the passion of Christ, and, 2) a proclamation into a spiritual darkness shrouding both Jew and Gentile alike. Consequently, the apostle's three missionary journeys to the Gentiles are not aberrations of God's law, but rather a clear submission to its dictates. In actuality, Paul is not the person on trial but rather, his accusers, for *they*, not he, have failed to recognize and yield to the Word of God.

Thus, if Paul sees the Old Testament being encapsulated in these two key themes (Christ/cross-cultural witness) then one should expect that these parameters will also guide the interpretation of the apostle's several letters as well as the other New Testament writings. Certainly, the New Testament authors believed that their literary productions were no less-inspired than the Jewish Scriptures.[7]

It is fair then to say that Jesus, and later Paul have provided us with a necessary set of hermeneutical

---

6. In Romans 1:1-3, Paul identifies himself as one who has been "set apart for the gospel of God—the gospel he promised beforehand through his prophets in the Holy Scriptures" (NIV)—an equally explicit claim that the Pauline message was one in essence with the Old Testament Scriptures.

7. Cf. 2 Peter 3:2,16.

lenses that enable us to read our Bibles in reasonably the same way that they read theirs. We can catch both the essence of the gospel in Genesis, as well as its inseparable partnering theme. Salvation is (and always has been) for *both* the Jew and Greek. Likewise, these two themes provide the modern reader considerable relief to pass through the "difficult" terrain of the "dusty" historical books. If the outline of the forest is first observed then finding one's way through the trees is much easier.

Origin of Key Themes

The kerygmatic theme (suffering, death, and resurrection of Christ for our sins) has long been recognized as existing in germ form in Genesis 3.[8] In the aftermath of the Fall, the Lord God pronounces a series of consequences ("curses") which will now be in the experience of those living in this sin-stained universe. The serpent is sentenced to a humiliating existence. The woman is to endure both the pain of childbirth and the hurt of male relationship. And, the man will work on earth that at times is more foe than friend (Gen. 3:14,16-19). In the middle of this cheerless pericope come these well-known words of hope:

> And I will put enmity between you and the woman, and between your offspring and hers; he will crush your head, and you will strike his heel (Gen. 3:15).

---

8. This recognition of the Gen. 3:15 "Gospel" is evidenced in the New Testament: More implicitly in the gospels (the birth narratives as well as the almost disproportionate space given to the "Passion Week") and quite explicitly by the writer of the Revelation, as for example, in his most artistic twelfth chapter. John tells the "Christ Story" with the precise characters who people the garden: the woman, her male child, and the serpent (dragon). One might even say that John has provided us with an "imaginative exposition" of Gen. 3:15.

Gospel in the Garden

These words introduce the first great biblical theme enumerated by Jesus and Paul—the suffering, death, and resurrection of Christ. Roger Hedlund put it well, describing the "Gospel in the Garden."[9] God's redemptive work in Christ is both predicted and preached. Indeed, the "coming of the seed of the woman" becomes the ultimate goal of the rest of Old Testament as well as its present "confessional base" for ones' salvation. This pre-history proclamation was nothing less than the gospel in its most rudimentary for. This saving message the apostle Paul later described as "the gospel in advance" when brought to Abraham (Gal. 3:8). The mention of Abraham, then, points us in the direction of a foundational text for the second key biblical text for the second key biblical theme (world evangelization)—Genesis 12:2,3:

> I will make you into a great nation and I will bless you; I will make your name great, and you will be a blessing. I will bless those who bless you, and whoever curses you I will curse; and all the peoples of the earth will be blessed through you (Gen. 12:2,3).

Covenant with Abraham

Walter Kaiser has referred to this passage as the "grandest of all missionary texts"[10] as it promises a nation to Abraham (Israel) which is called into being specifically for a missionary task. The comprehensive missiological character of this passage is clear. God reveals Himself as Yahweh to Abram (a missionary

---

9. Roger Hedlund, *The Mission of the Church in the World* (Grand Rapids: Baker, 1991), p. 25.

10. Ralph D. Winter and Steven Hawthorne, *Perspectives on the World Christian Movement: A Reader*, revised edition (Pasadena, CA: William Carey Library, 1992), p. 27.

revelation), extends to him His missionary grace, calls Abram to a missionary task ("be a blessing"), and sets forth a missionary goal ("all peoples," literally "families"). Furthermore, the call of Abraham signals the beginning of the Scriptural "history of salvation"—a story which demands a missiological hermeneutic.[11]

Clearly, one does not need to go beyond the first twelve chapters of Genesis in order to acquire the two-pronged, "cross-commission" perspective articulated by Jesus and Paul. Genesis 3 and 12 are very observable indicators that the ensuing biblical records will revolve around Christ and world evangelization.[12] Certainly, God's call of Abraham places the missionary obsession of the Careys, Taylors, and Townsends in a mandate twice as old as the familiar Matthew text; in

11. Mont Smith clearly recognizes the global implications of the Abrahamic Covenant in his most comprehensive work, *What the Bible Says About Covenant* (Joplin, MO: College Press, 1991). What is disappointing, however, in Smith's generally credible volume is his failure to see the "blessing to the nations" as any more than *predictive*; a "hint" of the New Covenant's "Great Commission" (198-200). Consequently, his treatment of the other major OT covenants also share in this missiological "deficiency," i.e., that Israel had an ongoing "commission" to evangelize the Gentiles.

12. This is not to suggest, as some would, that we have a "level" Bible, where apparent "distinctions from biblical era to biblical era are merely glossed over." Rather, as Charles Van Engen would describe it we have the same covenant permeating the pages of Scripture though one that is "contextualized" in its successive contexts (Gilliland, *The Word Among Us*, pp. 75-99). Therefore, when Paul refers to the salvation of the Gentiles as a "mystery" (Eph. 4-9), he is not implying that ethnic evangelism is a new or different course in God's age-old covenant. He is, however, celebrating the fresh "contextualization of the timeless will of God," a deeper and fuller revelation of God to His people (Ibid., p. 82). Van Engen summarizes the "continuity/discontinuity" issue in this manner:

"God's self-revelation never really gets beyond the most basic issue of God's triumph over evil (Adam), and God's election of a people for service as a blessing to all the nations (Abram) (see 1 Peter 2). God's law is never abrogated, nor are the promises of

actuality, "Make disciples" is the one, explicit order that God gives every beneficiary of His grace in both the Old or New Testaments. Yet, we can even go *further* back than Genesis 2, or even the "Gospel of the Garden" (3:15). The opening words of Robert Speer in this chapter beckon us to a missiological hermeneutic that is essentially grounded in the *person* of God *apart* from any explicit evangelistic commands.

God's Missionary Nature

The opening chapter of Genesis brings us into contact with a God who in his essential nature, is missionary. Several missiological characteristics are at least subtly implied (although these surely were more explicit to the Mosaic author's original audience).

God's "Global Nature"

First, God is introduced by a *global name* "Elohim" (1:1) rather than the more intimate and personal Yahweh (The latter name first appears in 2:4). The Supreme Being is not viewed as merely one of a number of tribal deities—Israel's exclusive god—but is presented as the one, true god of every tribe, nation, and language *regardless* of whether they acknowledge Him or not. His existence is presented as an undeniable reality and suggests a certain dimension of universal accessibility, what theologians refer to as "general revelation." Unlike the gods of other peoples, the Old Testament Elohim is in some way knowable to

---

David's eternal reign ever annulled. And yet in each new context something deeper and fuller is revealed. Paul exemplified this discontinuous continuity when he spoke of the fact that as in Adam all died, so in Christ, all will be made alive (Rom. 5:12-21)." (Ibid., p. 83).

every person. This is certainly the understanding of Paul in the first chapter of Romans.[13]

Submissive Creation

Second, a missionary God emerges as the creation narrative unfolds and the deities of an animistic worldview (i.e., rivers, sun, moon, stars, animals, etc.) are swept off their thrones and clearly placed in submission to Elohim.[14] They are not self-generated entities nor creators, themselves, but owe their very existence to the creative work of Elohim. A modern

---

13. Romans 1:19,20 where Paul contends that all peoples have been given "access" to at least two "divine truths": (1) God's eternal power, and (2) His divine nature, which are comprehensible through what he has made. In contemporary times, missionaries like Don Richardson have noted that there is presumably a monotheistic tradition in the "annals" (often oral) of every tribal people although such may be well hidden beneath centuries of animistic distortion (*Eternity in Their Hearts*, Glendale, CA: Regal, 1981).

14. It is interesting to note the parallels between the creation narrative (Gen. 1) and the record of the plagues (Ex. 7-11). The creation "characters" of the "Beginning" resemble the deities that are humiliated by Yahweh in the Exodus. I would suggest that the Mosaic writer is less concerned with giving his readers a precise, "scientific" account in Gen. 1, and is rather more oriented towards providing them with a polemic, which in turn exposes the subordinate and "non-godly"character of Egyptian animism (G. Hasel strongly argues this point in a journal article, entitled "The Polemic Nature of the Genesis Cosmology," 1974: Evangelical Quarterly 96). If this polemical understanding of Genesis 1 is correct—and I believe it is—then we can better understand and appreciate the Old Testament's ongoing presentation of a God who is intolerant of, and despises His lesser rivals: "You shall have no other gods before me" (Ex. 20:3) . . . "You shall not bow down to them or worship them" (Ex. 20:4) . . . "They have thrown their gods into the fire and destroyed them for they were not gods but only wood and stone" (Isa. 37:19). It is not surprising that Yahweh identifies Himself as a "jealous God" (Ex. 20:5; 34:14; Deut. 4:24, *et .al.*)—He alone is worthy of mankind's worship and devotion.

day missionary working in an animistic context can readily appreciate the evangelistic and redemptive power of the creation story. The animist believes him/herself to be a virtual prisoner in a dispassionate universe, in constant distress over whether the nature gods have been adequately placated. This belief system subjects the human spirit, then, to the impersonal forces of chance and magic as well as to the exploitative dictates of the mediators of this capricious universe, the witch doctor, shaman, or medicine man.[15] Furthermore, the writer argues that human beings are not merely misplaced entities in this vast universe, but rather the highest of all of God's creation, His unique "image" (Gen. 1:26-31). In verses 26 and 27 we read some of the most liberating words ever penned about humankind:

> Then God said, "Let us make make man in our image, in our likeness, and let them rule over the fish of the sea and the birds of the air, over the livestock, over all the earth, and over all the creatures that move along the ground." So God created man in his own image, in the image of God he created him; male and female he created them (Gen. 1:26,27).

Placed within the context of animism—either Moses' Egyptian forms or its many contemporary expressions—these words separate humanity from the rest of creation in dignity, value, ability, and purpose. In addition to this celebration of the human, any man-made distinctions/ barriers which are erected and set some people above others are implicitly challenged. Genesis 1:26 applies the common Semitic word, *tselem* ("image") to all humanity, not merely a select few (as was the case among Israel's neighbors).[16] All human

---

15. Gailyn Van Rheenan, *Communicating Christ in Animistic Contexts* (Grand Rapids: Baker, 1991), pp. 145-160.

16. Cf. D.J.A. Clines, "The Image of God in Man." *Tyndale Bulletin*, 1968.

beings—those of Egyptian nobility and those who were Hebrew slaves—share a common ancestor (the first couple) and their created dignity. Furthermore, the biblical writer defines "humankind" in verse 27 as encompassing both male and *female*, a notion quite foreign to the very sexist cultures of his day. (Such words explain why Hebrew women were treated considerably better than their ancient near eastern counterparts—they were viewed as humans!)

This statement rings out in bold critique against many contemporary cultures' treatment of women, as well—whether they are Asian, African, or Western. Consequently, Genesis 1:26-27 calls upon the followers of the one true God to repudiate racism, caste systems, cultural elitism and nationalism. This statement is a clear reminder to God's chosen people that they were not superior in value and intellect to their neighbors but rather recipients of divine grace (cf. Deut. 9:4-8). The "difference of man" from among the rest of creation is further accentuated by chapter two's more specific rendering of human creation. The narrative presents an intentional rehearsal of the human dignity theme. Genesis 2 is a most necessary part of the creation story, for its "microcosmic" look at the sixth day's final act provides the reader with an explanation for God's subsequent redemptive work on behalf of rebellious humanity.

This endeavor will require the death of His Son (one of the personages behind the "let us," in 1:26ff). The importance of the human creation to the Creator God is also implied in chapter 2 as we are introduced to Yahweh Elohim ("Lord God"). He is the cosmic God who chooses to reveal himself in a very personal manner to His "image." This name modification strongly indicates the missionary character of God. While Genesis 1 suggests that this one, true God may be known in part by all, this is hardly satisfactory to the Creator. The name *Yahweh* is a strong declaration that He desires a more intimate relationship with His cherished mankind, an intimacy that *He* must initiate and reveal.

God's Purpose for Humanity

God's purpose or plan for humanity is also revealed in the creation narrative. In Genesis 1, we are told that God "blessed" (*barak*) His creation: first, fish and fowl, then humankind. Blessing conveys the notion of God's favor or approval—a harmony between the Creator and His "good" creation.[17] This statement, coupled with the Lord's admonition to Adam in 2:16,17 ("to not eat from the tree of the knowledge of good and evil") clearly indicates a divine desire to dwell forever with people. This intention, of course, is "apparently" nullified with the advent of sin (Gen. 3) as Adam and his wife misuse their freedom, bringing not only a separation between themselves and a perfect God but an entire series of broken relations (cf. 3:12ff). Because of God's great attachment to His human creation, however, He offered His "Gospel in the Garden" (3:15). Thereby He offered the penitent a restoration of the intended blessing—partially in the present and completely in a day yet to come.[18] It is therefore, not surprising, that after this promise of undeserved hope, the term "blessing" reappears in

17. Cf. U. Becker, "Blessing," in C. Brown, ed., *The New International Dictionary of New Testament Theology* (Grand Rapids: Zondervan, 1975).

18. The "Missionary God" is seen immediately following the Fall, as He seeks after the disobedient, fearful couple (3:8-9). The questions "Where are you?" (v. 9) is not to be seen as an indication of the Lord's ignorance—He is all knowing—but rather a further demonstration of a God whose agenda is to rescue the lost (cf. Luke 15). Whereas the world's religions call upon humankind to seek after God—albeit in fear—the Bible, from the beginning—pictures Yahweh initiating the restored relationship.

Genesis. The genealogy of Gen. 5:2, the blessing of Noah and sons in Gen. 9:1, the promise of God's dwelling in the tents of Shem in Gen. 9:26, and the covenant to bless Abraham in Gen. 12:2-3—each involves making God's chosen man and his seed a vehicle of blessing to the world. The blessing theme becomes even more poignant when one notices the context of their appearance, i.e., following the death of Abel, the flood, and the presumptuousness of the Tower at Babel. This blessing repetition—especially when seen amidst a continual cacophony of sin—can only suggest that at heart our God is a missionary, truly desirous of restoring a broken relationship with humankind, a humanity which covers many nations (Gen. 10) and tribes (Gen. 12). The "Great Commission" mandate given to Abraham is a natural development given the picture of the missionary God that emerges in Genesis' preceding eleven chapters.

No Missions, No Bible

These early chapters suggest one further "divine missionary evidence," that is, in the very existence of these words themselves. The fact that we have the privilege of reading these narratives of creation, blessing, sin, promised redemption, and evangelistic mobilization (Abraham) is "proof" that God is a missionary. As noted above, the creation presentation of Gen. 1,2 stands in radical opposition, if not open antagonism to the animistic worldviews pervading the ancient (and modern) world. As the inspired text "demythologizes" divinity, cosmology and faulty anthropological notions, one cannot help but see such polemic as an attempt to liberate us from understandings of reality that preclude a relationship with the God of blessing. The Bible, then, is not simply a book about mission narratives, mandates or even about a missionary God. The Bible, rather, by its very existence is a ringing mission declaration; namely, that the one, true God is not an "unknown" deity (Acts 17:23) but one who makes Himself intelligible, ultimately in the Word become flesh (John 1:14). Furthermore, this written revelation has come to us in genuine human languages (Hebrew, Aramaic, and Greek) resplendent with a wide diversity of linguistic styles and devices—a "commonness" (*koine*) which communicates accessibility and a sincere desire to be comprehended. Earlier in the century, Wycliffe Bible Translators founder, Cameron Townsend, came to realize the *contemporary implications* of this "common language" revelation. As a young missionary in Guatemala, Townsend soon recognized that his Spanish translations of the Bible were not "speaking" to a majority dwelling in the villages of that nation. An Indian pointedly asked him, "If your God is so smart, why can't he speak our language?"[19] This inquiry brought in Townsend, a resolve to translate the Bible into the world's many tongues—a very fitting application of Scripture's essential nature as a missionary word from God.

Mission Consciousness of the Early Church

Henry Boer in his excellent 1961 volume, *Pentecost and Missions*, notes a somewhat surprising "fact" about the mission-consciousness of the first-century church:

> There seems to be no warrant to believe that awareness of the Great Commission played a role in the mind of the Church at Jerusalem when she undertook the great decision to acknowledge the equal share of the Gentiles in the gospel, and to validate Peter's baptism of the household of the Gentiles.[20]

19. Winter and Hawthorne, *Perspectives*, pp. 13-41.

20. Henry Boer, *Pentecost and Missions* (Grand Rapids: Eerdmans, 1961), p. 42.

While to some, the "omission of the commission" seems odd, if not perplexing, the reader of this chapter hopefully will realize that a solid biblical missiology is not dependent upon the words of the risen Christ. The early church had every reason to pursue an evangelization extending to the ends of the earth. She was reading her Bible (Old Testament) with the same hermeneutical lenses worn by Jesus and Paul—lenses that revealed a missionary imperative from first to last. Furthermore, these first generation Christians grabbed hold of a very fundamental truth: that the God who sent His Son, was in His essential nature, a missionary being. He expects those who have experienced the grace of this restored blessing to share that redemptive possibility with the worlds' "others." For these believers, the mandate to "disciple the nations" was in many ways a *postscript*, perhaps better stated, an *exclamation point*, to a biblical "essential" burned into the pages of Genesis–Malachi. May their understanding of Scripture, moreover, may their understanding of God, the *missionary*—become our own.

2
Israel and the Covenant:
Call and Commission

Paul McAlister

Is there, in fact, a missionary purpose for Israel? Is there a missionary intent within the "Covenant?" These questions have been met with conflicting responses throughout the history of the church. The issue is often confused in the minds of those who champion being "New Testament Christians."

Many Christians await for a missionary mandate until the last chapter of Matthew, the "Great Commission." This volume begins with a statement making clear that mission flows from the very character of God Himself. The goal of this chapter is to reflect upon the nature of God's missionary nature as it appears throughout the flow of history recorded in the Old Testament. Israel was called by God to reflect His nature, and that nature clearly implies a missionary character for Israel. Israel's relationship with God is tied to the covenant, and, the covenant relationship implies identity and purpose. God, through the covenant, calls the people to Himself, and commissions them to be a "Light to the Gentiles." To this understanding of the covenant we turn our attention.

The "Covenant" has been the subject of continuous discussion in the history of the church. Too often such discussion has not focused upon the dynamic nature of the covenant. The covenant has been seen as a static relationship, without careful attention being given to the contextual revealing of the covenant throughout the Testaments.[1] The Covenant was given to Adam, Noah, Abram, Moses, David, and Jesus. Each revelation of the "Covenant" presented a new manifestation, not simply a repetition. Each time the "Covenant" is revealed, it builds upon preceding revelations, but clearly presses beyond them. This means, not that the central content of the "Covenant" changes, but that it is expanded and intensified! Each new manifestation is like "new wine," in that it builds upon but looks beyond. We are able to more deeply understand the implications of the "Covenant," but, further, we are able to understand the nature of our God more fully as well.

Clearly, each new historical manifestation of the "Covenant" serves to intensify awareness of God's intent and nature. There is also a further issue for missions. Beyond the historical and, therefore, contextual revelations of the "Covenant," one may ask, does the implanting of the revelation of the "Covenant" in other cultures also serve to manifest more fully the nature of God, as the God of All Peoples? The static perception of the "Covenant" may lead to a myopia, a provincial view of God, and, therefore, miss the missionary intent of the "Covenant!" This is not a confused syncretism, but, the deepening of our awareness of the global intent of God's Covenant, and the recognition that the historical manifestations of the "Covenant" provides ever expanding awareness of His global concern, and deeper revelation of His nature. This pushes us beyond the narrowness of our own contexts and helps us see the "Covenant" as the dynamic revelation of God's intent as redeemer of all

---

1. For very helpful discussion of recent thinking, note the work of Van Engen in Van Engen, Charles, Dean S. Gilliland and Paul E. Pierson (eds.) *The Good News of the Kingdom: Mission Theology for the Third Millennium* (Maryknoll, NY: Orbis Books, 1993). The work helps focus upon the dynamic nature of the "Covenant."

peoples through Christ.[2]

The Mandate of the Covenant

Many have pointed out the variety of incidents and statements within the Old Testament which point to the involvement of Israel with peoples outside of Israel. Indeed, the list is extensive. Consider the following: Joseph was a blessing to Egyptians (Gen. 41:14-49). Moses had a Midianite convert: his father-in-law (Ex. 18:1-12). Joshua and the spies were a blessing to Rahab (Josh. 2:1-21). Naomi was a blessing to Ruth of Moab (Ruth 2:12). David reached out to the Gibeonites (2 Sam. 21:14). Nathan rebuked David because he had put a Hittite to death (2 Sam. 12:9,14). Solomon with Queen Sheba (1 Kings 10:1-9). The temple court which was dedicated to the Gentiles (1 Kings 8:41-43). Elijah and the widow of Zarephath (1 Kings 17: 7-24). Jeremiah was a prophet to the nations (Jer. 1:5). Daniel reaches out to Nebuchadnezzar (Dan. 2:47-49; 3:28-29). Jonah reached out to a Gentile city (Jonah 3:3-10). All of these examples are given in the context of pointing out the "bottom line" elements of God's blessing upon His people.[3]

---

2. While many helpful books are available concerning the "Covenant," many still do not deal with the dynamic nature of the Covenant as revelation of God's Global intent and His nature. The Covenant is critical for theology and mission. More could be done to highlight these areas of dynamic revelation which sees God at work in history, as well as God at work in various cultures manifesting His character and purpose. Perhaps more could be done to include these dynamic and recent discussions noting that more of the missiological significance of "Covenant" could be included in such works as that by Mont Smith, *What the Bible Says About Covenant* (Joplin, MO: College Press, 1981). We need to learn from Israel's failure to appreciate the missiological significance of the "Covenant" of God.

3. Robert Sjogren, *Unveiled at Last* (Seattle: YWAM Press, 1992), pp. 62-63.

An Obligation to the Nations

The above examples help us to see at least two major issues. The people of God throughout the Old Testament did have significant contact with the non-Israelite peoples. Also, the examples reflect the intention of God Himself. While many may believe such contact was incidental to the covenant, I would argue that such contact is, as Sjogren would say, the bottom line intent of the covenant. The covenant is often considered a contract offered by God to the people of Israel, guaranteeing their privileged status and exclusive blessings from God. The expression "top line/bottom line," points beyond this narrow and distorted view. From the very beginning of God's covenant relationship with Israel, the covenant had a dominating theme. That theme made clear that the top line blessings of Israel were intended to lead to a bottom line obligation to the nations.

All Nations to Receive Covenantal Blessings

The elements of the covenant may be described under three headings.[4] The covenant with Abraham included: Promised Land, a great nation of people, and, that he would become the source of blessing for all peoples. Genesis 12:1-3 provides us with the primary statement of the covenant to Abraham. This covenant was repeated in 18:18, 22:15-18; to Isaac in 26:3-4; and to Jacob in 28:14. Throughout these passages the three themes remain consistent. The thought that the covenant would become the source of blessing for all peoples is held central. Though different words are used to describe this blessing beyond Israel, the fundamental idea remains the same. In

---

4. David Filbeck, *Yes, God of the Gentiles, Too* (Wheaton, IL: The Billy Graham Center, 1994), p. 61.

Genesis 12:3, the promise is to the *mishpechoth*, peoples (NIV; other versions "families") of the earth. In Genesis 22:18, the word *goi[im]*, nations, is used. "Hermeneutically, in other words, both *mishah'oh* [sic] and *goi* together communicate that God's blessing through Abraham is for every size of group, from the smaller lineage to the larger nation."[5] It follows that all peoples, large and small, are the intended recipients of God's blessing! Genesis begins with a global view, it describes the curse upon all mankind as a result of sin. When God calls Abraham, against the background of God's judgment and division of the peoples in Genesis 10-11, He chooses one nation as the means of redeeming all nations.

The Law, given in Exodus 20, is preceded by a very important passage in Exodus 19: 4-6. The Law is often seen as that which defines Israel. In Exodus 19:4-6, a major part of Israel's identity often is overlooked. God reminds His people of His redemptive grace, and does so with magnificent beauty. However, God goes beyond the reminder of His blessing to project His purpose for His redeemed people. His people would be a "holy nation," and a "kingdom of priests." A contingency is stated clearly in verse 5. If the people are obedient, and keep His covenant (which contains the universal intent for all peoples), then, they will be His "treasured people." This word translated as "treasured," is a term from an old Akkadian word meaning "movable." The point would be that the term does not imply a static possession such as that which might refer to real estate. Wherever God's people would be they would be valued. But, note that the purpose of God for His people is intimately tied to the blessing. His people would be a "kingdom of priests." God's people are not, therefore, simply those whom God has finally favored over the rest of the peoples of the earth,

5. Ibid., p. 62.

rather they are called to represent God among those peoples. God's intent is overwhelmingly clear, and celebrated in such wonderful passages as Psalm 67. The first verse of this Psalm sounds very much like a "top line" blessing. The focus of the psalm is, however, shouts that God's salvation is to be known and rejoiced in throughout the nations!

Israel's Opportunity as a Light to the Nations

Israel had endless opportunity to be the "light for the Gentiles (Isa. 42:6-7). As early as the Exodus miracles, in Exodus 9:14-16, the opportunity for proclamation was present. Even the Land itself, the location of the Land, allowed for the nations to see the holiness of His people and His power (Deut. 32:8-9). God's power was being displayed throughout the history of the people of Israel, but, Israel had the responsibility to make clear God"s name to the nations. Too often, Israel became no different than the nations. God had called them to be a "holy nation." To be holy meant to reflect God's character and purpose, but they did not (note Ex. 34:33, Josh. 23:7-8, Isa. 26:18). God continuously called His people to purity in order to carry out His purpose. They seemed again and again to fail! The reasons for their failure must be addressed.

Failing the Call

What are the mistakes made by God's people which would not allow them to fulfill the mandate God had given them?

Disobedience

In the first place, the holiness of the people was destroyed by their disobedience. Consider the call for repentance which is repeated again and again (Amos

3:14-15; Isa. 3:8-9; 2 Kings 17:13, et. al.). Jeremiah also called for repentance (Jer. 7:3), as did Ezekiel (Ezek. 14:6). But as with Israel earlier, Judah would not listen (Jer. 25:7).[6]

The Land–A Place for Stumbling

The land itself became a problem for covenant faithfulness. The purpose of the land had been violated. Instead of a prominent model of the community God intended for His people, it was prostituted to the presumption of the people. It was no longer a model for all nations to see, but, rather, merely reflected the same pagan values which the nations already knew so well. It did not present an alternative! What about the land? Indeed the land was part of the covenant promise to Abraham. Unfortunately, the purpose of the land was lost. The land was intended to provide a place where the people of God could learn and demonstrate what holy community was all about. It was not intended as simply a symbol of political power, nor was it provided as an exclusive camp where the people could, with arrogance, praise themselves for deserving such blessings from God. In fact, the narrow interpretation of the land became a major stumbling block for efforts to reach out to other people.

The Land–A Symbol of Hope

God's intent for the land was not that Israel should hide her light from the nations behind her presumptuous arrogance. In fact, even within the Old Testament itself, prophecy depicts the inclusion of those who had no stake in the land. The land too, was meant to point beyond itself to a deeper and more global understand-

---

6. Ibid., p. 109.

ing of the people of God. Both Ezekiel 47:22f., and Isaiah 56:3-8, make clear that, in the new covenant, the land as a literal entity, would give way to something far grander. "In other words, the theological themes of security, inclusion, sharing and responsibility, which were once linked to the land, . . . are loosened from their literal, territorial moorings as the scope of salvation is widened to include non-Jews."[7]

The Land–A Place for Fellowship

The New Testament's discussion of fellowship captures much of the intent of what the land represented in the Old Testament. Note for example, the parallel between Deuteronomy 15:4 and Acts 4:34, where what was represented in sabbatical promise in Deuteronomy, is taken up in the "fellowship" of the early church in Acts 4. What the land stood for has been fulfilled in the community of the church. This section of Scripture in Acts presents a very interesting parallel to the prophecy in Isaiah 56. A time is viewed in which community would embrace all peoples! In the prophecy there is inclusion for the foreigner, in the church this fellowship, in which all things were *koina*, common, breaks down the barriers (Eph. 2:11-3:6). Israel missed the point and made the land a symbol of exclusivity, when God intended it to be part of the "light to the Gentiles." The parallel between the Old Testament "land," and New Testament fellowship, is suggestive.

The early church had to learn the same lessons which Israel was to have learned. The often ignored sixth chapter of Acts fits easily within the context of the expansive idea of God's community. If the church had become as narrow, and, in fact, ethnocentric as

7. Christopher Wright, *An Eye For An Eye* (Downers Grove: InterVarsity Press, 1983), pp. 95-96.

Israel had been, then the church could not have reached into the wider world as the covenant demanded and as Jesus commanded (Acts 1:8). After the nature of fellowship was exhibited in Acts 4, Acts 5 gives positive and negative examples of selfishness and selflessness. Israel had been selfish in her understanding of the land and her blessings; the church had to face the same challenge.

The Land–An Opportunity for an Internalized Focus

Chapter six of Acts presents us with internal conflict. This conflict related to the nature of the community and its ability to cross people barriers. It is as though the church is getting "pre-adoption counseling." If the church could not embrace the two groups, of Hebrew and Hellenist Jews, then, it would seem, that it would have been impossible to embrace the Samaritans, nor the Gentiles! The opportunity to exhibit the universal nature of the purpose of God was again tested as was the case in the Old Testament. The misunderstanding of the land in the Old Testament led to a provincial and arrogant refusal to be the light to the nations. That the land does not have the significance many feel that it should in the New Testament, can be seen in several ways. The land is not a part of the ministry of Jesus; in Stephen's speech in Acts 7, the promise seems to be intentionally represented as not limited to the land (note how often Stephen describes God's activity in other lands; also the Apostle Paul, in Romans 9-11, does not reference the land in what is a vital theological comment concerning Israel and her place in the purpose of God).

The Land–A Misunderstood Global Intent

God's gift of the land was misunderstood by His

people. It became a symbol of arrogance and exclusiveness. During the Monarchy, institutionalization of Israel's faith contributed to idolatry and ethnocentrism. Throughout this time witness to the one, true God was perhaps dulled, but God was not finished with His people or His purpose. God's global intent was still the driving force within Israel's history. This driving force, however, was not by the choice of His people; they were not completely active in this mission. God's resolute purpose to reach the nations would be carried out in spite of His people.

The Land–A Base for a Redemptive Community

The elements of the covenant, both the land and the issue of descendants, were challenged by God's action. Whereas the land was intended as a base for the development of the intended redemptive community, God drove the people out of the land into exile. Instead of the fertile soil of the land providing the context for the people to become strong and a blessing to all, the loss of the land became God's punishment for the failure of His people to reflect his name and holiness to the world. But, even in the midst of God's punishment of His people, and the clear disappointment of God Himself, His global purpose was still in the center of His concern. God forced His people into the world which she had refused to enlighten! The opportunity to carry out the mandate was provided by the exile itself. God's will would not be finally thwarted by His people's unfaithfulness. God was still at work in the midst of this difficult situation of bondage. God punished their failure, but, at the same time, provided the opportunity to become faithful to His purpose again.

God's Prevailing Purpose

God's purpose was resolute and there were clear events which help us see the success of His purpose during these days of exile and return. It is generally held that only around 42,000 people returned from exile. The majority stayed "among the nations." During the exile great examples can be found demonstrating that some were faithful to God's global purpose. The powerful and faithful ministry of Daniel stands as a beacon to the nations. Daniel's impact upon his captor, Nebuchadnezzar, is a powerful example of the "light to the Gentiles." Also, the establishment of synagogues, and the Sabbath observances help us to catch a glimpse of how God's persistent purpose was displayed.

Clear evidence shows a significant expansion of the Jewish faith in the days leading up to the coming of Christ. This expansion evidences the growth of the faith through proselytes, and perhaps God-fearers. Whether we speak of the centrifugal, or the centripetal force of the mission activity, the fact is that the nations were seeing the glory of the one God of all peoples. Imagine the power of observing the worship of the one true God taking place throughout the nations. The attractiveness of God could be seen in the worship and the community of faith. Even though the people did not always seek the expansion of the community, clearly some did at least partly. God was at work. Through the presence of God's people among the nations, people were being prepared for the marvelous work God was planning for the Messiah!

That God's purpose was planned from the beginning, and not subject to the whims of His people is clear from the ministry of His prophets. Even before the exile, the prophets made clear the reasons for God's punishment of the people. They had become tainted by their own arrogance, and reflective of the unholy, pagan attitudes of the nations. They had lost God's will for their own holiness, and had not recognized their "priesthood" to the nations. The people would never enjoy the salvation of God without recognizing the need to reflect His holiness and to reflect His redemptive concern for all people (Dan. 7:13-14; Isa. 11:1-10).

The prophetic message which captures the intent of God for His people corporately, and His ultimate plan to redeem all peoples through the Messiah, can be seen clearly in the prophetic declaration of the "Servant." The theology of the "Servant" can help us see God's intent unfold. There are numerous passages pertaining to the "Servant": Isaiah 41:8,9; 42:1,6-7,19,22; 43:1-3,10,22; 44:8; 49:3-6,22-26; 50:4-6; 53:3-12.

Note the first "Servant Song," Isaiah 42:1-4. Here clearly the servant, His people, would make known the God of justice. In the second song, 49:1-6, the servant assigned to the ends of the earth as "light." In Isaiah 50:4-9, it becomes clear that the "Servant" and the people are contrasted. In the great fourth Song, Isaiah 52:13–53:12, the "Servant" is clearly not the people, but Jesus. The New Testament so identifies the Servant with Jesus in Matthew 8:17; John 12:38; Luke 22:37; and Acts 8:32-35!

What has happened is that there has been a narrowing of God's people, perhaps the seed of Abraham, or, perhaps a narrowing or His redemptive "light to the nations." From Israel, to the faithful remnant, to finally, the Servant. It is by means of the Servant that the nations would receive forgiveness and redemption! This narrowing took place, not to exclude the peoples of the earth, but, rather to expand the peoples. Israel had failed to accept her role as a "light to the nations," even though this purpose was made clear to Abraham at the beginning. The driving purpose of the covenant could not be represented by the possession of land, nor could it be represented exclusively by the physical descendants of Israel. The comment of John as he called for the baptism of repentance of those who presumed to be the people of God, the children of Abraham, is telling. John said that: "out of these stones God can raise up children for Abraham" (Luke 3:8). The presumption of privilege was challenged with demand for faith, not biological but faithful identities!

Israel failed to accept the obligation which God gave to her to be a kingdom of priests. They refused to become the "light to the nations," they did not, therefore, honor the very covenant which they thought made them special. The covenant is focused upon God's missionary purpose. To understand the intent and nature of the covenant is to be captivated by the will of God to be a blessing to all the nations of the earth. Filbeck makes a careful and very important contribution concerning this point. The hermeneutic which alone comes to terms with the covenant is the hermeneutic which understands this missionary intent. In fact, the very reason why Jesus was rejected was likely His insistence that the intent of the covenant was global and that in fulfillment of God's purpose, He, the Messiah, had come to proclaim redemption to all. Throughout the Old Testament, the people of God had been called to give witness to the living God among the nations. The issues of the land and descendants continually became distorted so that Israel failed to be obedient to God's mandate. They were to be holy, set apart to Him, and they were to be distinct from the nations. This distinction was to show the clear contrast between YHWH and the gods of the nations. The very name YHWH implied the personal, living God, and, further, that YHWH was in fact Elohim. The Lord is God of all!

Whether we examine the Exodus, specifically noting Israel's impact upon the Egyptians, or the exile, we see God at work to see that His name would be proclaimed among the nations. God not only blessed the people by calling them to Himself, but, He commissioned them to be "priests" and a "light to the nations." The obligation was clearly theirs, the opportunity provided again and again. The people allowed their own desires and ethnocentrism to distort their understanding of God's covenant. Even though the people failed God remained faithful to His global purpose. The contemporary church faces similar challenges. God has mandated that we be His witnesses to the ends of the earth. When the Apostles asked Jesus about restoring the kingdom to Israel (Acts 1:1-8), they implied the same misunderstandings of the Old Testament peoples. The kingdom is not territory, nor does it pertain to those biologically descended from Abraham. The kingdom is the rule of God, manifested in Jesus and will be consummated at His return. But, this kingdom is to be proclaimed to all nations (Matt. 24:14). In fulfillment of God's covenant promise, we are mandated to be His witnesses to the ends of the earth, to every people!!!!!

3

The Church and the Covenant

Robert Kurka

A record of the genealogy of Jesus Christ the son of
David, the son of Abraham . . . (Matt. 1:1).

These unassuming words introduce the Gospel of
Matthew in a manner surprisingly pregnant with
missiological implications. Specifically, the Messiah
Jesus is clearly identified as the legitimate Davidic
King whose family tree includes Israel's greatest
monarch and the father of the nation, Abraham.
Coupling this opening verse of Matthew with the evangelist's concluding "Great Commission" statement in
28:18-20, a reader can hardly fail to recognize the
missionary theme that runs through this Gospel. The
words, *panta ta ethne*, ("all nations," v. 19) deliberately
echo God's promise to Abraham that the nations will
be blessed through him (Gen. 12:3; cf. also Gen. 18:18
and 22:18 where these exact words are found in the
Septuagint version). Unlike Luke who chooses to trace
Jesus' ancestry to the very first human being, Adam
(also a significant missiological statement!), Matthew
calls attention to Christ in terms of being the fulfillment of the divine promise to Abraham. Jesus was
then a descendant of Abraham who was to bless all
nations. Jesus, following His death and resurrection,
then commits His followers to the worldwide evangelistic task. Consequently, Matthew has set his presentation of Christ within a kind of "missionary inclusio,"

conveying that what we discover between the chapters one and twenty-eight is to be related to the Abrahamic covenant.

Missiological Motif of Jesus' Genealogy

This overriding "missiological motif" is immediately noted in the very presentation of the genealogy itself as Matthew not-so-subtly locates five women in this kingly line: Tamar (v. 3), Rahab (v. 5), Ruth (v. 5), the wife of Uriah ("Bathsheba," v. 5), and of course, Mary, the mother of Jesus (v. 16). Jewish genealogies rarely list women which makes this ancestral list remarkable in its culture. But we would be remiss if we failed to observe the *Gentile* bloodline of these females: Every one of these women were considered non-Jewish in their day, including Mary, who came from Galilee, whose inhabitants were regularly ridiculed by first century Judeans.[1] Matthew's inclusion of these five Gentile women is not so surprising, however, when placed within the context of a Gospel whose opening and closing verses are concerned with global evangelization.

Missiological Inclusiveness in Jesus' Genealogy

The name of "David" in the Matthean genealogy

---

1. See D. A. Carson's excellent discussion of the Matthean genealogy in: "Matthew," *The Expositor's Bible Commentary*, Vol. 8, Frank Gaebelein, editor (Grand Rapids: Zondervan, 1984).

Several scholarly interpretations have been offered concerning the inclusion of these women in the Messiah's family tree, among them that three of the five were involved in gross sexual sin, and the two exceptions (Ruth and Mary) would have been loosely associated with such a stigma. Lohmeyer's understanding of the Gentile ethnicity of the women seems to be the most plausible suggestion, especially in light of an apparent "all nations" theme to the first gospel, which climaxes with the "Commission."

also contributes to the author's missionary intentions. At first glance, the mention of this great king seems to play up the "Jewishness" of Jesus, for indeed, He is to be seen as the ultimate Davidic heir. In chapter two, the magi inquired of King Herod as to the location of the one "who has been born King of the Jews" (2:2), and the written charge placed upon the dying Jesus' crown carried the charge "the King of the Jews" (27:37). The evangelist Matthew, thus, makes no attempt to slight either Jesus' ethnicity or place within Israel's royal house. Jesus is nothing less than the genuine, promised Davidic successor. However, the genealogical notation of David is clearly ethnically *inclusive*, as well, in that David, the King of Israel, was also a recipient of a covenant from God, which was just as global in its blessing as Abraham's. In 2 Samuel 7:19, David recognizes that his everlasting house is, in actuality, a "charter for humanity."[2] David's kingly successors (a "new," more specific, understanding brought to the Abrahamic concept of seed) will not only reign in order to promote Israel's self-interests, but rather to promote universal, Gentile blessing. While it is arguable as to how much the immediate line of Jewish monarchs contributed to God's global witness (Solomon did, to some extent), nonetheless, the eschatological focus of the promise to David (7:12-16)—pointing to the ultimate ruler Jesus—removes any doubt as to the covenant's missiological interests. The Davidic covenant was but a further reaffirmation as well as amplification (the kingly theme) of the *panta ta ethne* mandate of Genesis twelve.

---

2. This is the rendering of 2 Sam. 7:19 given by Walter C. Kaiser, Jr. in *Toward an Old Testament Theology* (Grand Rapids: Zondervan, 1978), pp.149-164. Kaiser has elsewhere defended the "character" translation; cf. "The Blessing of David: A Charter for Humanity" in Skilton, John, ed. *The Law and the Prophets* (Philadelphia: Presbyterian and Reformed, 1974), pp. 298-318.

Universal Blessing in Jesus' Genealogy

Thus, when Matthew begins his genealogical record, connecting Jesus to the bloodline of both Abraham and David, he is not only calling attention to the Christ's role as the promised monarch in the kingly dynasty of Israel but even more importantly relating Him to the "larger" Old Testament covenant of universal blessing; a theme which was just as pronounced in the words spoken to the son of Jesse as they were to the son of Terah. Consequently, when the evangelist concludes his Gospel with the resurrection and commission of the King of the Jews, the mandate "disciple all the nations" proves to be a most fitting way to end a book that introduces itself by recalling God's earlier missionary covenants.

Abrahamic Covenant Fulfillment

The nineteenth-century German Old Testament scholar, Franz Delitzsch, devised an appropriate model to describe the progression of the Abrahamic covenant's fulfillment—from Genesis to Jesus (Matthew's genealogical time-frame) which is helpful in understanding how we as the contemporary "New Testament" church are both beneficiaries and participants in this missionary drama. Delitzsch's so-called "pyramid" (see Figure 1, p. 51) begins with a broad base, presenting the corporate people of Israel, in partial fulfillment of God's promise to Abraham that he would be the father of a nation. In pyramid-like fashion, the lines begin to slope inward as those who are not truly "Abraham's children" (Rom. 9:6,7) vacate the structure, leaving a much smaller "remnant" to represent the line of promise. Eventually, the pyramid reaches a singular peak which is the one, completely obedient Abrahamic descendant, Jesus.

The model does not end there, however, for a

second, upside-down pyramid begins to emerge from this point, with an ever-widening base. This second pyramid is intended to represent the church—"originating" with a few faithful (the apostles) and expanding into Jerusalem, Judea, Samaria, and eventually all Gentile nations (cf. Acts 1:8). The *broad* base of this upside-down figure calls our attention to the future vision of the Revelator as he sees gathered around the Lamb's throne, a great multitude . . . from every tribe, people, and language" (Rev. 7:9).

The Delitzsch model suggests two theological (and missionary) themes that are relevant to our purposes in this chapter: First, the "seed" of Abraham is *singular*. Corresponding to the earlier Genesis 3:15 description of the "seed of the woman," the promise to Abraham includes both a very unique "son" (ultimately, Jesus, the Messiah) as well as a corporate offspring ("Israel"—cf. Ex. 4:22,23, etc.). Israel is more a community of faith (and a multi-ethnic one, at that) rather than a Jewish bloodline.[3] The "seed/seeds" interplay is seen throughout the entire Old Testament, with the corporate line becoming increasingly dependent upon the faithfulness of the one *Messianic*, Abrahamic descendant, for the accomplishment of God's salvific plan.[4] In other words, Christ becomes

---

3. The word "seed" (Hebrew = *zera*) is a collective noun which can refer to both a single descendent or a multitude of descendants. In the Gen. 3:15 promise, we are told of the crushing of Satan—obviously the work of a singular (virgin-born) Deliverer—which in turn, benefits a large group of people, those who ally themselves with the Messianic figure. Likewise, Satan has a "seed" as well (those who follow the serpent's rebellious purposes) who, in turn, will share in his enmity towards the woman's seed as well as in his defeat (Kaiser, *Toward an Old Testament Theology*, pp. 36-37).

4. The "servant" figure in Isaiah refers to an individual as well as the corporate community. H . H. Rowley concludes that the four "servant songs" (Isa. 42:1-4; 49:1-6; 50:4-9; 52:13-53:12) first portray a missionary community, then, the individual Jew, and finally the

the faithful son that Israel never was, or ever could be. The Delitzsch pyramid, as the first figure comes to its final peak, reminds us of Paul's eloquent declaration, that "all the promises of God are 'yes' in Christ" (2 Cor. 1:20), as well as our Lord's own claim to be the *telos* (aim or goal) of the Law and Prophets (Matt. 5:17,18).

On the other hand, the inverted, second pyramid suggests the parallel truth: the seed of Abraham is *plural*. The Christ who, on the one hand, is the perfect *son* of God, makes it possible for those who believe in His name, to themselves become God's children (John 1:12), "sons" who are led by the Spirit (Rom. 8:14) and thus, form the "church (*ekklesia*) of the firstborn" (Heb. 12:23). Because of the Son's perfect obedience, we too have been "adopted" as sons (or, more specifically received the "Spirit of sonship," Rom. 8:15). This adoption brings with it the guarantee of bodily resurrection into a Christ-like immortality (Rom. 8:23; cf. also 1 Cor. 15:42). Along with the salvific privileges of sonship comes a son-like missionary imperative, as well: "As the Father has sent me, I am sending you" (John 20:21). Consequently, the second pyramid figure develops its "base" as it practices its missionary sonship.

The Delitzsch model, then provides us with a visible representation of the Gospel of Matthew: a redemptive story that reaches its apex in the coming of Christ (chapter one), but then proceeds from the promised Son to an worldwide aggregate of sons

---

future One who would complete the mission in a humiliating death (H.H. Rowley, *The Missionary Message of the Old Testament.* London: Carey Kingsgate, 1945, pp. 51-63). This individual/corporate duality of the servant is also the basis of the "Delitzsch pyramid" which is pictured in "Figure 1." This pyramid model was first suggested by Franz Delitzsch in his Isaiah commentary, co-authored with his scholarly cohort, C.F. Keil (cf. C.F. Keil, and F. Delitzsch, *Isaiah, Commentary on the Old Testament in Ten Volumes,* Vol. VII, translated by James Martin (Grand Rapids: Eerdmans, 1973), p. 174.

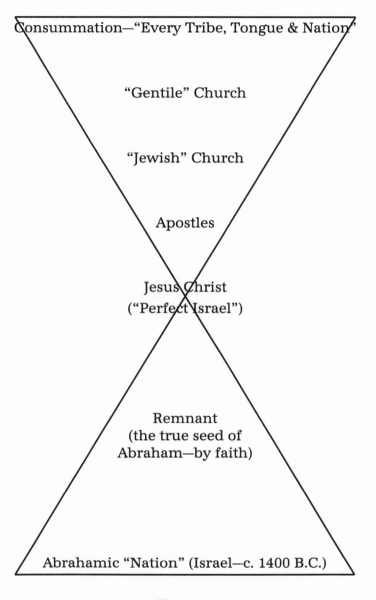

Figure 1
"Delitzsch's Pyramid"

(chapter 28). The overall "hourglass" shape of the twin pyramids further reminds us that we stand on the other side of a missionary people called into being some 4000 years ago; Old Testament children of God, who like their New Testament counterparts are united by a *common* person (Jesus), righteousness (by grace), and purpose. The covenant initiated with Abraham, codified in the Exodus, reaffirmed to David, and brought to completion in Jesus, thus, becomes our covenant as in faith, we become united to this "family tree." The "Great Commission"—both in its Old and New Testament renditions—runs directly to, and through Jesus.[5]

The Missionary Manner of Jesus

For no matter how many promises God has made, they are "Yes" in Christ (2 Cor. 1:20).

Paul's emphatic declarations about Christ—that He is the aim and fulfillment of God's promises—is an extremely intriguing one, given the missionary nature of those promises. Certainly, the death of Christ provides forgiveness of sin for all the world's peoples who believe (Acts 2:38,39); He is both the redeemer of the Gentiles as well as the Jews (3:22-30). This inclusive truth is quite obvious. However, what may not be so

---

5. Both Jesus and Paul suggest that the Biblical (Old Testament) message is centered around two key themes: (1) The Christ will suffer, die, and rise from the dead for the forgiveness of sins; and (2) This message of salvation will be preached to all nations (cf. Luke 24:46,47; Acts 26:23). Likewise, the Lord and His most effective apostle are adamant that this reading of Scripture is in no way at variance with the "prophets and Moses" (Acts 24:22; Luke 24:44)—a common Jewish accusation against Paul. These two themes are readily grounded in Gen. 3:15 and 12:1-3, respectively, and not only run throughout the Old Testament but permeate the New, as well, right up to the very end (cf. Rev. 5:12, 12:9, 20:10 with Gen. 3:15; and 7:9, 20:3, and 21:24 which deliberately corresponds to and fulfills the nations' blessing in Gen. 12:3).

apparent is how Jesus fulfilled God's "all nation" concern, *prior* to His sacrifice on the cross. What I am suggesting is that in Jesus' three-and-one-half year earthly ministry, He intentionally practiced the Abrahamic covenant, blessing not only the house of Israel but many non-Jewish people, as well.

Missionary "Manner" of the Life of Christ

Furthermore, I am convinced that the missionary *manner* exhibited in the life of Jesus later became a model for the later expressions of cross-cultural outreach seen in the early church. Jesus' life of righteousness which perfectly fulfilled the law's demands (Rom. 10:5) included a "neighborly love" which reflected His Father's global desires.[6] Using the Gospel of Luke, this time, let us briefly note how some examples from the earthly ministry of Jesus clearly demonstrate this "all nations" perspective.

Lucan Narrative

The Lucan birth narrative introduces us to a Messiah who comes into the lives of rather ordinary people on the "fringe" of Judaism: the country priest Zechariah; his elderly (and barren) wife, Elizabeth; and a *Galilean* teenager by the name of Mary. Mary would

---

6. In his Romans Commentary, C.E.B. Cranfield comments: "It is possible to understand Paul to be applying the words of Lev. 18:5 not to the impossible, hopeless task which men set themselves when they think to earn a righteous status before God by their own works, but to the achievement of the one Man who has done the righteousness which is of the law in His life, and above all, in His death, in the sense of fulfilling the law's requirements perfectly and so earning us His right a righteous status before God . . ." (Cranfield, *Romans*, Vol. I. Edinburgh: T. & T. Clark, 1975, pp. 522-23). This understanding of Rom. 10:5 makes good theological sense in light of the Old Testament "pyramid" that we have previously discovered.

have been regularly associated with the Gentile people in the minds of the Judean rabbis.[7] Whereas Matthew is fond of relating how Jesus frequently "fulfilled" Old Testament prophecy (cf. 1:22; 2:17,23; et. al.), Luke presents the first advent in the context of "new prophecy"—prophecy which often times comes from the lips of those *outside* the "recognized" Jewish religious circles.

Unpretentious Witnesses

Unpretentious men and *women* become God's mouthpieces in the Messianic era (cf. also Acts 2:17,18) —as His "Gentile" prophets celebrate Yahweh's faithfulness to the Abrahamic covenant (Luke 1:73) and its promised "light to those living in darkness" (v. 79). Furthermore, two additional "little persons" (Simeon and Anna) praise God's "light for revelation to the

---

7. Galilee was considered to be a "backward locale" by the inhabitants of Jerusalem (cf. Acts 2:7) and peculiar due to its strange sounding dialect (Matt. 26:73). It was populated by conservative rural people who were generally suspicious of Pharisaical traditions. The rabbis, on the other hand, were known to make occasional disparaging comments about their less sophisticated northern neighbors (Riesner, "Bethany Beyond the Jordan" in *Tyndale Bulletin* 38 [1987] 29-63). In Green, McKnight, and Marshall, the negative attitudes towards women in first-century Judaism is fairly well-attested in the writings of Josephus, Philo, and the apocryphal Sirach. Josephus, the historian, states that the Law teaches the inferiority of women in all things; therefore, females can no more than be submissive to their male superiors (Ag.Ap. 2:25 - An apparent first century tradition, records 201). A man offering three benedictions each day, including one in which he expresses his gratitude for not being made a woman (t. Ber 7:18). Josephus also notes the inadmissibility of female testimony in legal contexts (Ant, 4:815:219). (Scholer, in Green, McKnight, and Marshall, ed., *Dictionary of Jesus and the Gospels*. Downers Grove: InterVarsity Press, 1992, pp. 880-83) Given her "double negatives" (a Galilean female), it is not surprising to find the expectant Mary and her husband in a room occupied by the animals.

Gentiles" (2:32) as they marvel at the infant, Jesus, after his parents bring him to Jerusalem. The birth story proper also follows this inclusive theme. The *Bethlehem* entrance of the incarnate God is itself due to the decree of a Gentile ruler (2:1), while the first visitors to the divine infant are shepherds, among the most despised classes in Judea.[8] The "Messiah of the outsider" may himself have been the victim of cruel discrimination. A Jewish innkeeper would hardly sentence a "Jewish" mother to a barnyard maternity suite, but he might feel reasonably justified if such a woman betrayed Galilean origins.

Matthew and Luke Genealogical Differences

I have already noted the major difference between the Matthew and Luke genealogies: the former grounds the messianic line in Abraham, whereas the latter traces His origins to the first person, Adam. In this account Luke suggests a missiological motif just as pronounced as that of the first evangelist, especially in a context highlighting the non-Semitic characteristics of the incarnation.[9]

Luke's "All Nations" Perspective

The first three chapters of the Lucan account then

---

8. Strack-Billerbeck's *Kommentar zum Neuen Testament aus Talmud und Midrash* notes that as a class, shepherds were held in low esteem, often exhibiting a tendency to confuse others' property with their own—a "gypsy-like" characteristic (E. Earle Ellis, *The Gospel of Luke*. Grand Rapids: Eerdmans, 1974, p. 80).

9. Perhaps, the most obvious missionary feature of the third gospel is in the identity of its author and recipient (Luke, Theophilus)—both Gentiles. Luke was not an eyewitness to the earthly ministry of Jesus, but rather a non-Jewish convert, concerned about setting his Christ-narrative in the context of "secular" history (cf. 1:5; 2:1ff).

serve to prepare the reader for a messianic mission that will be marked by an ostensible, "all nations" perspective. Let us briefly survey some of these inclusive encounters.

Claims in Nazareth

In Luke 4:14-30, Jesus returns to His hometown, Nazareth ("Galilee of the Gentiles"—Isa. 9:1). There he claims personal ownership of the Isaiah 61 prophecy of the Lord's anointed who comes to bring a holistic redemption to the earth's oppressed. The crowd's incredulity at their local son's message prompts Jesus to recall the Old Testament ministries of Elijah and Elisha who, too, were not received well by their native people, but rather by more spiritually sensitive Gentiles (4:24-27). Walter Liefeld notes that the text does not necessarily call attention to Jewish unbelief, but rather that these prophets were deliberately "sent" (*epemphthe*) to these non-Jews.[10] Therefore, Jesus, likewise is calling attention to a Gentile intentionality in His mission, thus, enraging the "hometown folks" provincial concerns. This reaction reflects irony because these Nazarenes would have been considered outsiders by the Judean establishment.

References to Women

Another "all peoples" note is sounded throughout the third Gospel in the evangelist's many references to *women* involved with the ministry of Jesus. As cited above, the Gospel's first two chapters concludes with the *healing* of a woman (Simon's mother-in-law; 4:38-39). Luke 7 records the raising of a widow's son (7:11-15) as well as Jesus' anointing by, and subsequent forgiveness

10. Walter Liefeld, "Luke" in *The Expositor's Bible Commentary*, Frank Gaebelein, editor (Grand Rapids: Zondervan,1984), p. 869.

of, a "sinful woman" (v. 39). In chapter eight, Luke mentions Jesus' several female "disciples" (Mary Magdalene, Joanna, Susanna, etc., 8:3). Having female "disciples" would have been an aberration in the Jewish culture.[11] Furthermore, females play major roles in Jesus' parables (15:8-10; 18:1-9), His crucifixion (23:27-29), and perhaps, most significantly, as the first witnesses and heralds of the resurrection. This privilege would have defied the "political correctness" of first century Palestine, in that, a woman's testimony was inadmissible in a Jewish court of law.[12] Luke clearly intends his readers to see that our "all peoples" perspective transcends *gender*, as well as ethnic differences.

Self-Designated "Son of Man"

The characteristic self-designation of Jesus (recorded some 80 times in the four Gospels), "Son of Man," is unquestionably a title steeped in an "all nations" theology. Jesus' "Son of Man" understanding comes from the vision of Daniel in Dan. 7:13-14, in which an eschatological human-like divine figure is given authority, glory, and sovereign power" as well as the worship of "all peoples, nations, and men of every language."[13] Jesus couples this futuristic portrait of Daniel with Isaiah's servant figures, thereby establishing a very earthly, *ministry-oriented* dimension to the "Son of Man" concept (cf. Luke 9:44, et.al.). Many commentators have also noted the ambiguity that such a term would convey to Jesus' immediate hearers, who would have been more attracted to a "Messiah" vocabulary, as well as its contemporary nationalistic/political associations.[14] The term "Son of Man," then, was

11. Ibid., p. 905.

12. Ibid., p. 1049.

13. Ellis, *The Gospel of Luke*, pp. 105-106.

14. G.E. Ladd, *A Theology of the New Testament* (Grand Rapids: Zondervan, 1974), pp. 145-158.

less controlled by an unbiblical popularism and given the global context of the Danielic vision, most amenable to a Christ committed to an all peoples/all nations ministry.

Jesus' "All Nations" Teaching

Luke also records Jesus' "all nations" *teaching*; including such varied situations as the rebuke of James' and John's "racist" attitudes (9:51-56), and the cleansing of the Jerusalem temple (19:45-46) because its *inclusive* purpose and structure had been subjugated to Jewish nationalism and instruction about paying taxes due to Gentile rulers (20:20-25). Jesus augmented these didactic occasions with many parables, often featuring *non-Jews* as key characters (cf. parables of the "Good Samaritan," 10:25-37 and the "Tenants," 20:9-19), a "riddle" which predicts that the "vineyard" will be given to others. Christ's missionary instruction is also seen in His "commission of the seventy" (10:1ff) which symbolizes the seventy Gentile nations in the Gen. 10 "table of nations,"[15] as well as in His eschatological discourse which predicts the advent of the "times of the Gentiles" in the near future, an implied period of non-Jewish evangelism that will reach its intended goal (21:24; cf. also Matt. 24:14 and Rom. 11:25).

"Kingdom of God" for All Nations

Integral to the message and ministry of Jesus was His proclamation of the "Kingdom of God" (Luke 4:43, 6:20, 7:28, et al.). This theme had a clear "all nations" nuance as the coming of the kingdom (also known in the Old Testament as the "Day of the Lord") was

---

15. I.H. Marshall, *The Gospel of Luke: A Commentary on the Greek Text* (Grand Rapids: Eerdmans, 1978), p. 415.

understood to be a time when God's covenant would
reach its fulfillment, which, of course, included the
ingathering of the nations (cf. Isa. 11:64-66; Jer. 23:5-6,
31:31-34; Ezek. 37:24; Dan. 2:44, 7:13-14).[16] The eschatological orientation towards the kingdom of first
century Judaism is "expanded" in the life and teaching
of Jesus to include His present Kingdom inaugurating
work as well as the expected final perfection. Ladd
calls this perspective the "mystery of the Kingdom,"
i.e., the Kingdom will work in two different stages.[17]
The dynamic saving reign of God is now here in the
person of Jesus; thus, the future gathering of the
nations has *already commenced*. The gospel of the
Kingdom is related by Jesus to an *holistic* program of
redemption: the sick are healed, the demon-possessed
are cured, and sins are forgiven (cf. 8:1ff; 10:9ff;
16:16ff). This emphasis upon the total person apparently became the model for the early church's
outreach (Acts 4:32; 6:1ff).[18]

"All Peoples" Urban Mission

Jesus' "all peoples" perspective is seen in His urban
mission, as Luke not-so-coincidently records the

---

16. Arthur Glasser in particular, has seen the "Kingdom of God"
theme as much larger than the proclamation of the Servant Jesus.
The "Kingdom," according to Glasser, is the "particular diachronic
theme most seminal to understanding the variegated missions of
the people of God touching the nations" (Glasser, *Kingdom and
Mission: A Biblical Study of the Kingdom of God and the World Mission
of His People*. Unpublished course syllabus. Pasadena: Fuller
Theological Seminary, pp. 9,13).

17. Winter and Hawthorne, *Perspectives*, p. 69.

18. Paul Hiebert has aptly warned against a Western
Reductionism that often occurs in our understanding (and prac-
tice) of the Kingdom (i.e., the relationship between Kingdom-
Church-Evangelism). Hiebert reminds us that the *missio dei* begins
with the *dei*—the King determines the course of the Kingdom (Van
Engen, et.al. *Good News*, pp. 153-60).

Messiah's ministries to the cities: Capernaum (4:31); Nain (7:11); the various "cities and villages" (8:1); "town after town" (8:4). Cities were (are) not only the centers of population but of ethnic and cultural diversity as well.[19] Apparently, a key part of the Messiah's city itinerary included a stop at the local synagogue to teach on the Sabbath day (cf. Luke 4:15,31). This "program" evidently became the paradigm of Paul's own practice of urban missions (cf. Acts 13:14) as well as his "to the Jew, then to the Gentile" (cf. Rom. 1:16; 2:9) evangelistic sequence.

An "all peoples" perspective is gleaned as we note the assortment of Gentiles who are touched and/or participants in the Messiah's mission: the thankful *Samaritan* leper (Luke 17:16); the surrogate cross-carrier, Simon from Cyrene (23:26), an African; and the Roman centurion's "crucifixion-site confessional" and praise of God (23:47). Apparently, the evangelist Luke wanted his readers to appreciate how Jesus affected those on the "outside" of Judaism throughout His ministry.

Cornell Goerner has well summarized the message and ministry of Jesus:

> In all three sections of the Hebrew Bible, the books of Moses, the Prophets, and the Psalms, we found God's concern for all nations of the earth, and His plan for dealing with them through the Messiah. We believe that Jesus mentally "underscored" these passages in His Bible, and planned deliberately to fulfill them by His life, His death, and His resurrection. . . . We find in the Gospels that the words and actions of Jesus confirm this all-inclusive concept of His ministry. The New Testament flows right out of the Old with unbroken continuity. In the distinctive title He chose for

---

19. Cf. Harvie M. Conn, *A Clarified Vision for Urban Mission* (Grand Rapids: Zondervan, 1987).

Himself, in the strategy of His ministry, and in His clear teachings, it is obvious that Jesus undertook a mission for all mankind.[20]

As suggested earlier, Jesus' message to "all nations," as well as its accompanying inclusive attitudes and actions became the model for the early church.

Acts Perspectives

The book of Acts opens with a "forty-day seminar," in which Jesus instructs His apostles in the things concerning the Kingdom of God (Acts 1:3). Their inquiry concerning the "restoration" of the kingdom of Israel (1:6) indicates that these erstwhile followers of Jesus had not yet grasped the "all nations" orientation of a mission which *fulfilled* all that was written in the "Law of Moses, the Prophets, and the Psalms" (Luke 24:44). Consequently, the Christ spoke these explicit, evangelistic words to them as He was about to ascend:

> . . . and you will be my witnesses in Jerusalem, and in all Judea, and Samaria, and to the ends of the earth (Acts 1:8).

Slowly, reluctantly and with the help of the Holy Spirit, the global emphasis resident in the words and deeds of Jesus became the apostles' own: (1) In their preaching as Peter's sermon on the day of Pentecost proclaims a salvation which is for both "you and your children, and for all who are far off" (2:39); (2) In the infant church's concern for the physical welfare of their community. "They gave to anyone as he had need" (2:45). They brought the proceeds of house and land sales to the apostles for distribution to the "have nots" (4:34,35). And, they saw to the needs of their widows including the Grecian Jews as well as the native Palestinians (6:1ff).

---

20. Winter and Hawthorne, *Perspectives*, p. 75.

Beginning in Jerusalem

The commission to witness in *Jerusalem* was in many ways a resounding success. However, this was but an initial step in an evangelistic program of a much larger, multinational nature. This inclusive dimension of the Messiah's ministry and mandate was eventually learned through a series of rather "surprising" if not uncomfortable events. They included a Jerusalem persecution precipitated by the speech and subsequent martyrdom of Stephen (7:1-8:1), evangelistic encounters with Samaritans and Africans (chapter 8ff), a vision of all kinds of animals (10:11) which prompts Peter to genuinely "witness" to non-Jewish people, and a council in Jerusalem (15) which finally concludes that salvation in Christ *transcends* ethnic distinctions (15:12-21), yet does not obliterate them (cf. vs. 24-29).[21]

To the Ends of the Earth

This decision, then, allows the gospel message to freely move to the "ends of the earth" (cf. 28:26-30). Converts were simply asked to "repent and be baptized in the name of Jesus Christ" (2:38) in order to receive both the forgiveness of their sins and the promised indwelling Spirit (v. 39)—a "universal" faith that was transported from Jerusalem to Rome. Thus, a church which, at its inception, had called Jerusalem home, was now able to move its evangelistic "head-

---

21. At the Jerusalem Council, the question of a transcultural gospel message was settled in large part by an Old Testament quotation. The elder James, the half-brother of Jesus, as well as a most traditional Jew, assesses the testimony of the missionary apostles with the words of Amos 9:11-12. The eighth century prophet predicted a time in which a rebuilt "Davidic tent" would, in turn, bring together both Jew and Gentile—a reconciliation which, nonetheless, still protected an identifiable ethnicity.

quarters" to such Gentile cities as Antioch (11:26; cf. also 13:1-3), Ephesus (19:1-22), and eventually to Rome.[22]

The Epistles–Explaining the Gospel's Essential Message

Furthermore, the epistles of Paul bear constant testimony to attempts by both Jew and Gentile, to constrain the transcendent genius of the gospel. In 1 Cor. 15, the apostle reminds his primarily Gentile audience that they are saved only by a gospel that is at its core ("of first importance") the death, burial, and resurrection for our sins (15:3-5) all in accordance with the Old Testament Scriptures. J.C. Beker has called this the "coherent center" of the Pauline Proclamation: the fundamental themes of the gospel which were always

---

22. The book of Acts is structured around six church growth "panels"; each panel concludes with a summary statement concerning the progress of the Gospel. These six divisions (as well as their point of missionary advancement) are as follows:

(1) Acts 1:1-6:7: "So the word of God spread. The number of disciples in Jerusalem increased rapidly and a large number of priests became obedient to the faith" (Jerusalem).

(2) 6:8-9:31: "Then the church throughout Judea, Galilee, and Samaria enjoyed a time of peace. It was strengthened and encouraged by the Holy Spirit, it grew in numbers, living in the fear of the Lord" (Samaria).

(3) 9:32-12:24: "But the word of God continued to increase and spread" (Syria).

(4) 12:25-16:5: "So the churches were strengthened in the faith and grew daily in numbers" (Derbe).

(5) 16:6-19:20: "In this way the word of the Lord spread widely and grew in power" (Ephesus).

(6) 19:21-28:31: "Boldly and without hindrance he (Paul) preached the kingdom of God and taught about the Lord Jesus Christ" (Rome). cf. Longenecker, "Acts," *Expositor's Bible Commentary*, Frank Gaebelein, editor (Grand Rapids: Zondervan, 1981), pp. 231-35.

intact in the apostolic message.[23] This is the message that Paul preaches (v. 11). In his Galatians epistle, Paul decries the "different gospel" which is being shared by the sectarian Judaizers (Gal. 1:7,8). This adulterated gospel not only stands in marked distinction from the apostolic message but also from the gospel preached to Abraham (3:8): "that God would justify the Gentiles by faith." The transcultural gospel was to remain free from Colossian animistic accretions (Col. 1:15-20; 2:15) as well as from the "asceticism" which was threatening the church's existence at Ephesus (1 Tim. 4:1ff). In this way, the message of God's grace in Jesus could be accurately appropriated by every culture.[24]

The mention of this "apostle to the Gentiles" (Acts 9:15) calls us to embark upon one last task in this survey of the church and covenant, that is, to make some observations concerning Paul's missionary principles.

Pauline Strategy

The subject of whether Paul had a definite missionary strategy has long been debated by mission theologians. People like Michael Green and Roland Allen have argued no intentional mission strategy

---

23. Dean S. Gilliland, *The Word Among Us* (Dallas: Word, 1989), p. 57.

24. Dean Gilliland has noted that "the ministry of Paul provides us with the clearest of case studies for contextualization in the New Testament" (Gilliland, *The Word Among Us*, p. 55). This contextualization can be seen in several ways:

(a) Paul's "transitional terminology" (Phrasing theological concepts in several different ways).

(b) Use of mystery cult vocabulary.

(c) Application of secular language to spiritual concepts. (Ibid., p. 57)

Although Paul would readily adapt his message to the needs of the audience, there was always a "coherent center" in place.

exists in Paul's journeys; rather they "evolved" as the Spirit led the apostle to sometimes quite surprising destinations.[25]

The late mission scholar, J. Herbert Kane, begged to differ. In his classic volume, *Christian Missions in Biblical Perspective*, Kane noted nine strategic principles practiced by the New Testament's greatest missionary:

(1) He (Paul) maintained close contact with the home church base.
(2) He confined his efforts to four provinces.
(3) He concentrated on large cities.
(4) He made the synagogue the scene of his chief labors.
(5) He preferred to preach to responsive peoples.
(6) He baptized converts on confession of their faith.
(7) He remained long enough in one place to establish a church.
(8) He made ample use of fellow workers.
(9) He became all things to all men.[26]

Whether or not one accepts everyone of Kane's observations or his analysis in general, it is nonetheless, interesting to compare these "strategies" to the missionary life of Jesus. Not a few of Paul's "principles" relate directly to the "all nations/all peoples" perspective exhibited in the ministry of Christ. I

25. Roland Allen comments, "It is quite impossible to maintain that St. Paul deliberately planned his journeys beforehand, selected certain strategic points at which to establish his churches and then actually carried out his designs" (Allen, *Missionary Methods*, p. 10). In this writer's estimation, it is more difficult to believe that a certain degree of planning was not involved in the Apostle's missionary ventures. The definable characteristics of the Pauline mission (cf. Kane) are hard to account for in terms of purely spontaneous activity.

26. J. Herbert Kane, *Christian Missions in Biblical Perspective* (Grand Rapids: Baker, 1976), pp. 74-84.

believe that the above list mirrors the Messiah's own approach enough that some degree of intentionality has to be accepted.

Samuel Escobar, on the other hand, has suggested that the Pauline missiology is best understood as a fourfold enterprise. Taking Romans 15:11-33 as a "paradigmatic" text, Escobar sees a mission strategy which includes: proclaiming (vv. 17-22), envisioning (vv. 23-24), completing (vv. 25-29), and struggling (vv. 30-31).[27] This final observation ("struggling") is a poignant reminder about the *cosmic* dimensions of the mission—a consciousness that Paul manifests throughout his writings (cf. Eph. 6:10-20; Col. 2:8ff; 2 Thess. 2:3ff).

Another view of the Pauline mission is offered by C. Timothy Carriker in a provocative article entitled "Missiological Hermeneutic and Pauline Apocalyptic Eschatology."[28] Carriker argues that Paul's ambitious missions program is primarily fueled by an *apocalyptic* vision. This futuristic focus (salvation of his Jewish kinsmen) will come to pass only after the Gentiles have heard (Rom. 11). Consequently, the apostle is driven to preach the gospel where "Christ has not already been named" (Rom. 15:20). Carriker has brought to light an emphasis that is often ignored in our missions theology, perhaps due to a desire to distance ourselves from dispensational connotations. An objective understanding of the Pauline Mission must come to grips with the apostle's eschatological anticipation of Jewish converts (Rom. 11:25, 26).

In an attempt to synthesize and summarize the above analyses of the Pauline principles, let me suggest the following theses:

---

27. Charles Van Engen, Dean S. Gilliland, and Paul E. Piersom, eds., *The Good News of the Kingdom: Mission Theology for the Third Millennium* (Maryknoll, NY: Orbis Books, 1993), p. 57.

28. Ibid., pp. 45-55.

Paul was a "frontier" missionary. He determined that he would not build on another's foundations, but rather take the message of Christ where it was not known (Rom. 15:20).

Paul "championed" a missionary partnership between two discernible entities: the local congregation and the missionary band (cf. Acts 13:2). These structures were "descendants" of the Jewish synagogue and Jewish proselytizers,[29] and served to enrich and nourish each other. The missionary band (or its contemporary mission agency) was dependent upon the recognition, prayers, and finances of the local body of Christ. It was accountable to the sending church, yet maintained a certain autonomy to determine how the gospel would best penetrate its "foreign" culture.

Paul practiced a *missionary theology*, that is, he continually applied biblical doctrine to the changing contexts of the mission field. This last principle is actually an important hermeneutic application. It reminds us that he was less concerned about writing systematic theology than he was in "contextualizing" important Scriptural *principles* for emerging churches.[30] Paul was not a theological relativist, but rather one who made the absolutes of theology relevant to specific cultures and their missiological needs.[31] Thus, Paul could be more accurately called a "task theologian."

Revelation and the Covenant

We could hardly conclude this study about the Abrahamic covenant's New Testament "conscience"

---

29. Winter and Hawthorne, *Perspectives*, pp. 46-47.

30. Cf. David Hesselgrave and Edwin Rommen, *Contextualization: Meaning, Methods, and Models* (Grand Rapids: Baker, 1989).

31. On the occasional nature of epistolary literature, cf. G. Fee and D. Stuart, *How to Read the Bible for All its Worth* (Grand Rapids: Zondervan, 1992), pp. 45-60.

without turning to the words of the Bible's final book.

Prior to the opening of the final seal, the Revelator provided his beleaguered, and to some extent, "bored" Christian audience a picture of the outcome of their labors:

> After this I looked and there before me was a great multitude that no one could count, from every nation, tribe, people and language, standing before the throne and in front of the Lamb (Rev. 7:9).

The meaning of this vision was clear: the covenant that God had made with Abraham so many centuries ago—that he and his seed would bring blessing to all the world's "families"—was the same covenant that had become the church through Jesus. Furthermore, this covenant of universal blessing was guaranteed to succeed in all its fullness. This vision was to be firmly implanted in the readers' minds, so that when John could then call upon them to "overcome" the adversary and his allies, they would be faithful to their missionary obligations, even to the point of death.

Sadly, however, the apostles' impassioned summons largely went unheeded (if not in that generation, most certainly in a later one) as a contemporary, "spiritual map" of "Asia Minor" reveals a terrain largely foreign to the worship of the Son of Man. Today's lack of a Christian "East," in reality represents a breach in the church's contractual agreement with God. My hope and prayer is however, that our generation will not so easily forsake its covenantal obligations, as in the power of the Holy Spirit, we press on to "finish the task."

4
God's Determined Purpose

Stephen E. Burris

Look at the nations and watch—
and be utterly amazed.
For I am going to do something in your days
that you would not believe,
even if you were told.
—Habakkuk 1:5

Introduction

Beginning with Genesis 12:3 God clearly communicates his central character as a missionary God. Since God is a missionary God, a review of the expansion of Christianity should reveal the church fulfilling God's purpose and plan.

First, a preliminary overview of the history of the church shows how God moves through his people, using both strength and weakness. At times surprising individuals have made major contributions to the expansion of the world Christian movement. This employment is in direct fulfillment of 1 Cor. 1:26-29,

Brothers, think of what you were when you were called. Not many of you were wise by human standards; not many were influential; not many were of noble birth. But God chose the foolish things of the world to shame the wise; God chose the weak things of the world to shame the strong. He chose the lowly things of this world and the despised things—and the things that are not—to nullify the things that are, so that no one may boast before him.

Secondly, the Holy Spirit empowers God's mission. In Acts we see the Holy Spirit as the initiator of the mission movement. Examples include how Philip brought the gospel to Gaza, Acts 8; how Peter was used to introduce the gospel to the Gentiles, Acts 10; the Holy Spirit leads the Antioch church to "separate Saul and Barnabas," Acts 13; at the conclusion of the Council of Jerusalem, Paul and Silas are told to go West, to Macedonia, to Europe, Acts 15.

Thirdly, God's purpose is to reach all nations. Matthew 28:19 has been called the Great Commission. In fact this is a restatement of the Commission given to Abraham in Genesis 12:1-3. The Psalmist (67:2) reminds us that God "has made his way known upon the earth, his saving power among all nations." Paul in Romans 16:26 declares the gospel is to be made known "to all nations, according to the command of the eternal God." Revelation 5:9 and 7:9 give a glimpse into the throne room of heaven, a clear enough view to show representatives from every tribe and language and people and nation.

Fourth, God has ordained the church as the "body," "temple," "family," "people of God," to be the representation of God's love, the proclaimer of his kingdom among the nations, *laos tou theou* (people of God) going to *ta ethne* (the nations).[1]

One weakness in a study of history is cultural bias of the author. Church history or other history written by a Western scholar will almost invariably show a Western bias. Much of the historical record readily

---

1. See Charles Van Engen, *God's Missionary People: Rethinking the Purpose of the Local Church* (Grand Rapids: Baker, 1991).

available comes from the West. This bias leaves the impression that the early church grew out from Jerusalem to Judea to Samaria to the Roman Empire to Europe to England, the New World and so forth. The reality is Christianity went out from Jerusalem in virtually all directions. A careful reading of the peoples present on Pentecost gives evidence of representatives from Africa and the Middle East. While the biblical and historical record shows a greater emphasis on the West, we should be aware that the expansion of the world Christian movement was global from the beginning. This expansion included similarities with the patterns of expansion in the West such as periods of advance followed by setbacks.[2] Latourette asserts Christianity may have found its strongest numerical strength in North Africa and Asia Minor.[3]

One example is the Parthians, also known as the Persians. Representatives of this people were present at Pentecost, Acts 2:9. Foster writes, "For nearly 500 years, from 240 BC to AD 225, the Parthians, whose first home had been south-east of the Caspian Sea, ruled all the territory from Mesopotamia to the frontiers of India."[4] The written record supports a church being built as early as AD 135. Eddessa and Abiabene were key strongholds. Foster summarizes, "The *Chronicle* names seventeen sees (i.e., seats of a bishop's rule) which were established before the end of the Parthian period. Then follow these words: 'and there were bishops in other cities too.'"[5]

Another example comes from Africa. The Acts of the Apostles mentions representatives of peoples in

---

2. Pablo Dieros, Presentation, Jan. 1995.

3. Kenneth Scott Latourette, *The First Five Centuries* (Grand Rapids: Zondervan, 1970), p. 91.

4. John Foster, *Church History I: AD 29-500 The First Advance* (London: SPCK, 1972), p. 92.

5. Ibid., p. 95.

Egypt and the parts of Libya belonging to Cyrene (Acts 2:10). We also have record of the Ethiopian eunuch and Philip recorded in Acts 8. Ethiopia claims to be the oldest continuing Christian country in the world.[6]

With this expanded perspective in mind we turn to examine the expansion of the world Christian movement. This chapter examines the history of the church from Pentecost to approximately 1800 AD in three time periods. The division of these periods follow those suggested by Kenneth Scott Latourette in his massive seven volume work, *The History of the Expansion of Christianity*. It also assumes nine theses proposed by Paul E. Pierson. Pierson's theses include the following:

1) that God's redemptive mission has been worked out in history through the normative use of two structures,
2) that the renewal of the church and its expansion are interlinked,
3) that renewal and expansion happen when the historical/contextual conditions are right,
4) that renewal and expansion are frequently triggered by a key person,
5) that renewal and expansion are often accompanied by theological breakthroughs,
6) that renewal and expansion are often accompanied by new spiritual dynamics or re-contextualised forms of spirituality,
7) that renewal and expansion are contagious in contexts where information is easily distributed,
8) that renewal and expansion are often seen to have been accompanied by new leadership patterns,
9) that renewal and expansion are often seen to have begun on the periphery of the ecclesiastical structures of the day.[7]

---

6. Ibid., p. 107.

7. Paul E. Pierson, "Historical Development of the Christian Movement." Fuller Theological Seminary, syllabus and lecture outlines, 1990.

It is not our intention to attempt in one chapter to give a comprehensive overview of eighteen centuries of expansion, but to identify a few important movements and key individuals within those movements.

People's Movement, 1-500 AD

There were only a few prominent missionaries during this period. One is Ulfilas who in 350 became a missionary to the Goths and led a breakthrough to reach the barbarian tribal peoples. This breakthrough was the beginning of widespread evangelization. Specifically, Ulfilas stressed the importance of presenting the gospel to the hearts of the people. One way of accomplishing this was to speak the language of the people. Of his efforts Foster writes, "Ulfilas had grown up bilingual, so he knew what to do: take Greek letters to write Gothic sounds. And so he produced his Gothic Bible. It was the first book in the whole German family of languages, to which, later, English would belong."[8]

During this period, the movement was not led by missionaries, but by ordinary Christians moving from province to province, sometimes to escape persecution. Often this effort was outside the main stream of church activity.[9] Soldiers became Christians and carried the good news to the outposts of the Empire. It would be a mistake, however, to confine the movement to the lower classes. Justin Martyr is an example of the educated class accepting Christ. Clearly, Christianity had penetrated all social/economic classes, but the lower classes tended to dominate.

Persecution was important to the expansion of Christianity. Christians knew how to die nobly. Every Christian lived with the realization that at some point

---

8. Foster, *Church History I*, p. 122.

9. Winter and Hawthorne, *Perspectives*, pp. 845-857.

he or she might be killed. No church, however, was subjected to continuous persecution.[10]

In contrast to the general breakdown in society, the Christians demonstrated a new lifestyle. This lifestyle was characterized by Christian communities that demonstrated love and emphasis on the family. The Christians became known, even among their enemies, for their loving service and care for others, especially those in the church. More important than numbers was the character and quality of the Christians.

Rapid Growth of the Movement

Evidence suggests the apostle Thomas carried the gospel to India during the first century. We have evidence that the church was planted in Ethiopia from 325 AD.[11] Patrick expanded Christianity's movement into Ireland. Other countries and regions were introduced to the gospel during this first period.

Why has Christianity endured? Latourette suggests six reasons why Christianity expanded and stood in spite of incredible obstacles, including

the endorsement of Constantine. . .

the disintegration of society. . .

the organization which it developed. . .

its inclusiveness. . .

Christianity was both transigent and flexible. . .

Christianity supplied what the Graeco-Roman world was asking of religion and philosophy, and did it better than any of its competitors.[12]

---

10. See Stephen Neill, *A History of Christian Missions* (Baltimore: Penguin Books, 1964), p. 43.

11. Edgar J. Elliston, "An Ethnohistory of Ethiopia: A Study of Factors that relate to the Planting and Growth of the Church." Fuller Theological Seminary, M.A. Thesis, 1968.

12. Latourette, *The First Five Centuries*, pp. 163-165.

By the end of the first three centuries, in spite of the fact that Christianity was not officially recognized, all the main areas of the Roman Empire had an active Christian witness.[13]

In the year 311 Emperor Constantine issued the Edict of Toleration. At this time about 10% of the population of the Roman Empire was Christian. That the church was growing in spite of persecution is evidenced by the fact that in 250 AD the church at Rome had 30,000 members.[14]

A new situation existed after Constantine. The church is in culture, but the penetration is both ways. As both Pierson and Neill point out, this growth provided new opportunities to penetrate culture with the gospel, but it also opened the way for new temptations and dangers of cultural penetration of the church.[15] "With a new freedom, the Church was able to go out into the world; at the same time, a new and dangerous fashion, the world entered into the Church."[16]

Shortly after the Edict of Toleration, persecution began in Persia. This persecution had its roots in what Foster describes as foreign policy.

> In foreign policy, the Persians recognized the Romans as successors to the Greeks, i.e. as Persia's traditional enemy. So there began in 225 four centuries of Persian-Roman strife: disputed territory, frontier raids, invasion, [and] war.[17]

The Christians in Persia were vulnerable after Constantine because they were now suspected of

---

13. Ibid., p. 100.
14. Ibid., p. 95.
15. Pierson, "Historical Development," p. 11.
16. Neill, *A History of Christian Missions*, p. 47.
17. Foster, *Church History I*, p. 97.

belonging to the religion favored by the Romans. This situation was created as a Roman Emperor openly demonstrated his pleasure with the large numbers of Christians in Persia. The reaction of the Persian authorities was predictable. The obvious question was, whose side are the Christians on, Rome's or Persia's? The most surprising aspect is the length of time it took the Persian authorities to begin the persecution.[18]

The resulting persecution beginning in about AD 339 perhaps surpassed any the church suffered in the Roman Empire.[19]

Importance of Church Leaders

Several important church leaders emerged during this period. The first was Justin Martyr. Justin Martyr's most enduring contributions include his *Apologies* and *Dialogue with Trypho*. In contrast to the immorality associated with some religious rites, he stated that the *Logos* was made flesh in order to free individuals from evil. In his *Dialogue with Trypho* Justin places Christianity in the stream of Jewish thought, and its successor.

Tertullian, as another influential leader, formulated what came to be knows as the Trinity formula. In the process he maintained the Messianic character of the Son and His atoning work on the cross.

Origen was a third important leader. As part of the school in Alexandria, he insisted on scholarship in the church. He believed that knowledge contributed to the understanding of truth that culminated in theology. Some consider Origen as the greatest scholar in the history of the church.

Augustine impacts Christianity to this very day.

18. Ibid., pp. 97-98.
19. Ibid., p. 99.

Augustine was a champion of the doctrine of grace. His *Confessions* and *The City of God* are considered among the world's great books. In *The City of God* Augustine contrasted two cities, the church and the world, and showed how they were in opposition to each other. He suggested that events work out for the good of the church. Following Romans 8:28, Augustine showed what the world considers to be bad can be used by God for good. Foster notes "The teaching of the *City of God* is that the Church, on pilgrimage through history, is that which gives meaning to history, and that the end of its pilgrimage is *beyond* history, the Church Triumphant."[20]

Neill lists several human factors that contributed to the spread of Christianity during this first period, a period he notes as miraculous.

> First and foremost we must reckon with the burning conviction by such a great number of the earliest Christians were possessed. . . unshakable assurance that in face of every obstacle men can be won and must be won for Christ, which was the mainspring of the whole enterprise. . . Thirdly, the new Christian communities commended themselves by the evident purity of their lives. . . . Finally, we must consider the effect of the persecution of the Christians on popular opinion about them.[21]

Middle Ages, 500-1500 AD

This period has been labeled the "dark ages" because of the fall of the old civilization known as Rome. Additionally, a new foe, Islam, would also appear and threaten the Empire and the church. Latourette summarizes the problem as both internal and external.

---

20. Ibid., p. 129.
21. Neill, *A History of Christian Missions*, pp. 39-42.

The Roman Empire suffered from both internal weaknesses and external pressures. We have already noted that the weaknesses in part ante-dated the coming of Christianity, that they were for a time allayed by the imperial system inaugurated by Augustus Caesar, but that from the end of the second century they began again to be apparent, were aggravated, and multiplied. The external pressures were by invaders who took advantage of the internal decay to overrun most of the Empire.[22]

Breakup of the Empire

Two important invasions usher in this period and help bring about the fall of Rome. The first, in 410 AD, was by the Visigoths. The second, in 455 AD, was by the Vandals. The church appeared to gain ground, however. Some historians give credit to Leo I, also know as Leo the Great. He centralized the government of the Western Church and had influence on the Eastern Church. Under Leo and his successors the church was the most stable institution and provided security during a time when the Roman Empire was breaking up.

Islam

The setback initiated by Islam is the greatest in the history of the church. Not only did large areas convert to Islam but the very advance of Christianity in other regions was threatened by surrounding the Christian strongholds. As a result many countries were permanently lost to Christianity such as Christian strongholds including Syria, Palestine and North Africa.[23]

---

22. Kenneth Scott Latourette, *A History of Christianity* (New York: Harper Brothers Publishers, 1953), p. 270.

23. John Foster, *Church History II AD500-1500: Setback and Recovery* (London: SPCK, 1974), pp. 11-12.

Islam enjoyed two periods of great success. The first was in the seventh and eighth centuries when the Arabs controlled Arabia, Syria, Mesopotamia, Persia, Palestine, Egypt, North Africa, and the Iberian Peninsula. The second was at the end of the thirteenth and the beginning of the fourteenth century when the Mongols of Chinese Turkestan adopted Islam. This effectively shut off the peoples east of the Euphrates to Christianity.[24]

While attempts to regain what was lost to the Muslims were launched, most notably the Crusades, in most areas the loss was permanent.

Mongols

Christianity appears to have faded from China about 900. The Nestorian version of Christianity had spread out across Central Asia and by 635 Christianity had reached China. Beginning at this point and continuing until about 900 China was probably the wealthiest and most civilized empire in the world.[25]

Monasticism was very influential in China. A significant difference is obvious in this form of monasticism, however. Unlike Europe where the monk was likely the most highly educated, and perhaps one of few literate individuals, in China the monks lived among a highly civilized population and in competition with other religious systems, most notably Buddhism.

When the Mongols appear, an important change takes place in the way missionaries conduct their work. The Mongols were nomads. If the missionaries were to evangelize these peoples, they would need to adopt a nomadic way of life as well.

---

24. Kenneth Scott Latourette, *The Thousand Years of Uncertainty* (Grand Rapids: Zondervan, 1970), p. 288.

25. Neill, *A History of Christian Missions*, p. 95.

Genghis Khan, considered by some to be one of the most remarkable conquerors in history, set out to invade China in 1211. On the positive side, he decreed that deference be shown to all religions.[26] Foster reports that under Kublai Khan the Mongol Empire was the "widest that the world had ever known, stretching from the China Sea westward to the river Danube, and from the Ural mountains south to the Himalayas."[27]

Christianity missed an incredibly important opportunity during this period. Kublai Khan, Genghis Kahn's grandson, requested that the Pope send a hundred missionaries. In response Pope Gregory X sent two Dominican Friars, who travelled with Marco Polo, but turned back before reaching China.[28]

Not all was lost, however. One notable breakthrough came through the efforts of a Franciscan missionary. By 1294 John of Monte Corvino, perhaps the first missionary to reach China, arrived in Khanbalik (Peking). He was allowed to build a church and by 1305 he claimed to have baptized 6,000 persons. The report of John's success provided motivation to send additional missionaries to China.[29]

Summarizing this important period Foster writes of what might have been if the Pope had sent a hundred missionaries.

> If it had happened, Christianity would have been reinvigorated by this mission-of-help, and might have spread from Mongols and other non-Chinese peoples to the Chinese themselves and so have survived in China. It might even have spread to the Mongols of central Asia, before Babar led them over the

---

26. Ibid., p. 120.

27. Foster, *Church History II*, p. 80.

28. Ibid.

29. Latourette, *Thousand Years*, p. 332.

Himalayas in 1526 to found a kingdom in Hindustan, and permanently plant their religion there. The history of all Asia might have been different.[30]

Crusades

The Crusades were not primarily for the spread of Christianity or for regaining the peoples lost to Islam. Pope Urban II stated the objective as rescuing the holy places in Palestine, defending Christians in the East, and pushing back the Islamic conquest.[31]

The purposes of the Crusades were only partially fulfilled. One negative result was the growth of bitter feelings between the Muslims and Christians. These feelings exist to the present day. Not all was negative, however. For the first time the Crusades attempted to bring Christians together to act in a cause. Also they opened the routes to the East.[32]

Celtic Missionaries

The great contribution of the Celtic monastic movement is evidenced in its fervent missionary activity and its commitment to learning. The Celtic church was unique. The center was the monastery. In spite of the episcopal nature of the Irish church, the abbot was clearly the key leader, not the bishop.[33] Two individuals stand out as a key to understanding this movement and its contribution to the advance of the church.

At the age of 40 Patrick decided to return to Ireland. During the next 30 years he organized 200 churches, and is credited with 100,000 converts. He contributed to the organized structure of the churches on Northern

---

30. Foster, *Church History II*, p. 171.

31. Latourette, *Thousand Years*, p. 317.

32. Foster, *Church History II*, pp. 76-77.

33. Neill, *A History of Christian Missions*, p. 57.

Ireland and to some degree he helped establish relationships with churches on mainland Europe. One important characteristics of the monasteries during this period was their missionary achievement.

Columba settled on the tiny island of Iona and built a very simple monastery. According to Latourette, Columba spent his time with study, prayer, writing, fasting, and watching. Describing the monastery Latourette says, "It was more in the nature of a centre in which missionaries could be trained and from which they could conveniently be sent forth."[34] Columba was involved in the training of Celtic Missionaries. He also made frequent missionary journeys to Scotland.

Roman Missionaries

Pope Gregory the Great was instrumental in bringing the English Church into fellowship with Rome. He worked to set up dioceses similar to the pattern on the European continent. England, in turn, sent out missionaries to the European mainland, particularly to Holland and Germany. Several orders were founded for the purpose of expanding Christianity. While several orders were organized for the purpose of teaching, others were formed for missionary purposes. Creative ideas were employed to enlist the laity in missions. The most widespread was the Society for the Propagation of the Faith. Boniface stands out during this period of advance.

Many consider Boniface, also known as Winfrith, the greatest missionary of this period. He planned and calculated, strategized that the gospel should be preached to those still considered barbarous peoples.[35]

---

34. Latourette, *Thousand Years*, p. 53.
35. Neill, *A History of Christian Missions*, p. 74.

Boniface was instrumental in developing rules and practice of penitential discipline.[36]

Reflecting on the status of the expansion at this point Foster writes,

1. The conversion of northern Europe was almost completed by about 1000. 2. The first answer to the challenge of Islam was offered about 1100. The answer was neither decisive nor fully Christian, but at least western Christendom had sufficiently emerged from the Dark Ages to feel that it could do something about the Muslim menace. 3. The Friars found a more excellent way, soon after 1200. Better than the Crusades, this movement of renewed Christian zeal came to express itself in mission in North Africa and the east. 4. The chance given to win the Mongol rulers of Asia, just before 1300, seems to have been one of the biggest missionary opportunities of all time.[37]

Reformation/Pietistic Movement, 1500-1800 AD

Several advances are noteworthy during this third period. As in the previous two sections, individuals tended to lead the way, and often outside the main stream of the church's activities.

Francis Xavier

Xavier is considered by many to be one of the best known Roman Catholic missionaries and one of the most successful missionaries in history. At the heart of his missionary activity Xavier taught followers three important documents: The Ten Commandments—

---

36. Ibid., p. 77.

37. John Foster, *Beginning From Jerusalem* (New York: Association Press, 1956), p. 52.

Morals; The Lord's Prayer—Devotion; The Apostle's Creed—Doctrine.

Neill writes concerning an incident early in Xavier's life.

> To a passionate but disciplined nature, profound devotion, and an eager longing for the salvation of souls, Xavier added the wide outlook of the statesman and the capacity of the strategist for organization on a large scale. He went to India in 1542, not as an ordinary missionary but as the representative of the king of Portugal, armed with considerable powers, and with the right to correspond directly with the king.[38]

Matthew Ricci

Ricci was largely responsible for pioneering the Jesuit mission work in China. Early he realized that in order to gain a foothold for Christianity he needed to gain the favor and friendship of the ruling classes. He was able to accomplish this goal through several means.

> Indeed, it was through their scientific knowledge and mechanical skill, especially in the realm of mathematics, the making of maps, and the regulation of the calendar, that the Jesuits were henceforth to acquire and to hold most of that respect which assured to them and to missionaries of other orders whatever opportunity was theirs to propagate the faith in the Middle Kingdom.[39]

Ricci's methods bear a surprising contemporary perspective. He adopted the dress of a Confucian scholar and attempted to contextualize his message

---

38. Neill, *A History of Christian Missions*, p. 148.

39. Kenneth Scott Latourette, *Three Centuries of Advance* (Grand Rapids: Zondervan, 1970), p. 340.

and the worship to fit the Chinese milieu whenever possible. This approach was not lost on those he sought to influence. "He had become Chinese in dress, manners, and speech, and had won friends among the officials by his wide knowledge, so different from their wholly literary education.[40] Of this strategy Latourette writes,

> Thus he rendered it possible for one reared in the Confucian tradition to become a Christian without being disloyal to two institutions esteemed by the Chinese as basic. Ricci was, in other words, endeavoring to meet the solid opposition offered by the structure of Chinese life by maintaining that Christianity was not antagonistic either to the family or the state, and that it was congenial to much in the Classics. Ricci wished, too, to adapt for Christian uses the pagoda, prominent in the Chinese landscape, and to have the form of Christian worship as nearly Chinese as possible.[41]

Ricci enjoyed great success. He established a mission in the capital and had access to the very center of the Empire and to those in authority.

Robert De Nobili

Using a similar strategy to that of Ricci, Nobili believed that if the higher classes were brought to Christ the common peoples would follow. This contextualized strategy included the following elements:

> So far as he could do so without what he believed to be compromise of essential Christian principles and practices, he adopted Indian methods and customs and accommodated himself to Indian prejudices. He lived like an Indian holy man or *sannyasi*, and later,

---

40. Foster, *Beginning From Jerusalem*, p. 88.
41. Latourette, *Three Centuries of Advance*, p. 341.

more like an Indian *guru*, or teacher. He adopted the vegetarian diet deemed by the Hindus consistent with the religious profession and employed a Brahmin cook. In conformity with the custom of the Indians, he admitted only Brahmins to his meals, although he would eat with other missionaries.[42]

He was criticized for the use of these methods, primarily from other missionaries. Nobili's methods were successful. He baptized more than a thousand adults each year.[43] While he concentrated on the Brahmin class, the majority of the Christians were from the lower classes.

Reformers and Missions

Not much missionary activity took place in the early years of the Reformation. Foster cites two reasons why the church was slow to respond.

First, the Reformation affected the small weak countries of northern Europe, still concerned about their own independence, rather than the great powers reaching out over the world for trade and empire. . . . Second, in most countries Protestants had to struggle so long in self-defense against Roman Catholics in power that they grew accustomed to an attitude of self-regarding.[44]

One notable exception was the Moravians. In its early years this movement was composed of refugees. Nicolaus Ludwig, Count of Zinzendorf provided a place for these refugees to settle at Herrnhut. Ludwig was a Pietist and had been educated at the University of Halle. Several factors make this group unique.

---

42. Ibid., p. 260.
43. Ibid., pp. 261-262.
44. Foster, *Beginning From Jerusalem*, p. 74.

Herrnhut developed its own form of pietism, with a deep devotion to the crucified Redeemer and an intense and strenuous demand for total surrender and consecration to his will. Under the leadership of Zinzendorf this small Church was seized with a missionary passion which has never left it. The Moravians have tended to go to the most remote, unfavorable, and neglected parts of the surface of the earth. Many of the missionaries have been quite simple people, peasants and artisans; their aim has been to live the Gospel, and so to commend it to those who have never heard it.[45]

The beginning point for missionary activity was in 1732 and the Greenland mission. Foster reports that "this small denomination has maintained the highest standard of missionary giving in Christendom."[46]

The influence of the Moravians is seen in other areas besides missionary activity. John Wesley was greatly influenced by his contact with this group. They also contributed to worship through a distinct liturgy and hymnology.[47]

Others, such as Spencer, Francke, Ziegenbalk, and Plutchau, also contributed but space does not allow a summary of their activities. It is sufficient to suggest that Pietism leading to the Great Awakening had great impact on the missionary activities of the church at the close of this period.[48]

The Roman Catholic mission efforts of this period were not terribly creative. The missionaries, for the most part, came from the monastic orders, most of which had developed in Medieval Europe. Most of the

---

45. Neill, *A History of Christian Missions*, p. 237

46. Foster, *To All Nations*, p. 19.

47. Latourette, *A History of Christianity*, p. 897.

48. See Max Ward Randall, *The Great Awakenings and the Restoration Movement* (Joplin, MO: College Press, 1983).

gains in membership came as a result of inclusion of tribes or castes incorporated as European dominance spread out over the rapidly expanding colonial lands.

Conclusion

Throughout the history of the expansion of Christianity four missiological principles emerge. The first is the church and school work together. Missionaries were more often than not at the forefront of education, literacy, translation and other activities that brought learning along with the gospel. As the church expanded schools opened centering on the particular needs of the people. In cases like Ricci education was used as a strategy to open doors of opportunity.

The second principle is the Bible is in the language of the people. From the earliest periods putting the Bible in the language of the people or the heart language has been evident. We have only noted a few examples, but the history of the expansion of the Christian movement is full of translation activity, beginning from about the middle of the third century A.D.

The third principle is that preaching is aimed at conversion and on the needs of the people. The incarnational model is clearly evident. Ricci and Nobili both underscore the importance of contextualizing the gospel message. While this is commonly accepted today, these pioneers, as well as others, were instinctively applying high level missiology.

And finally an indigenous ministry is developed as soon as possible. Missionaries realized the importance of leadership development. This along with the emphasis on education helped to secure the gains, often beyond the life and work of the missionary or mission.

While the history of the expansion of Christianity is a story of advances and setbacks, we can clearly see that in every age key individuals appeared who understood that God is a missionary God and attempted to expand Christian influence. Often our picture as been distorted since we haven't seen the entire landscape clearly. While Christianity might be experiencing setbacks in the West, often in those places out of the spotlight, such as China or India, fresh and exciting new developments were taking place.

5
Modern Waves of Expansion

Stephen E. Burris

Background

Thomas Kuhn in his landmark work, *The Structure of Scientific Revolutions*, provides a helpful model in understanding the development of the modern missions period. Kuhn suggests that change is often caused by a "paradigm shift." A paradigm is an accepted model or pattern that provides understanding in a particular situation or within a given set of circumstances. In this way Kuhn talks about the conceptual transformation that takes place during a paradigm shift. A conceptual shift also produces a shift in practice. Kuhn, writing about science, maintains that paradigms have two basic characteristics:

> Their achievement was sufficiently unprecedented to attract an enduring group of adherents away from competing modes of scientific activity. Simultaneously, it was sufficiently open-ended to leave all sorts of problems for the redefined group of practitioners to resolve.[1]

This chapter describes the paradigm shifts that have occurred during the approximately 200 years of the "modern missions" period. It builds on Ralph

---

1. Thomas S. Kuhn, *The Structure of Scientific Revolutions* (Chicago: University of Chicago Press, 1970), p. 10.

Winter's landmark work "Four Men, Three Eras, Two Transitions: Modern Missions."[2] In light of Kuhn's model, it is helpful to see Winter's "three eras" as "waves" or "paradigms." Each wave was produced by a paradigm shift that not only changed the focus of mission work, but also helped clarify the unfinished task of world evangelization. Each paradigm shift sought to touch regions untouched by previous missionary activity. The impact of a shift of this magnitude is described by Kuhn.

> That is why a new theory, however special its range of application, is seldom or never just an increment to what is already known. Its assimilation requires the reconstruction of prior theory and the re-evaluation of prior fact, an intrinsically revolutionary process that is seldom completed by a single man and never overnight.[3]

Each wave also produced a paradigm shift within the sending church. In the first wave the understanding centered around continents. In the second wave countries located in the interior of the continents began to dominate. In the third wave "unreached peoples" or socio-linguistic distinctions were the center of attention. In the fourth wave the internationalization and urbanization issues come into focus.

Similarities appear in each wave as well. Education, for example, is present in each wave. The development of local leaders has been a key to the expansion of the world Christian movement throughout history. Bible translation is a another example. Bible translation, while highlighted in the third wave, was present in the other paradigms. Translation is still a priority in the emerging fourth wave. A third example is Winter's four stages of mission activity present

---

2. Winter and Hawthorne, *Perspectives*, pp. B33-B44.

3. Kuhn, *Structure*, p. 7.

in each wave of missionary activity. Winter lists the stages of mission activity as:

> Stage 1: A Pioneer stage—first contact with a people group. . . . Stage 2: A Paternal Stage—Expatriates train national leadership. . . . Stage 3: A Partnership stage—National leaders work as equals with expatriates. . . . Stage 4: A Participation stage—Expatriates are no longer equal partners, but only participate by invitation.[4]

Other examples could also be cited. It should be carefully noted that although there are numerous similarities between the various waves there are also distinct differences. Each paradigm produced a "conceptual transformation" resulting in a practice shift. It is the review of this shift that we now turn our attention.

First Wave: Focus on the Coastlands

William Carey challenged the popular notion that world evangelization was not binding on the church of his day. In fact the Reformers said very little about the evangelization of the world. Stephen Neill cites Johann Gerhard, the dean of Westminster, who proposed that "the command of Christ to preach the Gospel to all the world ceased with the apostles: in their day the offer of salvation had been made to all the nations; there was no need for the offer to be made a second time to those who had already refused it."[5] Carey challenged the church to use "means" for the conversion of the heathen. This position was in direct opposition to the paradigm of the day that can be summarized as follows: "the conversion of the heathen would be the Lord's own work in his own time, and that nothing could be done by men to hasten it."[6]

---

4. Winter and Hawthorne, *Perspectives*, p. B47.

5. Neill, *A History of Christian Missions*, p. 222.

6. Ibid., p. 261.

Carey was not the first Protestant missionary. The Moravians are a notable example of others who were seriously involved in missionary activity before Carey. However, the involvement of the English-speaking world is usually attributed to Carey. The English-speaking world would account for the predominant number of missionaries and also the majority of the funding for modern missions. This pattern remained true for about 180 years.

This paradigm was greatly influenced by a rising awareness of geography. Carey was significantly influenced by Captain Cook's writings. The Great Awakening had significant impact as well.[7]

Winter identifies two structures at work within the church. According to Winter these structures are evident from the New Testament period to the present. The first is the church structure itself that Winter calls a "modality." The second is what is popularly known today as a "parachurch" structure, "apostolic band" or what Winter calls a "sodality."[8] These sodalities were voluntary organizations organized for a specific purpose. In Carey's case the "means" became a missionary structure or sodality. Stephen Neill calls this the great age of societies.

> In many cases the Protestant Churches as such were unable or unwilling themselves to take up the cause of missions. This was left to the voluntary societies, dependent on the initiative of consecrated individuals, and relying for financial support on the voluntary gifts of interested Christians.[9]

---

7. For additional information see J. Edwin Orr, *The Eager Feet, Evangelical Awakenings 1790-1830* (Chicago: Moody Press, 1975), and *The Flaming Tongue* (Chicago: Moody Press, 1973). Also refer to Max Ward Randall, *The Great Awakenings and the Restoration Movement.*

8. Winter and Hawthorne, *Perspectives,* pp. B45-B57.

9. Neill, *A History of Christian Missions,* p. 252.

In this wave most of the sodalities were connected to denominations.

The paradigm shift Carey introduced focused on the geographical continents. Carey was able to form a sodality for the purpose of using "means" for the conversion of the heathen. As a result Carey and his family left for India under the umbrella of the Baptist Missionary Society. Soon other sodalities in Europe and North America were formed for the purpose of world evangelization. Carey's work produced within Protestant leaders an awareness that they needed to understand the process of world evangelization. The result was a paradigm shift resulting in a church awakened to the unfinished task of world evangelization.

Second Wave: Focus on the Interiors

Hudson Taylor challenged the church to think of the unfinished task in more specific ways, to go beyond the wave produced by Carey and others. Geography was also an important ingredient in this wave as Taylor, like Carey, spent time studying maps. Taylor ushered in a new paradigm in mission activity as he challenged the church to consider the interiors of the continents. During Taylor's day a notion was circulating that the job of world evangelization was nearing completion. After all the church was planted on every continent and so by definition the church had gone into "all the world." Taylor raised the church's awareness of the still large areas known as the inland regions that still did not have the gospel or the church. Taylor was interested in reaching the interior provinces, particularly in China. This produced a new wave of mission practice in Asia and Africa.

The paradigm shift produced by Taylor included several characteristics. First Taylor located the headquarters for his mission in China rather than with the sending church. While following the shift introduced by Carey of organizing a sodality, Taylor believed that those closest to the work and most intimately involved were in the best position to make decisions regarding the direction and future of the work. Second, he believed in the faith principle regarding the support of the work. This principle ushered in what is now known as "direct support" or "faith missions." Taylor believed that "God's work, done God's way, will never lack for God's supply." While sodalities were already present, Taylor produced a new interdenominational type of sodality. Third, he allowed married women as full partners with their husbands and single women to be involved in the work. Fourth, the missionaries would wear the dress of the local people, in Taylor's case Chinese, and identify with the local people whenever and however possible. Fifthly, the primary aim of the mission was evangelism. Sixthly, opportunity of service was provided for those of little formal education.

A key in this wave was the Student Volunteer Movement. This movement, the largest student movement in history, provided the personnel and the funding during this second wave. John R. Mott was a key leader. This movement produced 100,000 commitments from students with about 20,000 students going to the field while 80,000 stayed behind to pray and support those who went out.

Third Wave: Focus on the Unreached Peoples

The third wave was influenced by both geography and culture. A relatively new discipline, anthropology, became influential in this wave. This paradigm highlighted linguistic and cultural differences. While Bible translation work had been going on for some time and was a prominent component of William Carey's work, a heightened awareness of the place of linguistic and cultural difference is present in this wave.

The new field of psychology was also having an impact on the Western mind. Specifically what some have called the "self-centered self" began to emerge. One effect of this was the movement in Western thought toward the individual. This created the tendency in the West to interpret from an individualistic perspective. Yet, the majority of the world continues to be group oriented.

Two individuals served as a catalyst in this third wave. Cameron Townsend went to Guatemala in the 1930s to distribute the Bible. He noticed that the majority of the people did not speak Spanish. Townsend became aware of the linguistic distinctions that separated peoples. As a result of Townsend's efforts Wycliffe Bible Translators was born.

Donald A. McGavran focused on cultural distinctions and similarities. In India, with its caste system, McGavran noticed the cultural differences in the nearly 3,000 subgroups. McGavran called these groups "homogeneous units." "The *homogeneous unit* is simply a section of society in which all the members have some characteristic in common."[10] McGavran suggested that the key to discipling a homogeneous unit was within that unit. "In leading peoples to become Christian the Church must aim to win individuals in their corporate life. The steady goal must be the Christianization of *the entire fabric which is the people,* or large enough parts of it that the social life of the individual is not destroyed."[11] On another occasion McGavran said it

10. Donald McGavran, *Understanding Church Growth* (Grand Rapids: Eerdmans, 1970), p. 85. For a more complete discussion of the homogeneous unit principle see C. Peter Wagner, *Our Kind of People*, Atlanta: John Knox Press, 1979, and Stephen E. Burris, "The Biblical Basis for the Homogeneous Unit Principle." Lincoln Christian Seminary, M.A. Thesis, 1980.

11. Donald McGavran, *The Bridges of God* (New York: Friendship Press, 1955), p. 16.

this way, "Men like to become Christians without crossing racial, linguistic, or class barriers."[12]

During this third wave homogeneous units have popularly been called "people groups." In this paradigm a new way of looking at the world is present. The common missiological focus is not continents or countries, but unreached peoples. In this sense to speak of an "unreached people" generally means to speak of a tribe, clan, extended family or close knit community.

Several additional characteristics are present in this paradigm. The first is the rise of "majority world"[13] missions. World evangelization is becoming less of a "Western" activity. Traditional mission fields such as Korea, Philippines, Japan, Guatemala, and many others are now sending missionaries. This trend is more fully in view during the fourth wave.

A second characteristic is the rise of new nations, beginning with Israel and India in 1948. This has resulted in the collapse of the colonial apparatus so prominent during the first and second waves of modern missions.

Another characteristic is the rise of independent churches. This is the result of the four stages mentioned earlier at work during the past 200 years, and the successful completion, in many cases, of those steps. The work of evangelization has resulted in churches across the majority world moving from the Pioneer Stage to the Paternal Stage to the Partnership

---

12. McGavran, *Understanding Church Growth*, p. 198.

13. I am using the term "majority world" missions rather than the more common "two-thirds world" and "third world" terms, following the use employed by R. Daniel Shaw in various courses taught at the Fuller School of World Mission. This is an attempt to see the world in proportion and acknowledge the growing number of missionaries and mission agencies outside of the West. The term "majority world" may better communicate the internationalization present in the fourth wave of mission activity.

Stage to the Participation Stage. This is the reason most missionaries went out in the first place—to plant an "indigenous church." This is cause for celebration.

The unreached peoples paradigm of this third wave may still be helpful in the emerging fourth wave. While McGavran's original definition of homogeneous units is general enough to include the paradigm shift of the fourth wave, it has often been applied narrowly to families or clans, and usually in a rural setting. However, in order for the unreached peoples characteristic of the third wave to be helpful in the fourth wave resistance to a narrow definition is necessary. It is at this point that a dynamic tension has caused a rethinking that leads to a fourth wave or a new paradigm shift.

Fourth Wave: Focus on the Cities

In this fourth wave two ideas are in focus. The first is the internationalization of the Christian movement. Today two-thirds or more of the Christian population live in Africa, Asia, and Latin America. The West, Europe and North America particularly, while dominating the first three waves, will not dominate in this fourth wave of modern missions. This change requires a redefinition of missions. For over 200 years missions has been synonymous with the Western church sending out missionaries to the majority world. Today, this definition is no longer appropriate. A new definition setting forth the twin tasks of communicating the gospel and forming the church must be emphasized. In other words the church is in the mission business. McGavran said it this way, "We may define mission narrowly as an enterprise devoted to proclaiming the Good News of Jesus Christ, and to persuading men to become His disciples and dependable members of His Church."[14]

---

14. McGavran, *Understanding Church Growth*, p. 34.

A second focus is urbanization. The mass migration to the cities of the world has been underway for some time, particularly since the 1950s. Evangelical missions have been slow to meet the challenge of the shift in population to the cities. Social concerns such as crime, disease, illiteracy, poverty, among other problems, are clearly present in virtually all urban centers. However, as Paul Hiebert suggests,

> Cities also offer tremendous opportunity. They are the centers for world communication, and the source from which ideas spread to the countryside. One reason for the rapid spread of early Christianity was its movement through the cities. We desperately need to look more closely at modern urban dynamics in order to understand how change takes place, and then to apply these insights to today's mission planning.[15]

This wave, while influenced by geography and culture, is also influenced by sociology.

Hiebert asks important questions:

> The rapid urbanization of the world raises many questions for those concerned with church growth. What is the societal structure of a city and how does this structure influence communication and decision making? How do changes take place in the highly mobile and varied city society?[16]

The answers to these questions will suggest strategies appropriate for this fourth wave of modern missions. Likely these strategies will continue to account for the unreached peoples emphasis of the third wave, but increasingly strategies targeting the city will be added. These new strategies will consider

---

14. McGavran, *Understanding Church Growth*, p. 34.

15. Paul Hiebert, "Social Structure and Church Growth, in Winter and Hawthorne, *Perspectives*, p. C33.

16. Ibid., p. C32.

societal structures that are unique to the urban milieu.

What type of societal structures are present in the city? Unlike the third wave that centered on families or clans, people groups, the urbanization process has created new webs of relationships. Harvie Conn suggests that these webs "are more and more defined in terms of macrostructural social classes, the social groups structured around wealth, power, and prestige."[17] Relational webs are organized on a more voluntary basis. People groupings are only one of the distinctions and therefore one way of establishing the church among those in the city. Networks and geographical groupings are also important ways to reach the previously unreached. In an urban setting the use of media becomes an important tool. When considering the city Conn writes,

> In the city, however, family networks are only one method of socialization among many. Personal relationships and a sense of belonging can be created out of commonly shared residential territory (a neighborhood). You build relationships with the mechanic who lives next door, the barber down the street, your child's teacher in the house on the corner. Vocation can bring non-neighbors together. You socialize with your fellow factory workers, the teachers in the same school where you work, the woman selling apples in the stall next to yours in the market. The city spawns such networks in much larger array than the village and rural cultures. People create an identity from a plural set of groups.[18]

The second is the growing influence and participation of majority world missions. Current estimates range as high as 55,000 missionaries from over 2,000

---

17. Conn, *A Clarified Vision*, p. 17.
18. Ibid., p. 197.

agencies based in the majority world.[19] This may be the most important missions phenomenon in the modern missions era.

Pate using statistics up to 1990 states,

Our research demonstrates that the growth of the non-Western Protestant missions movement continues to be phenomenal. While the growth rate of the Two-Thirds World evangelical churches is a remarkable 6.7 percent per year, the Two-Thirds World missions movement (which our studies identify as almost entirely evangelical) is growing at 13.3 percent per year. This projects to a phenomenal 248 percent increase every ten years![20]

Pate provides data that suggest a needed paradigm shift in the way Westerners think of missions and the mission field in this fourth wave. This is a clear indication that the majority world missions continue to emerge as full partners.

This establishes the fact that the Two-Thirds World Protestant missions movement has assumed a major portion of the church's responsibility for world evangelism. As of the end of 1990, Two-Thirds World missionaries comprised 35.6 percent of the total Protestant missionary force in the world! These missionaries are not mere statistics. They are living, suffering, struggling, sacrificing, witnessing, and often very effective cross-cultural missionaries, who very well may make a greater impact than their counterparts from the Western world . . . . If both the Western missionary force and the Two-Thirds World missionary force continue to grow at their current

---

19. This estimate is provided by the Mobilization Division of the U. S. Center for World Mission as of December, 1994.

20. Larry D. Pate, "The Changing Balance in Global Mission," in Winter and Hawthorne, *Perspectives*, p. D230.

rates, the majority of the world's Protestant missionaries will be from the non-Western world by the year 2000. The number of Two-Thirds World missionaries would overtake the number of Western missionaries some time in 1998."[21]

A third factor is the rise of tentmaking ministries, non-resident missions, and other creative ways of entering a country. Ruth Siemens defines tentmakers as "mission-committed Christians, who, like Paul, support themselves in secular work, as they engage in cross-cultural ministry on the job and in their free time."[22] Siemens goes on the give six practical reasons for tentmaking:

1. Tentmakers can gain entry into restricted-access countries. . . . 2. Tentmakers can serve in needy open countries. . . . 3. Tentmakers help solve the problem of the cost of missions. . . . 4. Tentmakers help solve the problem of personnel. . . . 5. Tentmakers are ideal workers for emerging mission agencies. . . . 6. The international job market itself is an argument for tentmaking, because it does not exist by accident, but by God's design.[23]

Examples include teachers, engineers, business persons, and others.

A fourth characteristic is the availability and use of technology. Technology provides unprecedented opportunity for world evangelization but also raises serious questions. To what extent should a mission be involved in the use of technology? What does it mean to be "human" in a technological age? What is the risk of technology altering the message? What contextual considerations affect our choice among various

---

21. Ibid., pp. D233-D235.

22. Ruth E. Siemens, "Tentmakers Needed for World Evangelization," in Winter and Hawthorne, *Perspectives*, p. D246.

23. Ibid., pp. D248-D249.

technologies? Charles Kraft's emphasis on "receptor oriented" approaches may hold a key to the answers to these and other questions.

C. Peter Wagner has written describing another characteristic, Post-Denominational Churches. Wagner defines this term as

> A generic term that covers the rapidly expanding segment of Christianity including independent charismatic churches, house churches in China and elsewhere, African independent churches, apostolic networks, urban megachurches (charismatic and non-charismatic) central "mother" churches surrounded by numbers of satellite churches, and others. These churches are characterized by indigenous leadership, contemporary worship, concert prayer, power ministries and mutual affiliation based on spiritual rather than legal and bureaucratic ties.[24]

Wagner states that these churches are "by far, the most rapidly growing segment of Christianity on all six continents."[25]

Christian community development is characteristic in this paradigm. Elliston has treated this subject more adequately in chapter 10 of this book, but I should at least mention some of the concerns in an attempt to more adequately understand the present wave of mission activity. Balance will likely be the key in the future as it has been in the past. This is not an either/or situation, evangelism and church planting vs. Christian community development, but a both/and approach. The church must be aware of and give a Christian response to the growing disparity between rich and poor, basic social services such as food, shelter and health, education, social witness, and a variety

---

24. C. Peter Wagner, "Those Amazing Post-Denominational Churches," in *Ministries Today*, July/August 1994, p. 50.

25. Ibid., p. 49.

of other issues we might lump under the term social action.

Issues for the Future

The future calls for a new model of mission activity that seriously considers this fourth wave of modern missions. Paul Pierson suggests a beginning point for a new model.[26] This model incorporates the elements of this new paradigm in mission activity, and contains the following elements.

New Model of Missions

1. The church must be the base—no return to earlier autonomy of the missionary organization or structures. This is a return to the New Testament pattern. Antioch sent out Paul and his missionary band. Paul was given a great deal of latitude in deciding the where and how of the work. Paul remained accountable to Antioch, however.

2. The "base" cannot be the end of mission; mission is not "inter-church aid." The mission station approach that dominated the first and second waves often produced a limited response to the gospel. This fact was clearly pointed out by McGavran,

> Indeed, the largest, most famous missionary medical centres seem to have grown up where there are no great growing churches. Where great populations have not turned to Christ, there are great hospitals; and where great populations have turned to Christ, there are few great hospitals. Thus the Mission Station Approach, frustrated by meagre response, turned to secondary aims.[27]

---

26. Pierson, "Historical Development," pp. 90-91.
27. McGavran, *The Bridges of God*, p. 53.

In this fourth wave the "base" must give attention to first priorities, church planting and discipling, other important, worthwhile activities will follow.

3. The end of mission: "That the world might believe." In this fourth wave a new affirmation to reaching the whole world with the gospel is in order. "And this gospel of the kingdom will be preached in the whole world as a testimony to all nations, and then the end will come" (Matt. 24:14). In some places the nations will include families, tribes and clans. In other situations, especially in urban settings, the nations may include webs of relationships.

Spiritual Power

An examination of the discrepancy existing between our theological interpretation and validated field experiences concerning spiritual power is overdue. This danger is often present both in historic settings such as seen in Palestine at the time of Christ and in contemporary cultures influenced by a Western worldview. We need to keep an open discussion on the theological presuppositions governing our beliefs of what God can or will do. Documented examples of God demonstrating His power in miraculous ways create a tension with a "closed" theology. A clear exegesis and re-examination of all of the relevant, not just our favorite, passages is necessary.

At least two issues demand our careful attention. One concerns our view of the biblical text and the other concerns our experience. We hold a high view of Scripture. At the same time, how do we make sense of the biblical text, as we have been taught from a Western perspective, and honestly account for undeniable experience? The problem is further complicated as Kraft explains. "In spite of our suspicions of the validity of experience as a measure of truth, we accept as fact very little that does not fit our experience."[28] Every person's interpretations are closely connected to his/her experience, or lack of experience and therefore contribute to this tension. The often pointed to dichotomy between Scripture and experience is a "red herring." Scripture is interpreted in terms of and related to experience and experience to Scripture. Yes, we can go too far—experience without Scripture. Without balance we not only risk missing the truth of the gospel but may also miss what God is actively accomplishing in the world today.

Mission Tension

An urgent issue requiring immediate attention is the tension that exists between missionaries who are operating under one paradigm or another, often in close proximity. Transitions are seldom easy. This is especially true today as several of the paradigms may be simultaneously present in the same geographical location. Kuhn understood this and referred to paradigm shifts as revolutions. Kuhn suggests that, "When, in the development of a natural science, an individual or group first produces a synthesis able to attract most of the next generation's practitioners, the older schools gradually disappear."[29] This trend is also evident in missions. The primary difference is that the old may be held on to for a longer period of time even though the new is proving to be a more helpful paradigm.

Two additional factors contribute to mission tension. First, paradigms are human activities. We devise paradigms as an attempt to understand and explain. We look at situations and circumstances and try to bring meaning. Therefore more than one

28. Charles Kraft, *Christianity With Power* (Ann Arbor: Servant, 1989), p. 44.

29. Kuhn, *Structure*, p. 18.

paradigm may exist at any given time, and they often overlap. This is the basis for tension on the field and in the sending church. Secondly, God has made himself known but we do not exhaustively know Him. There is room for reasonable people to disagree. God's plan is the same, however. Even in our desire to know God's plan and be involved in what God is doing, our interpretation is fallible. Attempts to complete the task of world evangelization are not exempted from this problem.

Steps to Reduce Tension

Building on Harry Larson's suggestions the following five steps may provide a means of reducing tension in the mission community.[30] Missionaries, mission agencies and supporting churches will do well to seriously consider the implications of these five steps.

1. Continue to support and honor the veteran missionaries who are working at a different task. Great care should be exercised in our communication. In our enthusiasm we should not make those who have labored long and hard in the difficult places of the world to feel that they are unfaithful, irresponsible, or out of touch. Those involved in a different type of work may not be working at a less strategic task. And they may be exactly where God has called them to work. However, this is not an excuse to be out of touch with current strategies or to the nature of new paradigms of mission practice.

The missionary, mission executive and supporting church continually needs to stay current with mission trends. This serves to alert when paradigms are chang-

---

30. Harry Larson, "Eras, Pioneers, and Transitions," in *The World Christian Movement*, ed. by Jonathan Lewis (Pasadena, CA: William Carey Library, 1994), pp. 23-25.

ing. In this way the missionary can evaluate the local work in light of current missiological developments.

2. Educate concerning the nature of the task. We need to be involved in a variety of mission tasks. Given the circumstances at the local level the task may well be different from one field to another, particularly when comparing a rural and urban situation. The "strategic mix" is critical. The sending church should not be placed in a position of choosing between one type of activity or another without careful analysis of the local situation. With this field analysis in hand, the sending church can assist in the development of strategies that make sense in the local context.

The more evangelization has moved forward, the more necessary it has been to carefully define targets, so as not to waste effort. The church has often been slow to grasp the new waves of mission activity. The tendency has been to hold onto the old ways.

3. Allocate new resources and missionary personnel to the most strategic task. Given the local circumstances this may involve emphasis from each of the waves in modern missions. Clearly the key priority is cross-cultural church planting. Virtually, all other worthwhile work grows out of this single strategy. Decisions must consider this central strategy as the key to the success of other emphases. In some cases this will involve church planting among unreached peoples. In other cases it may involve church planting across cultural barriers within the city.

4. Share a new vision with present missionaries. Many need to "re-tool" in order to be informed concerning new methods and strategies. In some cases a broader base is needed. In other cases a different paradigm is needed. This will likely include a variety of approaches including additional formal training as well as a mix of informal training such as seminars and conferences and reading in current missiological books.

5. Maintain a strategic balance among different types of missionary work. This may be the key in the reduction of tension. In partnership with the missionary the sending church should intentionally consider what goals and plans should be implemented. This will serve as the overall "grid" through which decisions can be filtered as to their strategic importance. Key questions may include: 1) Are we praying and seeking God's guidance regarding our missions program? 2) Are we satisfied with the "strategic mix" in our missions program? 3) Where should *new* resources be allocated? What priority do we give to cross-cultural church planting?

Conclusion

Wagner suggests that missions have come "full circle" (Acts 11:19-13:3). By following the pattern in the book of Acts Wagner suggests that the circle consists of the following major phases.

90° Mission to go, evangelize, and plant churches
180° Fruit—church planted
270° Church gains autonomy
360° New church gives birth to a mission—Antioch.[31]

Have we come full circle? Roland Allen suggests,

St Paul's theory of evangelizing a province was not to preach in every place in it himself, but to establish centres of Christian life in two or three important places from which the knowledge might spread into the country round. This is important, not as showing that he preferred to preach in a capital rather than in a provincial town or in a village, but because he intended his congregation to become at once a centre of light.[32]

---

31. Pierson, "Historical Development," p. 89.
32. Allen, *Missionary Methods*, p. 12.

In the fourth paradigm that focuses on urban centers, it would appear that we have come full circle. And a renewed study of the methods used in the Acts of the Apostles is in order. Much remains to be learned regarding the strategic choices to be made. This includes strategic points and identification of homogeneous units or webs of relationships within those strategic points.

As we continue to transition between various paradigms we should be sensitive to the following: 1. Continue to support and honor the veteran missionaries that are finishing a task associated with a different paradigm. 2. Educate the local church as to the nature of the transition. 3. Allocate new missionary personnel to the priority tasks described in a new paradigm. 4. Share a vision of a new paradigm with present missionaries. 5. Determine a strategic balance for the sending church between different types of missionary work.

The Holy Spirit has always raised up individuals and movements that help articulate a new paradigm and thereby clarify the remaining task of world evangelization. At the close of this millennium it is critical that the church recognize the global nature of the missionary enterprise and become involved in more clearly defining the remaining task in order to complete the task of discipling the nations, *ta ethne*, that our Lord commissioned us to do.

6
Finishing the Task

Rondal Smith

In the previous chapters we have viewed the unfolding of God's purpose for mankind, His mission, as recorded first in the Bible and then in the history of the expansion of the church. We understand that the task God has given His church is to be a part of His mission to the end that the Good News of salvation through Jesus be proclaimed to every person on the globe and that there be disciples of Jesus in every ethnic group on earth.

A short summary of the salient lessons learned from the biblical as well as the historical chapters that have been covered up to now can be summarized as consisting of at least the following key strategic points that we might well call *God's Historic Global Ethnic Strategy*: (1) God's intention is global: *persons* from *every* ethnic group *on earth* (Matt. 28:18-20; Rev. 5); (2) God's Strategy is a *people group strategy*: "persons from every *family* (= clan, Gen. 12:1-3), *tribe, language, people, and nation* (= ethnic group)"; (3) God's purpose is *directed toward Closure*: "as a testimony to every ethnic group and *then the end will come*"(Matt. 24:14).

At this point in our study we need to pause and ask: To what extent has this task already been completed? What is involved in finishing the task?

The Magnitude of the Unfinished Task

What a revolution might occur if the church today could view the world from God's perspective! Just for a moment let us mentally imagine standing on the moon like the first astronauts in the late 60s. From this perspective we can view the earth rising dramatically over the horizon with its white swirling clouds over the blue, brown and green globe, capped by snow at both poles. On this living sphere there are 5.3 billion people scattered across the continents and oceans. Of this vast population one third or 1.62 billion consider themselves to be Christian at least in a nominal sense. The best estimates suggest that about one out of every ten persons on the globe or 540 million persons are currently active evangelical believers who take the Great Commission seriously.

That perspective alone shows us one of the great truths we need to know: That while the gospel has spread extensively within the world's population, an overwhelming number yet need to hear and to respond before the task of world evangelization is finished. With the world's population exploding and the sheer numbers of unbelievers growing ever larger, the task seems even more impossible to imagine completing.

But this perspective of sheer numbers alone is not a complete picture of our task. As we imagine peering at this marvelous earth other questions arise. Where on the earth are Christians located? What is the current relationship of the Christian to the non-Christian population? What kind of avenues of communication exist between these two populations? What are the barriers to communicating the Good News of Jesus to the non-Christian population? What countries, what languages, what cultures are Christians and non-Christians a part of? What will it take for the nominal Christians to become active, evangelical, Great

116

Commission Christians? What resources are needed and available among the ten percent who are active evangelicals for carrying out the task of extending the gospel to those yet unreached? What kind of strategy will enable Christ's people to finish the task?

A Strategic Issue

Because missiologists in the last two decades have been developing answers to these questions we now are able to begin envisioning both the enormity and the feasibility of finishing the task in a more realistic way. Answering these questions enables us to develop a strategy based both on the Biblical mandate as well as upon the sociological and linguistic divisions of the world's people. If we can identify those segments of the world's population within which communication flows freely because of the lack of various barriers to communication, a strategy could be devised for reaching each of these segments with the gospel. Such a strategy suggests there would be a limited number of "bite size" pieces to which the church could allocate its resources and thus distribute the task to the world-wide body of Christ for completion. Theoretically, every person on earth is within reach of Christian radio. AM, FM, and short wave now reach most people on earth. An optimistic goal of the producers of the *Jesus* film is to have it produced in enough languages so that every person can understand it.

Geographic Barriers

Geographic separation among peoples creates barriers to communication. The world's people are distributed throughout the globe on all continents (with Antarctica being the only exception) and most islands of the seas and oceans. They are separated from each other by the oceans, lakes and streams, mountains, jungles and deserts which divide the earth we live on into many types of living environments. Furthermore, these global land masses on which people live has been carved up into 149 geopolitical countries and territories. Though we could not see the political boundaries of these countries from the moon, missiologists have determined that in all but 29 of these geopolitical entities is the population more than 1% Christian.

Religious Barriers

Another set of barriers important to seeing the world from God's perspective are those created by large blocks of peoples who espouse various non-Christian religious traditions. As already mentioned, 1/3 (32.8%) of the world's population claims to be Christian, divided into Orthodox, Catholic, and Protestant-Evangelical-Pentecostal. Almost one fifth (19.6%) espouse Islam, while 18.6% are Non-religious or Atheist. Hinduism in its various shades dominates over one eighth—13.5%. Buddhist and Eastern Religions account for 11.6% and Animists/traditional religions account for 2.7%. The remaining percents consist of Jews, Sikh, Baha'i and other minority religions, each with its own barriers challenging the spread of the gospel.

The major religious populations have centers of concentration on the globe. However, these religious commitments cut across many different geographic and political boundaries. The distribution of believers in these faiths is further complicated by the large scale immigrations that have taken place in the last two centuries as well as by missionaries who are spreading some of these faiths. Christian believers are most diversely scattered. Two centuries ago Christians were primarily concentrated in Europe and areas colonized by Europe. But, the density of Christian believers in the last two decades has shifted to non-Western countries in the Eastern and Southern hemispheres.

The secularized non-religious and atheist populations are mostly concentrated now in Europe, the former Soviet Union, China and North America, all industrialized and urban nations of Europe, Asia and the Americas. Islam is centered in North Africa, the Near and Middle East, Central Asia and Indonesia. Hinduism's focus is in India. Buddhism and Eastern Religions are in Southeastern and East Asian nations including Japan. Animistic peoples are found everywhere, often in small enclaves of indigenous peoples especially in Africa, Latin America, Oceania and parts of Asia or in immigrant groups from these areas. Animistic folk religions are also common in many parts of North America.

Linguistic Barriers

Linguistic barriers separate the world's populations even further, dividing continents, dialects and literate versus non-literate. Even though global literacy is optimistically claimed by the various governments of the world to be at 79% worldwide (if some degree of literacy in a second language is considered), the majority of the mother-tongue languages of the world are still unwritten. As an example of great challenge for world literacy consider that by mid-1993 only over 2,000 languages had some portion of Christian Scriptures published in them, and yet fewer, only 300 plus languages, have the Bible in its entirety published in them. These facts are significant in that during the last two centuries most languages for which literacy has been developed had that happen as a result of the translation of the Christian Scriptures. At present worldwide only just over 1,199 languages have Bible translation and literacy programs currently active within them.

Other significant cultural factors include the barriers that divide the world's populations into rural versus urban, technologically more advanced versus less advanced, economic disparity, sociological segmentation into levels, worldview differences, aesthetic expressions and preferences, living conditions, poverty and wealth, particular historical traditions and lifestyle.

On the other hand, when such factors as geographic proximity, political boundaries, religious tradition, language, and the like, are shared they thus give a people a sense of identity providing coherence to a group thus facilitating communication between its people. Such a group, sharing a sense of identity and common culture, constitutes a *people group*. It is within such groups that the fewest barriers to communication exist.

God's Ethnic Strategy

God made His promises to Abraham and his descendants in terms of people groups (Gen. 12:1-3). God promised Abraham He would bless him and his descendants and that they would be a blessing and that "in Abraham's seed (descendant(s)) every nation (ethnic group) will be blessed." Two thousand years later, that distant promised special "seed of Abraham," Jesus, commands His followers to carry the blessings of salvation to all people groups when he sends them out to make "disciples of every nation" in Matt. 28:18-20. The vision of the victorious Christ in Revelation 5 pictures heavenly creatures and saved mankind gathered all around the throne of God and the Lamb singing the victory song of the Lamb, "you were slain and with your blood you purchased men for God from every tribe and language and people and nation." This mission to bless all nations we can aptly identify as *God's ethnic strategy*: God intends that His people make disciples of individuals from within every distinct people group in the world.

The ethnic or people groups became the focus for evangelization during the third era of the modern mission history. Both William Townsend and Donald A. McGavran helped us understand that such groups must become the focus for development of a strategy to complete the task. Later missiologists have identified unreached people groups by other names: (1) *Hidden People Groups* emphasizing that the groups have not been identified as needing to be reached, since they often exist side by side with reached groups within the same country; (2) *Frontier People Groups* emphasizing the fact that the groups need to yet be pioneered by cross-cultural missionaries, and (3) *Unpenetrated People Groups*, emphasizing that the groups have had no missiological breakthrough that has produced an indigenous, contextualized church within it.

Thus if we are to see the world as God sees it, then, we would have to have God's *"people group vision."* With God's perspective we can see the global sphere of the earth as the multifaceted mosaic of ethnic diversity that it is. Thus seen the earth is divided into tens of thousands of diverse people groups. Once we begin to use the "people group" as a unit as pointed out both by the Biblical mandate and by communication requirements, we are immediately presented with a relatively simple and clear means of developing strategy to finish the task of world evangelization. We are now faced with a new set of questions: What, more particularly, is an ethnic or people group? When can a people group be considered strategically reached? What people groups have already been strategically reached? What groups need to be reached in order to complete the task of discipling the nations?

People Group Definition

First, an ethnic or people group can be defined anthropologically as "a group of people who share a common life, common culture and common language and who have a sense of being one people." It is the unique combination of where the people live, how they gain a living from their environment, their means of economic distribution of goods and services, their various social and political and legal systems, their religion and worldview and many other aspects of a learned and shared system of behavior that make a people unique. Secondly, a missiological, strategic definition would define it as a "group of people within which the gospel can travel without encountering any significant barriers of language or culture." Political boundaries and the people group boundaries seldom coincide.

Stages of Evangelistic Strategy

Two stages to evangelistic strategy can be deduced from the nature of discipling people of different people groups. The first one is crossing the ethnic-linguistic boundary that defines each group. This is a difficult task of communication because of the inherent differences between the source culture—that of the cross-cultural agents, in which the gospel already exists—and the target culture. The second stage is that of evangelization of the target culture by agents within that culture who know and share its cultural features. These evangelists are agents of change of their home culture through the preaching of the gospel and evangelism.

"Reachedness:" A Definition

A culture or people is strategically reached as a group when outside agents are no longer needed to evangelize this culture. More technically we define a people as having been "reached" as that point when they have "a *cluster of viable, growing congregations with the resources to reach the remaining individuals within that people group without outside assistance*, i.e., without cross-cultural missionaries."

From another perspective we can say that a people group is reached when a missiological breakthrough has occurred, so that the gospel is seen as, in some sense, a fulfillment of needs in that culture and the church is accepted as an institution in that culture, not threatening that culture's existence. Such people groups often have, or have had within them a people movement, where rather than isolated decisions by individuals there are multi-individual decisions involving families, extended families and other significant groupings within the culture over a time that eventually reaches large portions of a particular group.

"Reachedness:" A Strategic Factor

Some confusion has continued at the popular level by missiologists' use of the terms "reached" and "unreached people groups." To clarify we should first note that we are referring to a group as a whole being strategically reached, not to reached or unreached individuals. The Adopt-A-People Clearing House suggests five conditions of a people that mark it as unreached: (1) The people group has not heard the gospel; (2) The people group has not responded to it; (3) The people group does not have a church movement in it; (4) The people group does not have the word of God translated into their mother tongue or (5) The people group does not have the word of God readily available.

From this list we can conclude that two bottom-line conditions are considered necessary for a people group to be considered reached:

1. A cluster of congregations are planted within the people group and are *indigenous and contextualized,* i.e., a church exists in a form that does not present unnecessary borrowed cultural patterns from the missionary that would be considered foreign but rather the life of the church is expressed within cultural patterns adopted and adapted for its life. Therefore, the church can be considered a legitimate expression of the new host group without compromising or syncretizing the gospel.

2. The cluster of congregations have access (through literacy or at least audiocassette) to a *Bible version in the language they understand best (almost always the mother tongue of the people group)* so that no barrier of understanding exists either for evangelizing the remainder of the group or no barrier stands in the way of the people nourishing themselves on God's Word in their personal and church life.

A people group is considered *"strategically reached"* even though it almost always will have within it many unreached individuals. But because of the church's strength, cultural adaptation, established pattern of growth and use of its own mother-tongue Scriptures, no cross-cultural missionary is deemed necessary for the continued evangelization of the group. It is thus considered a reached group.

An *Unreached group* may have Christians from other groups living among or adjacent to it. The group may, indeed, even have missionaries and possibly a missionary church established in it. However, even though the church established in it may even be composed, at least partially if not entirely, of individuals from the group itself, if that church does not yet meet both of the two conditions mentioned above it is not yet a reached group.

The Task Remaining

What is the extent of the World Christian movement? Or more specifically, to what extent has the Christian movement discipled the nations? Winter's estimate sets the total at 24,000 people groups in the world. Of these, there are approximately 13,000 that are strategically reached with the gospel which leaves about 11,000 that are strategically unreached, the target for the cross-cultural mission of the church. *Targeting these unreached people groups is a goal with highest priority for the completion of the mission of God in the world.*

So, we attempt in our imagination to see the earth from God's perspective and gaze at the earth rising over the horizon of the moon. With our new people group oriented vision, we see a diversified mosaic of people groups covering its surface. Over half of the mosaic pieces are now identified as strategically reached with the gospel of Jesus Christ, because they have within them a significant group of disciples of Jesus no longer needing outside help for evangelizing their group. However, almost half are as yet unreached —the targets of the mission God calls His people to find their role in.

The 10/40 Window

Now we can ask the next important question in our quest for understanding the unfinished task: Where are the unreached people groups? Unreached people groups are found around the world but there is a heavy concentration in an area of the globe helpfully dubbed the 10/40 Window by Luis Bush. It is the area on the globe stretching from the Atlantic in the west (just west of Spain and North Africa) to the Pacific in the east (just east of Japan and the Philippines) between the 10th degree latitude north of the equator and the 40th degree north of the equator. It includes the countries of North Africa, the Near and Middle East, South Asia, East Asia, and the part of Europe bordering the Mediterranean.

Geopolitical areas and countries of the 10/40 Window that are among which the highest proportion of unreached groups are found:

Europe: Albania, Bosnia, East Europe and the Former Soviet Union (FSU)

North Africa: Guinea, Guinea-Bissau, Gambia, Senegal, Mauritania, Mali, Western Sahara, Burkina Faso, Niger, Chad, Sudan, Ethiopia, Libya, Algeria, Morocco, Central African Republic, Algeria, Tunisia, Egypt, Djibouti, Somalia, Benin, Togo, Nigeria, Cameroon

The Near East: Turkey, Lebanon, Syria, Jordan, Israel, Iraq, United Arab Emirates, Oman, Qatar, Kuwait, Yemen, Saudi Arabia

Middle East: Iran, Afghanistan, Pakistan, Bangladesh, etc.

South and Southeast Asia: India, Tibet, Nepal, Bhutan, Burma, Thailand, Laos, Kampuchea, Vietnam

East Asia: The Asiatic Republics of the FSU, Mongolia, China, Japan, North Korea

Within these countries of the 10/40 Window there are large clusters of unreached people groups defined by their religion and culture: the Muslims, the Hindus, the Buddhists, Animists and the Han Chinese. The large majority of the groups listed in the following table of unreached people groups are found in the countries of the 10/40 Window:

Animists: 2700 groups

Muslims: 3800 groups

Percent Evangelical

- 0 to 0.62
- 0.62 to 4
- 4 to 9.8
- over 9.8
- Not Available

94% of the people living in the 55 Least Evangelized Countries live in the 10/40 Window

Source: Provisional listing of P. Johnstone, 2/92

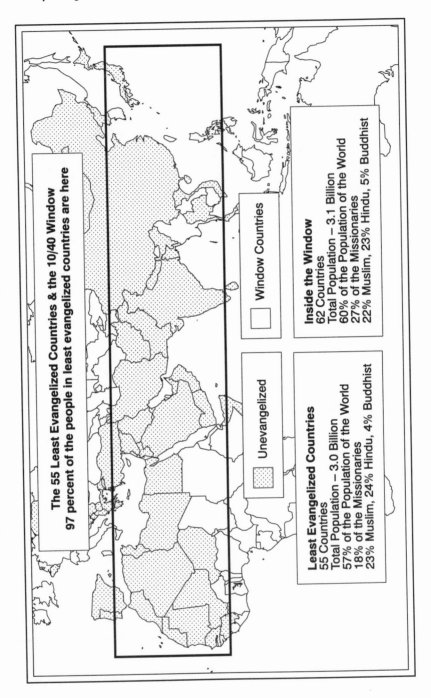

The 55 Least Evangelized Countries & the 10/40 Window
97 percent of the people in least evangelized countries are here

Window Countries

Unevangelized

Inside the Window
62 Countries
Total Population – 3.1 Billion
60% of the Population of the World
27% of the Missionaries
22% Muslim, 23% Hindu, 5% Buddhist

Least Evangelized Countries
55 Countries
Total Population – 3.0 Billion
57% of the Population of the World
18% of the Missionaries
23% Muslim, 24% Hindu, 4% Buddhist

Hindus:	1800 groups
Han Chinese:	900 groups
Buddhists:	900 groups
Others:	900 groups

Thus when we can see the world from God's perspective we realize there are about half of the world's people (2.43 billion) living within 11,000 unreached people groups, people groups within which there is no contextualized cluster of growing churches nor is there a mother-tongue translation of God's Word. Most of these peoples have representatives now living in cities.

The task before the church today is to mobilize the resource of people, their expertise and training, finances, prayer and all that God has placed within our hands in stewardship. Individuals within the church thus need to find their role in His mission in the world. In order to finish the task of world evangelism a two stage evangelistic effort is required. The first stage is to see that every unreached people group is engaged by cross-cultural missionaries in order to be used by God to make the group strategically reached. This stage, the most difficult, is designated the *Frontier Mission Stage*. The second stage is the preaching of the gospel by the churches within each respective people group that is reached in order to evangelize all of the individuals within it. This stage, in which the most powerful form of evangelism occurs, is designated *Evangelism* when it is carried out by the agents of the church within their own home culture or *Regular Missions* if agents from another culture are present to assist the indigenous church in this task.

Because the most powerful form of evangelism in the Ordinary Evangelism Stage cannot take place until the Frontier Mission Stage has occurred, there is a special and therefore *top priority* urgency placed on cross-cultural mission efforts. The fact that almost half of the world's population lives in almost half of the world's people groups which are unreached should only increase our sense of urgency to see that these groups are engaged. What it means is that almost half the world's population cannot hear the gospel in the language they understand best nor see its love and hope in patterns they understand clearly. At best, if at all, they can only hear the gospel in a second language and see it lived out in a culture with which they do not identify to any significant degree.

The Nature of the Task Remaining

As the church worldwide approaches the Frontier Mission Stage of engaging and strategically reaching the unreached groups, it needs to realistically recognize the barriers that this Stage presents. Recognizing the barriers enables us to choose and train appropriately the cross-cultural agents that are sent.

Preparation of Cross-Cultural Workers

The initial stage of engagement means establishing a positive Christian presence among the targeted groups. This may involve as little as moving to live in a different part of an urban area where members of the targeted group dwell. It characteristically has involved crossing both geographic and national boundaries. Above all it always involves, by the very definition of missions, moving into a culturally different people from that of the people group of church sending the agent. Cross-cultural adaptation therefore is always required of the cross-cultural agent. Any foreknowledge of the target group's cultural system is always of great help in the adjustment and effectiveness of the missionary going to evangelize cross-culturally.

Often, there is a language barrier to cross as minor as dialectal differences in the target group. The missionary may share a common trade language with the people of the target group or may have to learn one. Missionaries almost always find it necessary to learn the mother tongue of the group or at least to see that an understandable, natural, and accurate translation of the Christian message takes place as early as possible in the task of reaching the targeted group.

Cross-Cultural Nature of the Task

Almost always barriers implicit in the culture complicate the task, especially if the sending culture is urban, Western, wealthy and powerful politically on the world scene. The positive or negative reception of the cross-cultural agent may well be to these factors rather than to the inherent message of the gospel itself.

Worldview Differences

Above all the sending church and its missionary need to recognize that the target culture to a large degree does not know nor understand to any degree the message of the gospel that is being introduced. The target culture has its own indigenous system of worldview and belief regarding the spiritual world and will contain elements that will provide points of contact as well as points of conflict with the gospel.

Spiritual Power Differences

Furthermore, the Biblical message clearly indicates that Satan has established his own counter-kingdom among humankind and that all people before they accept Jesus as the Messiah Savior sent by God are in rebellion against God and in subordination to Satan's power. This presents the missionary with the task of not only dealing with the unbelief of the individuals in the target culture but the resistance of institutionalized aspects of their unbelief and behavior in the culture.

The Bible clearly indicates that the Christian faces a spiritual battle against the very forces of Satan. Active engagement of these forces must be undertaken in a ministry of intercessory prayer by the sending church and the missionaries alike.

Resources for Finishing the Task

The unprecedented growth of the church in the 20th century should encourage us that the task can be finished within the foreseeable future, even from our limited human perspective, not counting God's unlimited resources. The growth in the church during the 19th century was remarkable due to the missionary expansion of the church giving it the designation "The Great Century." The growth of the Christian movement in the 20th century has far surpassed all expectations in spite of the dire predictions of both Christian and non-Christian world affairs observers. The pessimism of its growth was based on the power and wide distribution of the world communist movement, post-industrial secularism in the West and the resurgence of some of the major traditional regional religions throughout the world.

As we consider the magnitude and nature of the unfinished task of world evangelization and particularly the growth of evangelical Christianity in Africa, Latin America, and major centers of Asia, viz. China, Indonesia, Korea: In these areas the gospel has been extended into new people groups that were dominated by traditional African animism, Buddhism, Chinese traditional religion and Islam.

Ralph Winter has done us a particular favor by pointing out that the portion of the Christian population throughout the ages who have been concerned about obeying the great commission and extending the Christian movement to all people groups has

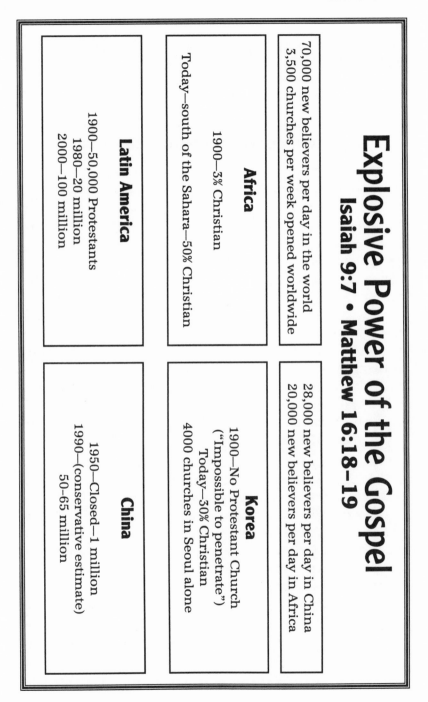

Explosive Power of the Gospel
Isaiah 9:7 • Matthew 16:18–19

70,000 new believers per day in the world
3,500 churches per week opened worldwide

Africa

1900—3% Christian

Today—south of the Sahara—50% Christian

Latin America

1900—50,000 Protestants
1980—20 million
2000—100 million

28,000 new believers per day in China
20,000 new believers per day in Africa

Korea

1900—No Protestant Church
("Impossible to penetrate")
Today—30% Christian
4000 churches in Seoul alone

China

1950—Closed—1 million
1990—(conservative estimate)
50–65 million

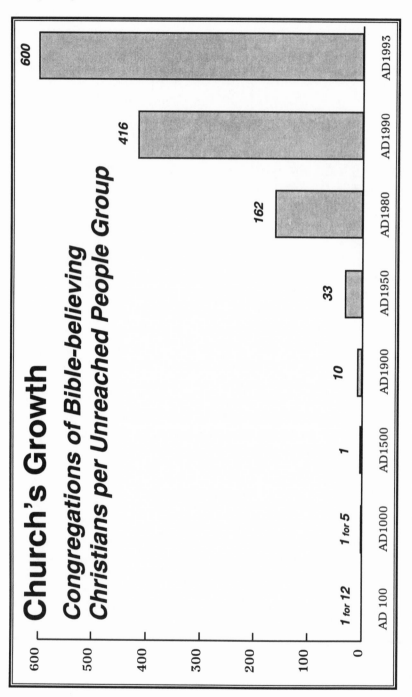

Church's Growth

Congregations of Bible-believing Christians per Unreached People Group

AD 100	1 for 12
AD1000	1 for 5
AD1500	1
AD1900	10
AD1950	33
AD1980	162
AD1990	416
AD1993	600

increased steadily and sometimes dramatically. Not only should this growth, especially since 1430 AD, be encouraging; it has also provided increasing numbers of Christians with resources in an increasingly wider geographic distribution for reaching the remaining unreached groups. Furthermore, the resources of God in His church for finishing the task become even more overwhelming when the number of congregations throughout the world are compared with the number of unreached groups.

The number of majority world missions will soon be sending more cross-cultural missionaries than all of the nations around the North Atlantic region. Korea, India, Nigeria, and Indonesia are only a few of the nations of the newly emerging missionary sending countries. North America, the 10/40 Window and peoples closer to home are among the recipients of these new mission efforts. Some of these missions are of world class size such as the ECWA mission with more than 600 Nigerian missionaries. These missions are taking new forms and often demonstrate outstanding success such as the Deeper Life Church in West Africa. Beginning in Lagos, Nigeria this church has now sent missionaries to 20 African nations and established more than 2000 new congregations.

Conclusion

Perhaps most encouraging is that Christians around the world are seeing the strategic possibility of fulfilling the great commission of Jesus in the foreseeable future. The Lausanne Continuation Committee, the A.D. 2000 Committee, the U.S. Center for World Missions and others have all devoted their resources toward a big push to challenge the church worldwide to complete the task of at least engaging in evangelism the remaining 11,000 unreached groups, as well as pray for and work for a breakthrough to the establishment within them of contextualized indigenous church movements. The heart of this push to complete the task may summed up by the motto "A church for every people by the year 2000." The challenge of mobilizing for the task to use the adequate resources God has provided through the church requires faithfulness on the part of individuals, congregations, agencies, and denominations. For the mission to succeed, God must superintend. Even so—Lord lead us.

A Covenant for Prayer and Action to Finish the Task

In light of:

The magnitude of the unfinished task,

The unprecedented growth of the church worldwide, and

The fact that Christians are seeing the strategic possibility of fulfilling the commission now,

It is our conviction

That our churches must participate more fully in what God is doing in the world to complete the task of world evangelization, and

That God is calling us to an intentional strategy of prayer and activity to facilitate greater involvement among our churches in global evangelization.

Therefore we invite all of like mind to covenant with us,

To pray faithfully for the mobilization of Christ's church,

To encourage, assist and equip the local church in its active and sacrificial involvement in world evangelization, and

To promote unselfishly the welfare of God's Kingdom above the welfare of our own institutions, agencies and personal interests.

7
Strategy for World Evangelization

Rondal Smith

Introduction

Once objectives are established then a plan can be devised for reaching those objectives. One of humankind's defining traits has been that of a tool maker. Tools are devised to help achieve an objective. Such tools are used in a sequence of planned actions that enable a person to achieve his or her objective. On November 23, 1977 while I was using a spade to cultivate my garden I struck a rock which drove home for me the unique planning and tool-making character of human beings. I wrote of that experience:

"On finding an Arrow-head while working in my garden, I mused: Some ancient craftsman chipped this stone, flake on flake—by precious skill learned from his father. From a rough rock with its special flaking character His transforming act showed man's own unique stature."

David, the ancient Hebrew shepherd-poet, goes even deeper into humankind's nature as he looks at the wonders of the creation of God seen in the night sky and then turns to reflect on humankind's unique role in the universe (Psa. 8:3-8):

When I consider your heavens,
the work of your fingers,
the moon and the stars which you have set in place,

what is man that you are mindful of him,
the son of man that you care for him?
You made him a little lower than the heavenly beings
and crowned him with glory and honor.
You made him ruler over the works of your hands;
you put everything under his feet:
all flocks and herds and the beasts of the field,
the birds of the air and the fish of the sea,
all that swim the paths of the seas.

The ancient American Indian craftsman-hunter reaching across the centuries struck a deep chord of identity with me through his finely crafted arrowhead. Here was a man very different from me in lifestyle, culture and time of existence, but underneath those centuries of difference he was a person like me: he had objectives, obtaining game for food, and a plan for achieving them, a sequence of hunting actions and skills that included the use of this special tool, the arrowhead. Here was a person like you and me who was endowed with a God-given dominion over nature —over all creation. The wonder of this is that because we are made in the image of God, we have this capacity to take leadership in our role by envisioning objectives as well as the capacity to manage achieving those objectives by using resources and skills available to us by planning a sequence of actions and devising tools for reaching those objectives. The use of these God-given capacities is what is meant by strategizing. A *strategos* historically referred to a general of an army and *strategy* was the art of planning and deploying his army to achieve military objectives.

In this chapter I want to propose that God has given men and women in His church the responsibility to use their God-given capacities in developing strategies to work with him for finishing the task of world evangelism. Furthermore, we will consider what that strategy might be like based upon the nature of the task presented us in Scripture as well as the nature of the peoples yet to be reached. We will consider strategy under the following headings: the need for strategy, aligning ourselves with God's people-group strategy, strategic planning that brings closure, and mission strategy for spiritual warfare.

The Nature of Mission Strategy

Can we really presume to develop strategies for the evangelization of the people groups of the earth? Is not that presumptive at best as well as ultimately futile for human beings to enter into this process of managing resources to achieve the objectives that God himself has set?

Strategic Planning: A Paradox of Grace

We must ask that question especially when we consider the doctrine of grace as exposited so masterfully in the Epistle to the Romans: that human redemption stems from God's gracious action, not on the works of humankind which have only demonstrated our fallenness and propensity to evil. Yet near the end of that same Epistle, he outlines his past plan and activities and affirms that "It has always been my ambition to preach the gospel where Christ was not known, so that I would not be building on someone else's foundation"(15:20). Then he gives his future plans to visit the Roman believers, "I plan to do so when I go to Spain. I hope to visit you while passing through and to have you assist me on my journey there"(15:24). Here we are faced with the paradox of God's sovereignty and man's free will to purpose and dispose. We plan, depending on God to lead through our discernment. We act, depending on God to prepare the way and to guide us at every step. A great mystery.

In the Epistle to the Ephesians Paul refers to God's plan for human redemption as "the plan (*oikonomia*) of God who works out everything in conformity with the purpose of his will"(1:11). This is "the mystery of his will . . . to be put into effect when the times will have reached their fulfillment—to bring all things in heaven and on earth together under one head, even Christ"(1:10).

God is here pictured as a manager (*oikonomos*) who has a plan for achieving (*oikonomia*) His own envisioned objectives for human salvation. Later yet Paul describes himself using the same basic vocabulary of being a manager and planner when he says later in the Epistle, "Surely you have heard about the task of managing (*oikonomia*) God's grace that was given to me for you [Ephesians], that is the hidden plan (*mysterion*) regarding the Messiah which was not made known to men in other generations as it has now been revealed . . . that through the gospel the Gentiles . . . are sharers in the promise of the Messiah Jesus. I became a servant of this gospel . . . to preach the gospel to the Gentiles . . . and to make plain to everyone the plan (*oikonomia*) i.e., this hidden plan (*mysterion*). . . . His purpose was that now through the church, [it] should be made known to the [spiritual] rulers and authorities in the heavenly realms" (3:2-8, passim). It is a mystery to us, yet a clear biblical teaching that God is the sovereign and the master strategist, planner, and manager and yet he has given human agents a responsible role as strategists, planners, and managers.

Strategic Planning: An Issue of Sovereignty and Free Will

This mystery of God's sovereignty and our free will to respond pervades the whole New Testament. Jesus lays out God's vision and objectives in a command given to his followers for world evangelization of all

the world's people groups in Matthew's Gospel (28:18-
20). The strategy for carrying out this task is not given
here nor elsewhere in any great detail. The Gospel of
Luke (24:47) and Acts (1:8b) do give some detail as
Jesus instructs his followers to wait in Jerusalem for
empowerment for their task by the Holy Spirit and
that "repentance will be preached in my name, beginning at Jerusalem" and again "You will be my witnesses in Jerusalem, and in all Judea and Samaria, and
to the ends of the earth." In the Gospel of John (20:21)
some hint of strategy is perhaps suggested when Jesus
tells them "As the Father has sent me, so send I you."

The book of Acts then unfolds for us the how the
gospel spread from Jerusalem. Only after a persecution
in Jerusalem did early Christians take it to Judea and
Samaria and later on to even Gentiles in Antioch of
Syria. It took a special revelation to Peter to get him to
take the gospel to a Gentile Roman centurion in
Caesarea. Finally, Paul is brought into the picture as
the Apostle to the Gentiles, people who belong to non-
Jewish people groups. In this task Paul eventually car-
ries the gospel all the way to the Roman people
groups' capital at Rome. Paul is a critically important
figure in the spread to non-Jewish people groups. It is
Paul who develops the powerful arguments (see the
Jerusalem Council in Acts 15 and the Epistle to the
Galatians) that reinforce the special revelation that
God made to Peter regarding the legitimacy of evangelizing the Gentile people groups. He becomes a missionary to the various non-Jewish people groups
throughout the eastern Mediterranean world. He prov-
identially finally arrives in Rome where he preaches
the gospel as a prisoner but nevertheless "without hindrance" to Jews and non-Jews alike (28:31).

God Directs

Luke in Acts of the Apostles makes it clear that
God is directing and empowering his agents of mis-

sion through His Holy Spirit, but parallel to that we see plainly that human beings continue to plan and strategize. In 15:6-10 the interaction between our planning and God's direction is very clearly portrayed. "Paul and his companions traveled throughout the region of Phrygia and Galatia, having been kept by the Holy Spirit from preaching the word in the province of Asia. When they came to the border of Mysia, they tried to enter Bithynia, but the Spirit of Jesus would not allow them to. . . . During the night Paul had a vision of a man of Macedonia standing and begging him, 'Come over to Macedonia and help us.'" After Paul had seen the vision, we got ready at once to leave for Macedonia, concluding that God had called us to preach the gospel to them." Following this event Paul's mission band carried out a strategy to preach the gospel in Macedonia which we are left to presume they devised.

People Responsible

The need for God's people to assume the responsibility for devising particular strategic plans for world evangelization and then for implementing them, clearly emerges from the history of the expansion of the church. After the reformation in Europe, two centuries passed before the evangelical Protestant churches seriously undertook the carrying out of the Great Commission of Jesus to disciple all people groups. One cause for this long delay has been traced to the strong teaching of Calvin regarding the total depravity of man and a kind of sovereignty of God that seemed to negate the responsibility of man to get involved in strategic mission planning and execution. That negation of human involvement in developing strategy was challenged by William Carey. His booklet on missions called *An Inquiry into the Obligation of Christians to Use Means for the Conversion of the*

Heathen brought about a paradigm shift in the way the evangelical churches in England and North America thought about missions. This work helped launch Carey himself as well as the multitude who followed his example into the tremendous missionary outreach of the 19th and 20th centuries. The point he made was that Christians are obligated to use means, that is develop and implement strategies, to evangelize people groups not yet penetrated by the gospel.

"Work . . . Until I Return"

Jesus in his parable of the ten minas (Luke 19:11ff.) takes us to a new level of understanding of the responsibility for devising strategy for the growth of the kingdom. Here different people are pictured as being given various sums of money and told "Put this money to work . . . until I come back." Then each person who received money as a steward was judged by whether he had adopted a strategy for multiplying that money that brought growth or not. Humankind is also pictured as a manager (*oikonomos*) with capacities and responsibility for devising strategies. An example is from the parable of the shrewd manager (often translated the unjust steward) from which Jesus applies the lesson for his followers with the statement "For the people of this world are more shrewd in dealing with their own kind than are the people of the light. I tell you, use worldly wealth to gain friends for yourselves, so that when it is gone, you will be welcomed into eternal dwellings" (Luke 16:9). Is not the wealth of resources placed in the hands of believers then to be used strategically for the completion of the task of world evangelism?

Essentially, God expects us to act upon His commands and promises. Jesus said, "All authority in heaven and on earth has been given to me. Therefore go and make disciples of all nations, baptizing them in the name of the Father and of the Son and of the Holy Spirit, and teaching them to obey everything I have commanded you. And surely I am with you always to the very end of the age." Developing a strategic plan to accomplish world evangelization is obeying this command. When God's people develop a strategic plan to disciple every people group they are aligning themselves with His mission and discovering the particular roles they each can play using the gifts and skills that God has given them.

Three Approaches to Strategy

Christians then need to commit themselves to developing strategies that will help finish the task of world evangelism. Dayton suggests that in the past Christians have adopted one of three approaches for beginning cross-cultural strategy in an unreached people group: (1) The Standard Solution, (2) Being in the Way and (3) The Unique Solution.

Strategy: A Standard Solution

The first is essentially doing the same thing for every person in every culture, e.g., distributing tracts of Christian literature to every person. This kind of strategy, of course, in some respects may be valid for certain elements in the evangelism process. For example, the Bible makes plain that the goal of making disciples is establishing a body of worshipping believers within a people group. Developing a means of getting to that point must be clearly adapted to the nature of the group being targeted. While the gospel, Christ, God the Holy Spirit, humankind and the world we live in are constants, the means we develop must vary according to time, place, and persons we are communicating with.

Strategy: Being in the Way (No Plan)

The second approach essentially says that no explicit plan will be devised ahead of time. The person adopting this approach sees himself or herself as simply responding to each situation as he or she thinks best or as the Spirit leads at the time. Two weaknesses of this position immediately surface. Those who adopt this approach usually have no plan at all in mind, but simply deny it or do not want to take the time to think it out clearly. This second approach also falls short in that it makes it difficult if not impossible to join into group efforts for getting a task accomplished. Explicit plans shared with others are the basis for synergistic achievement by groups.

Strategy: A Unique Solution

The Unique Solution approach is recommended then as the most effective. Using it requires taking into account as many of the particular circumstances of the targeted people as possible as well as the nature of the gospel and the one whom it is presenting. Thus a strategic plan can be devised to communicate with them and demonstrate the love of Christ to them in culturally appropriate and tangible ways.

In the section that follows on the process of strategic planning, five objectives or means are envisioned to stimulate specific planning for every individual group. A unique solution using adaptations of various means must be developed to fit the cultural and linguistic circumstances and needs of each targeted people group.

Aligning Ourselves With God's People Group Strategy

In the previous chapter, it was suggested that God

has outlined for us the basic objectives of a strategy in some of the key passages, such as the Covenant Promise to Abraham, the Great Commission of Jesus and in the Vision of the Victorious Risen Christ in the book of Revelation. In these key passages the elements which we called *God's people group strategy* were found to be a constant. We also concluded that the people groups of the world are identified as the appropriate bite sized pieces or units into which the world has been divided for the sake of evangelism. There we presented the commonly used definition of a people group, which is:

"From the viewpoint of evangelization this is the largest group within which the gospel can spread as a church-planting movement without encountering barriers of understanding or acceptance."

A short time of reflection will lead to the conclusion that the people groups are the natural and logical choices for communicating with the individuals within them. Even though these individuals differ from each other in unique ways they nevertheless have much in common attitudinally, behaviorally and linguistically. By definition communication flows in regular structured ways among those within the group. Our task as agents bringing a new message is to work with those who so desire in order to discover how to communicate the message of Christ in their code, categories and channels of communication.

Obviously when other domains of unreached individuals than the people group are chosen as the focus for evangelism, such as continents, countries or even cities, success or failure depends on the extent to which the strategy adopted fits the needs of the various homogeneous people groups within that domain. When cities or countries are targeted as units, either multiple approaches including one adapted to each of the various groups must be used simultaneously or one must discover an approach that utilizes cultural and linguistic behaviors shared by each of the groups involved. What must be constant in such an approach is the principle of adjusting the media and translating the message for the audience receiving the message.

To finish the task of world evangelization, then, many missiologists today are developing strategies for missions that begin with identifying unreached people groups. As stated in the preceding chapter, a common definition of an unreached people group is:

"A people group among which there is no indigenous community of believing Christians with adequate numbers and resources to evangelize this people group without requiring outside (cross-cultural) assistance."

The Process of Strategic Planning

Dayton has suggested a cycle of five stages for strategic planning by Christians who seriously undertake the targeting of an unreached people for evangelization. Five questions serve to elicit crucial strategic planning information: What people is to be reached? What are they like? Who should reach them? How should they be reached? What will be the result when they are reached?

What People

First, then, "What people is to be reached?" Since we have already defined what is meant by "unreached," the next important step is to begin to compile a list of who and where the unreached peoples of the world are. Our assumption is that we should take the good news to all of the unreached peoples while giving priority to the ones who are more receptive.

The most recent edition of *Operation World* by Patrick Johnstone suggests a list of unreached peoples as does the database of the Adopt-People-Clearing-House in Colorado Springs, Colo.

What Are They Like?

The second stage of the planning cycle asks, "What is the people group like?" A reliable cultural demographic profile of information is needed. While one may question undertaking the project of "spiritually mapping" the world, clearly the spiritual condition of the people, their spiritual commitments and their engagements with the spirit world must be understood. A historical and geographical perspective as well as an understanding of the different spiritual commitments is critically important. Some information may be available from databases. By far the best information comes directly from trained people who have researched the people themselves.

Basic kinds of information are helpful in getting to know the people. Who are they? By what name(s) are they known? Where are they located geopolitically? What is their religion or religions? To what extent are they satisfied by their traditional religion(s)? What are various cultural attitudes and behaviors that relate positively or negatively to their accepting Christ? What language do they speak? What are the external influences of surrounding groups and of the government(s) of the country(s) in which they live? Social and economic conditions, geographic accessibility? Are there any indications of receptivity or resistance to the gospel? What is the present mission activity or lack of it among the people? If so, what mission agencies and/or other Christian groups from the outside are already doing work among the people?

Who Should Reach Them?

Thirdly, the question to be asked is "Who should

reach the people?" In an unreached people there may already be believers, there may be cross-cultural evangelists, there may be a fledgling body of believers or there may be a reached people geographically adjacent or even living in the same geographic region as the unreached group, e.g., in a city. Physical proximity does not necessarily mean that a person or a group would be the best group to engage the unreached people. Many factors may have a bearing on this question. For example, if a neighboring people group which may have been reached has a history of violence or mistrust with respect to the unreached group, then perhaps a cross-cultural evangelist from another group which has a positive relation to the unreached group might better reach the target people. Winter has proposed two scales by which we can measure the cultural difference between reached and unreached individuals. The first describes the cross-cultural evangelist as he/she enters and engages the people in evangelism. The second details the unreached people in respect to the cultural distance to the nearest indigenous church. What is the cultural distance between an evangelist and the unbelieving persons targeted?

E-0 Nominal believers needing renewal of the same culture as the evangelist

E-1 Unbelievers in the same culture as the evangelist

E-2 Unbelievers in a near-neighbor culture similar to the evangelist's

E-3 Unbelievers in a distant culture very different than the evangelist's

What is the cultural distance between unbelieving persons and the nearest indigenous body of believers?

P-0 Nominal believers are present in the same culture as the unbelievers

P-1 Active believers are present in the same culture as the unbelievers

P-2 Active believers are present in a near-neighbor culture similar to the unbelievers

P-3 Active believers are present in a distant culture very different than the unbelievers

As believers considering the targeting of an unreached people it is important to consider the cultural distance between the agent chosen to reach the people and the people themselves. The most powerful evangelism is almost always that undertaken by a person of the same culture who is committed to Christ and empowered by His Spirit and His Word. But until a real cultural, contextualization breakthrough is made that empowers a church planting movement, other sources outside the culture are needed for agents of evangelism.

How To Reach Them

The fourth stage in the process of strategic planning to reach a people is, "How should they be reached?" The gospel itself and the guidance of the Holy Spirit help construct a unique solution to communicate with the particular cultural, linguistic and spiritual nature of the targeted people. The Holy Spirit will lead the evangelist and individuals of the target culture together to work at constructing a bicultural bridge of trust and understanding across which the message of the gospel can freely flow.

In planning it is helpful to understand the complex process involved in cross-cultural evangelization. Five steps are identified in the progress of establishing a church planting movement among a people. Each of these stages may involve a great amount of time in both building positive relations of trust among the people as well as the evangelist learning to appreciate and use the cultural and linguistic channels of communication in ways that demonstrates the love and power of the good news of Jesus Christ.

Steps of Evangelization
Step 1: Presence
Step 2: Proclamation
Step 3: Persuasion
Step 4: Planting Churches
Step 5: Propagation

The first three steps may well be called evangelism, that is, the focus is on the process of bringing the gospel of Christ, but steps four and five are the ones that can lead to the evangelization of all the individuals within the people group. So that a group is not considered reached until the church planting movement within it has the resources to evangelize their own group without outside cross-cultural help.

What Will Be the Result?

The fifth and final stage of the strategic planning process asks, "What will be the result of the people being reached?" While it is impossible to know ahead of time it is very helpful to imagine what kind of church God through His word and Spirit might build in the cultural and life circumstances of the target people. Especially is it important to realize ahead of time that like the translated message of the Bible the form of the church enculturated in the targeted people will be different than the form of the church enculturated in the people group from which the cross-cultural workers have come.

Closure: An Essential Element of Strategic Planning

If the church worldwide is to be mobilized the reality of the coming end of the age must become a permanent part of our thinking. We must understand that we live in an age which will at some decisive point come to an end. Can we not just assume that our responsibility is just to enter into the process of world evangelization and not really plan to see that it will actually be completed? Do we as believers not have any time limit on the task of preaching the good news of Jesus to every people group? Theologically have we adopted a view of the end times that either Jesus has already come or that the Second Coming is only in the mythological future?

Serious strategic thinking, then, means planning to actually complete the task in the two stages. We must first reach every people group with their own translated Word of God and with their own planted cluster of contextualized self-propagating congregations equipped with the capacity for the evangelization of that people group. Second, the contextualized churches in each people themselves must complete the evangelization of their own group.

The sense of need for closure and urgency from the last days thinking (eschatology) in Jesus' teaching and in the message of the early church must be recovered. It will provide the background and deeper motivation for our undertaking the almost overwhelming task. It will also certainly give us a great sense of hope that the task can and will be completed.

Examining a few key passages of Scripture that exhibit the certainty and urgency of the last days is important. From these passages one can see the vital role Jesus' return must play in motivating us to plan strategically to complete the task of world evangelization.

Let us reflect briefly then on the strategic implications of these three theological facts for missions. First, planning to finish the task will mean that *we must communicate with other Christians*: We cannot know where to go unless we know where others have or have not been. We cannot know when we are done until we know when others are done. Only when God's people practice the unity of Christ's body in very concrete ways such as by communicating and planning together will the task be completed. It is for this kind of unity in practice that Jesus prayed in John 17, "My prayer is not for them alone [his disciples]. I pray also for those who will believe in me through their message, that all of them may be one, Father, just as you are in me and I am in you. May they also be in us so that the world may believe that you have sent me."

Secondly, our evangelization must not be restricted to a narrow understanding of the preaching the gospel. Rather *we must develop a strategy of reaching through evangelization and social action.* We must care for and respond to human needs as we proclaim the coming of Jesus who both preached and did good deeds that were evidence of the good news that God's kingdom has broken into human life. It brings a transformation from the inside out as individuals with new hearts and minds now exhibit behavior that influences the families, neighborhoods and finally the social structure and nation of which they are a part. We cannot forget the radical call for justice that God's reign brings with its presence. Jesus' announcement of His ministry's nature to His home congregation in Nazareth pointed out clearly that His good news was not only proclamation of a message but that as the Messiah He was calling for social justice: "The Spirit of the Lord is on me, because he has anointed me to preach good news to the poor. He has sent me to proclaim freedom for the prisoners and recovery of sight to the blind, to release the oppressed, to proclaim the year of the Lord's favor" (Luke 4:18-19).

Thirdly, *mission strategy must be understood as waging spiritual warfare* against the demonic forces of Satan who have established spiritual strongholds to be overcome by the power of Christ in this world. Men and women are bound by Satan's power and are waiting for Christ's church to bring His power to free them from captivity.

Adopting a Theistic Worldview

In order for the church to be effectively mobilized to enter into this strategic spiritual warfare, it will be necessary for the biblical view of life and the world to be recovered. Many Christians in urbanized Western culture have accepted a pared down view of reality. God is believed on as a reality, but in practice His existence and exercise of power is restricted to that of a Creator who does not interfere with his creation except in a psychological sense. They are practical deists who may theoretically believe in the existence of demons and angels, but who do not expect them to affect everyday living in the real world.

The middle or intermediary sphere of demons and angels between God and Satan who are spiritual realities and the real, natural world with its laws of action has been excluded from many a Christian's worldview. We should not neglect the reality of science as the study of God's handiwork and as a valid and necessary aspect of life. It is to deny, however, that the science of natural phenomena is absolute and autonomous from the revelation of God concerning other realities beyond nature. Therefore, recovering the excluded middle is necessary, if we are to plan strategically to complete the task of world evangelization: "Our fight is not against people on earth, but against . . . the spiritual powers of evil in the heavenly world" (Eph. 6:1ff). Not only should we recognize this spiritual dimension, we should actively engage to use the spiritual power available to us.

Nor, should this reality of Satanic powers that are arrayed against the church's mission be the occasion for fear. Jesus has already promised His church "I will be with you even until the end of the age." He has also pictured the church as on the spiritual warfare offensive. "On this rock I will build my church and the gates of Hades shall not prove stronger than it" (Matt. 16:18).

Prayer, a Strategic Weapon

Such a strategic concern seen in the light of the spiritual reality of the warfare leads us to rediscover the critical role of united corporate intercessory prayer. Jesus has already demonstrated His own commitment to pray for unbelievers as He prays for "those who will believe in me through their (his disciples') message." Prayer is the vital action along with resistance to Satan that believers are exhorted to do in the Ephesians 6:18 passage after the description of the spiritual armor that believers are provided: "And pray in the Spirit on all occasions with all kinds of prayers and requests." Jesus assures us that corporate prayer has its own promise and power. "Wherever two or three of you are gathered in my name there will I be among you and whatever you ask in my name agreeing I will grant."

Furthermore, Jesus not only exhorts His followers to acknowledge "The harvest is plentiful, but the laborers are few," but He continues by telling them "Ask the Lord of the harvest, therefore, to send out workers into his harvest field" (Matt. 9:37-38). Prayer for more evangelists both within a people group and cross-culturally then must be a further aspect of the strategic planning that takes into account the spiritual nature of the battle.

The current movement of prayer among believers has just such a strategic focus. David Bryant, one of its leaders, points out that at the beginning of the mission movement in the 18th century there was a prayer movement initiated by Jonathan Edwards that called on Christians to unite across sectarian lines to pray for two things: (1) the renewal of the church (2) so that the great commission of Christ might be completed. Such prayer is thus a vital element in any strategy to complete the task today.

Conclusion

Currently, evangelical believers throughout the whole world have engaged in a concentrated effort to complete the task of world evangelization. One of those efforts suggests that the first phase of our strategy, the effort to plant a cluster of indigenous churches within every currently unreached people group, be accomplished by the turn of the millennium, the year AD 2000. This raises interesting questions.

First of all, the question is raised, "Should it be done?" Can we as believers give ourselves a deadline for accomplishing such an immense task of engaging and effectively planting an indigenous cluster of contextualized evangelizing churches within currently unreached groups? Even when we realize that many of the unreached groups are already engaged and some may well have many congregations among them, but they do not yet have all the resources they need to classify them as reached, dare we presume to set such a time deadline?

We recognize several cautions. The actual transformation of a person's or a people's heart is a work of the Holy Spirit not subject to human projections or timetables. The uncertainties of world geopolitical conditions and the accessibility of many of the unreached groups certainly raises questions about feasibility. A further theological problem is raised by our under-

standing that the completion of the task of discipling
even a few persons from every people group is some-
how tied to the Second Coming of Christ. Might not
we seem to be, in some sense, presuming to bring
about the Second Coming by our activity of completing the task of world evangelization of every people
group? Debate continues whether our action would
influence the time of the Second Coming. Jesus
promised that He would return when the gospel is
preached to all nations (Luke 24; Matt. 24). He also
warned His disciples about date setting (Acts 1:7).

Granting all these valid reasons for not assigning
any certainty to a set time for completion, I would like
to suggest that, nevertheless, we should set a tentative
date at least for the *engagement* of every people group
with cross-cultural agents of Christ's church to begin at
least an active Christian presence if not proclamation
of the good news of Jesus. Certainly active intercessory
prayer for the unreached people groups and for laborers equipped appropriately to reach them is not only
acceptable; it seems to be the only way for a church
committed to the Lordship of Christ to respond. No
strategic plan is complete without a projected time of
completion. We know that it is God's will "that not any
perish." Granted that it takes time to carry out the task
of engaging, establishing relationships with, communicating in culturally and linguistically appropriate
ways, we must nevertheless envision an end point to
the process and prayerfully work toward its completion, always letting our strategic plans be subject to the
modification and transformation of the Holy Spirit.

Yes, we should set a date. So why not aim toward
the year AD 2000 realizing we can only propose and
that it is God who disposes of our plans. We need to
make plans strategically that will bring glory to God
and such a mobilization of the church certainly would.

"Can it Be Done?" is the next question that imposes

itself upon our thinking as we explore the proposition: "A Church for Every People by the Year 2000!" If we go beyond our basic assumption that "with God anything is possible," that resources for such an undertaking in God's providence are unlimited, can we on a purely human level envision how such an undertaking might occur? What would be needed from a human perspective is enough personnel appropriately equipped to go cross-culturally with the physical, social and emotional means and spiritual backing to accomplish the task of engaging the remaining unreached groups for evangelization. The previous chapter on "The Unfinished Task" has set forth the tremendous growth of the church worldwide demonstrating that one out of every ten persons on earth is an evangelical believer and that there are over 600 congregations among believers worldwide for every one of the unreached groups. The resources of people and means are available if the church mobilized them by catching the vision of finishing the task now.

8
To Reach the Unreached

Doug Priest Jr.

Introduction

We have entered the last five years of the second millennium since the birth of Christ. Ours is a time of unprecedented activity and opportunity for the spread of the gospel. Noted Restoration missiologist Donald McGavran was fond of saying, "We live at the sunrise of missions." Surely he was right. In these last years of the 20th century the center of Christianity has shifted from the Western world to the Two-Thirds world. More than half of today's Christians live in the non-Western world. There are more Christians in Latin America than any other continent, and Africa has the fastest growing church.

Living in the Information Age gives us access to the size and growth of the church anywhere in the world. The recently published new edition of *Operation World* by Patrick Johnstone (1993) is one of many databases from which we can draw. The last several decades have seen a tremendous amount of research being undertaken so that we can make a fairly accurate assessment about the church anywhere. Specialized databases have been developed by many different groups involved in missions. Relief agencies, Bible societies, denominations, mission agencies, and even theological schools have their own tailor-made research files that assist them in fulfilling their ministries.

Much of the research that has been undertaken is geared to the macro-level, encompassing the entire globe. It is research that is painted in broad strokes, giving a generalized picture of various countries and geographical areas. But to be able to narrow one's focus to a specific people, city, village, or segment of society is also important. Micro-level research must be undertaken in order to customize our efforts to a specific group so that the gospel is seen as truly good news to them. Failure to do basic and thorough research about a people prior to commencing missionary work among them can result in costly mistakes that might rob the people of their opportunity to inherit the kingdom.

God Wants the Lost Found

God wants the lost of the world to be found. Paul wrote to Timothy, "God our Savior wants all men to be saved and to come to a knowledge of the truth" (1 Tim. 2:3-4). We do not doubt for a minute that all the unreached peoples of the world need to be brought to faith in their Father through Jesus Christ. The question that consumes us all is, "How do we best cooperate with our sovereign Lord to reach the unreached?"

The Lahu Come to Faith

The ongoing mission effort among the Lahu people in northern Thailand illustrates conversion taking place as a result of a group decision. We are grateful for this information from third-generation missionary Jonathan Morse, who has lived in Asia all his life.[1]

---

1. Jonathan Morse, personal prayer letter, 1993, and "Forging a More Responsible Lahu Alliance," 1994, unpublished.

The Lahu are a tribal people living in Southeast Asia and numbering more than half a million. Well known for their hunting skills, they currently live in agricultural villages in Thailand, Burma, China, Laos and Vietnam. While originally living in Burma and China, the Lahu were forced to move to surrounding countries following persecution by the Communists.

In northern Thailand the Lahu are a mountain tribe, living at the mid-level elevations. Occupying this middle ground, they lie sandwiched between the Lisu people who inhabit the ridge tops and the Karen people who live along the valley floors.

Work among the Lahu in Burma began at the turn of this century as a mission outreach of the American Baptists. Some Lahu believers emigrated to Thailand in the 1950s and 1960s, and today the Baptists have an ongoing work with some 120 Lahu villages there. However, there are 140 Lahu villages in Thailand that have yet to be evangelized.

The Lahu are divided into different subgroups, and two of these groupings, the Lahu-Sheleh and the Lahu-Nyi, have been resistant to the gospel. It is among these subgroups that Morse recently began initial evangelistic efforts. The Lahu-Sheleh and the Lahu-Nyi are group-oriented. Though many villages have been exposed to the gospel, the villages are waiting for their leaders to make a decision about whether to become Christian.

The Lahu-Sheleh are at a significant crossroads concerning their decision for Christ. Jesus is being heatedly debated in every Lahu-Sheleh village. It is our firm expectation that when the gospel does finally break into this group, they will turn to the Lord in a solid block. In the mean time, they have paused at the very edge of the valley of decision. . . . I don't think we can say that the Lahu-Sheleh represent stony ground.

It is more a case where for some reason the fruit has just not yet ripened on the tree.[2]

While the Lahu-Sheleh debate, some of the Lahu-Nyi villages have decided to become Christian. Morse tells of the "wonderful surprise when nearly the entire Lahu-Nyi village of Na Ngai decided to place their faith in Christ. The villagers were led to make this dramatic move by the simultaneous conversion of both the village chief and the village shaman. A total of fifty-five persons became Christian."[3]

In the last few months at least four more Lahu-Nyi villages made the same decision as did the village of Na Ngai. Today there are some 300 new Christians. It is the village leaders, not the foreign missionary, who are leading the way to Christ. The people movement among the Lahu-Nyi is on the verge of encompassing many other villages, not only in Thailand but also in Burma and China.

The Lahu-Sheleh have not moved as far along towards conversion as have the Lahu-Nyi. But we can trust that they too will follow their distant relatives in making their decision to submit to the Lordship of Christ.

Becoming Christian

As we examine the early church of the first century recorded in the Acts of the Apostles we can learn how people became Christians. Often our study of this process is focused on the steps which people took as they showed their obedience. The steps recorded for us in Acts included hearing the good news of Jesus Christ, repentance from sin and turning to Christ in belief, obediently following the command of baptism and all

---

2. Morse, personal prayer letter.

3. Ibid.

other commands of the Lord from that day forward.

In our evangelistic efforts we often try to duplicate this pattern. Directing our attention on the proper order of these steps seems for us a theological and a methodological necessity. In individualistic Western society, this evangelism is usually attempted "one on one." We do home visitation, ask people to accept Jesus as personal Lord and Savior, give the invitation at the bonfire in our church camps and share a tract with someone. All of these methods are geared to the individual.

Following such methods, we often miss the sociological element of conversion as recorded in the book of Acts. Perhaps we have allowed our culture's bias towards individualism to blind us to the fact that Biblical decisions to follow Christ were almost always made as group decisions. In fact, throughout history, the majority of people who have become Christian have done so as a part of a group decision rather than an individual decision apart from the group.

Conversion in the Book of Acts

As we scan the book of Acts looking at incidents of belief, we find that of the thousands upon thousands of recorded conversions, only Saul and the Ethiopian official are given as individual ones. The rest are recorded as large gatherings, individuals together with their households, and groups of people in various cities.

Decisions that are made in the context of a group should not be linked with notions of mob justice or mass hysteria. Group decisions are simply the way many cultures throughout the world choose to determine things. What often happens is that the group will meet together, discuss an issue, strive to reach consensus over time, and then act on the decision when everybody is ready. If there is strong opposition towards the decision in the group, the decision is not made. Group decisions are really multi-individual decisions made together at the same time. Perhaps a common example would be when the people at a sporting event all participate in "The Wave." While each person acts in concert with the others, it is the group activity that is noted. People are not carried along against their will—they freely participate.

When conversion takes place as a group decision it is called a "people movement."[4] In non-individualistic societies, people movements represent the preferred conversion mode. If conversions are individualistic in these societies, very often there are severe consequences for the person as well as the spread of the gospel. Individuals may be disowned by their families and ostracized by their society. The further flow of the gospel may be hampered because the individual went against the wishes of the group.

Of course we are not suggesting that those who sincerely love the Lord should be discouraged from acting on their commitment. Far from it! Rather, we are suggesting that in our evangelistic methods, we target groups rather than individuals. When individuals show an openness to the gospel, we need to encourage them to speak to the group and encourage the group along towards a decision. If in the end the group refuses to participate, then by all means we must not hinder individual decisions.

People movements are best suited towards societies that are group-oriented and tight-knit. They do not occur in societies that are individualistic because in those societies people make decisions in different ways. Seeking group approval is not required in indi-

---

4. See McGavran, *The Bridges of God* and *Understanding Church Growth*.

vidualistic societies. Western societies are primarily individualistic, and urban societies around the world are rapidly becoming more individual-oriented.

Conversion As A Process

Western culture follows the Greek cultural notion of dualism. We tend to view our world as made up of pairs of opposites: man and woman; right and left; black and white; up and down; light and darkness; salt and pepper. An implication of this common view is to be found in our theology as it relates to conversion. Normally we classify people as either Christian or non-Christian, and we assume that moving from one category to the other takes place in a short amount of time. This quick movement is only possible if one is at the point of conversion.

Much must take place, however, in bringing a people to the point of conversion. Some missionary thinkers have found it helpful to see conversion not as an instantaneous occurrence, but as a process that takes place over time. Viggo Søgaard has developed a scale of ten points that begins with a people having no knowledge of God.[5] As that people progresses in their knowledge of God, they move farther along the scale. It is only when they reach the final point that they are ready to move from the category of non-Christian to Christian.

When Peter spoke to the Jewish people on the day of Pentecost he was not speaking to pagans. No, he was speaking to Jewish people who were well-grounded in their faith in God. They were already acquainted with the idea of an expected Messiah. How different these people were from people in Thailand who link divinity with a golden statue of Buddha.

---

5. John D. Robb, *Focus: The Power of People Group Thinking* (Monrovia, CA: MARC, 1989), pp. 43-50.

Through the use of Søgaard's scale, we can see that there is a gradual movement towards conversion. We can also see that it is possible to tailor our message to where people fit along the scale. For example, it would do no good to begin with a group of idol-worshippers by telling them to "repent" from idolatry when they view their idol worship as a good thing; a way of revering their ancestors by maintaining traditional family values. We should begin with the level of awareness of God that our audience understands. Since the Søgaard scale allows us to see the progression towards conversion, we can be encouraged with the steps a people are taking even before they are converted.

Open and Closed Countries?

Restoration missionary scholar Tetsunao Yamamori shares some sobering statistics: "The number of unreached people groups is said to be 5,310 located in 145 countries. In 1995, there will be an estimated 3.88 billion non-Christians within these countries—96% of the world's non-Christians."[6] These 145 countries can be considered as either "open" or "closed" to foreign missionary activity. Some of these countries allowed foreign missionaries to live and minister within their borders while others did not.

Those countries that allowed missionaries were the open countries, and the others that did not allow full time missionaries were the closed countries. It was assumed that the only way to minister in closed countries was through various media finding their way into the country. Hence, if one could not evangelize in Russia or China, at least Christian radio programs could be broadcast into these countries, or perhaps

---

6. Tetsunao Yamamori, "Forward," in *Working Your Way to the Nations: A Guide to Effective Tentmaking*, ed. by Jonathan Lewis (Pasadena, CA: William Carey Library), p. i.

Bibles could be smuggled across the borders.

Within the last twenty years, this notion of "open" or "closed" countries has given way to a much more useful understanding. Nowadays we no longer talk about "closed" countries because we have expanded our definition of missionaries to include those who are Christian professional workers. Countries that are closed to the traditional full-time missionary are now known as either "restricted access" nations or "creative access" nations.

It is possible to enter countries which are closed to the traditional missionary role. But we must be creative in doing so. Christians who practice a secular profession are usually welcome in those countries. While it may not be possible to enter Pakistan or Saudi Arabia as a missionary, it is definitely possible to enter those countries as a business person or as an oil worker. Similarly, most any country in the world can be entered if one has a background in teaching English as a second language.

How can we best reach the unreached peoples in countries where traditional missionaries are not welcome? There are numerous ways, but we will just highlight three. Through these creative strategies, access to restricted countries becomes possible.

Partnership

Even restricted access nations have some Christians living in them. While missionaries may not be able to secure visas to work in these countries, they can form partnerships with local Christians so that the gospel can be proclaimed. The local partners provide a way for the foreign partners to minister in the country. The foreign partners provide fervent prayer, sharing of Christian lesson materials, and usually some form of financial assistance. This aid may be used to pay preachers' salaries, provide building materials, or be used in relief and development projects.

Presently the country of Myanmar, formerly known as Burma, will not allow Christian missionaries within its borders. But my home church in Singapore is contributing assistance to Lahu evangelists based in Thailand who are able to minister in Myanmar. In Thailand these evangelists receive salaries and Biblical training. They can either then train Myanmar Lahu in two to three day teaching sessions at the Thailand-Myanmar border, or they can enter Myanmar for short periods of training local believers. In this way we are partners in assisting the work of reaching the unreached Lahu villages in Myanmar.

Non-Residential Missionaries

Another strategy to reach the unreached in restricted access nations is to become a non-residential missionary—while living in one country you are a missionary to another! A non-residential missionary need not be in full time service. After identifying the country, the non-residential missionary works to gather as much information about the country as possible. He or she then begins earnestly praying for ongoing ministries within that country. As opportunities present themselves, the missionary will network with others who share the same burden, perhaps forming an alliance of non-residential missionaries. They form contacts with Christians from within the restricted access nation and may form partnerships with them. Some non-residential missionaries work diligently through means of radio, Christian literature or Bible translation so that the people in the restricted access nations can hear the gospel.

Periodically the non-residential missionary will make trips to the country, entering on a tourist visa. These trips may serve the purpose of orientation, fact finding, and providing ministry assistance through preaching or teaching if feasible. Such short term mission trips can best accomplish desired results if made in cooperation with local believers.

Traditional American missionaries are not welcome in India. But a preacher friend of mine has made several preaching trips to India and has helped with the training of dozens of local evangelists. His church offers financial assistance so that some of these evangelists can devote themselves full time to preaching and teaching in unreached areas. My friend is correct when he calls himself a non-residential missionary to India, though he lives in Wichita, Kansas.

Bivocational Missionaries

Yet another strategy for entering supposedly "closed" countries is to enter as a bivocational missionary or a tentmaker, as was the Apostle Paul. A tentmaker is "a Christian who works in a cross-cultural situation, is recognized by members of the host culture as something other than a 'religious professional,' and yet, in terms of his or her commitment, calling, motivation, and training is a 'missionary' in every way."[7] The advantages of being a bivocational missionary, in addition to getting into restricted access nations, are that they can supplement the work of local Christians (and other missionaries if working in "open" countries), and they can have access to local people who do not want to be associated with traditional missionaries.

Unreached People in Bangkok

Without doubt, one of the world's most unreached

7. Donald Hamilton, in *Working Your Way to the Nations*, Jonathan Lewis, ed. (Pasadena: William Carey Library, 1993), p. 1-2.

major urban areas is Bangkok, capital of the Kingdom of Thailand. By night Bangkok has some eight million residents. By day the number rises to ten million with workers pouring into the city from outlying areas. Playing catch-up with the other thriving and thoroughly modern cities of Asia, like Singapore, Tokyo, and Seoul, Bangkok is rapidly becoming a world-class city. Not a week goes by without a new skyscraper being completed.

The major religion of Thailand is Buddhism, and the few Christians of the country come primarily from the north. Thailand is only 1% Christian, so it is appropriate to say that there is no reached group in Thailand except for those who attend Bible college! In Bangkok, one need not worry about planting churches in already reached areas—there are none. The most current listing shows that there are 115 congregations in the city, meaning that there is only one church of any sort for every 87,000 people.

To attempt to list the various unreached people groups in Bangkok would be an exercise in futility. Whoever has the most creative imagination would come up with the longest list. Suffice it to say, Bangkok is full of unreached people. There is no dearth of opportunities for evangelism, church planting and Christian social work in this Buddhist stronghold.

How are Christian workers attempting to minister in Bangkok? We will identify only three such efforts as illustrative of the creativity that is required in reaching the unreached. Many more innovative approaches could be cited.

The Traditional Bible Study Approach

The most common approach to church planting in Bangkok has been the traditional Bible study approach. Missionaries enter the country and spend one to two years in learning the very difficult Thai language. Once sufficient mastery of the language and culture has taken place, the missionary moves to a section of the city, making contacts which are then drawn into a home Bible study. The emphasis on this approach is that the missionary becomes identified as a member of the community, participating in as many community events as possible. Unfortunately, in urban areas where life is very complex, it is difficult to become known throughout the community.

As the Bible study grows, with members inviting their friends, soon it becomes necessary to rent a small building for weekly worship services. Local leadership is trained. More people become involved, and eventually a church building is constructed. Land prices being what they are in Bangkok, often the funds for such a building must be subsidized with contributions from the missionary.

The Incarnational Approach among the Urban Poor

While Bangkok is rapidly becoming modernized, the city has many slum areas. Those who inhabit the slums may be the very destitute who have no jobs, lower class people with menial jobs, or even upwardly mobile people such as clerical or factory workers who choose to save rental money by living in slum areas until they can move into better surroundings. In Bangkok, different from other urban areas around the world, it is not correct to simply label every slum dweller as homeless or destitute.

Several missions have targeted Bangkok's slums for ministry outreach. Their approach is termed "incarnational" because the missionaries move into the slums, living shoulder to shoulder with the people. Besides giving up the modern conveniences of running water, electricity, and privacy, they live in small rooms or shacks for two weeks at a time. They then take a break for several days, staying in a large modern house with an older couple who serve as their pastors and counselors. On these breaks they can read, study, do their laundry, go out to eat at a restaurant—basically they get their batteries recharged to return to the slums for the next two week period. With such a strategy, they are able to continue living in the slums for a longer period than one who simply stays in the slum, but "burns out" after a few months or a year.

These missionaries, often single or married couples without children, become well known throughout the limited slum area. They are strangers to no one, carry their water, and use the same communal facilities as the rest of the people. Through their contacts they not only witness and lead discussions, but also serve as educated advocates for the slum-dwellers in relating to the authorities. They initiate local development projects, such as putting in a sidewalk to keep people from having to walk in the mud or initiating a cardboard recycling business. Through their contacts, the missionaries can also encourage physicians to visit the slums and offer cheap medical care. Viv Grigg's book presents an excellent resource for those willing to consider such a needed ministry.[8]

The Cell Group Approach

The approach that has achieved the most success in reaching the unreached in Bangkok is the cell group approach, as capably outlined by Ralph Neighbour.[9] The largest churches in the world are cell group churches, and the Hope of God Church in Bangkok is the largest

---

8. Viv Grigg, *Companion to the Poor* (Monrovia, CA: MARC, 1990).

9. See Ralph Neighbour, *Where Do We Go From Here? A Guidebook for the Cell Group Church* (Houston: Touch Publications, 1990).

church in Thailand with some six thousand members.

Groups of people usually meeting in homes on a weekly basis are the key to the cell group approach. It is within these groups that evangelism, teaching, edification and encouragement occur. Within the small group, usually not more than twelve to fifteen people, people can share openly with one another. They minister to one another's needs, and outsiders are attracted to a small caring group.

Cell group churches are unabashedly evangelistic. They believe that the unreached will respond best in an intimate setting rather than in an anonymous worship service. While many large congregations are based on programs, cell group churches place their emphasis on the people in the cell group. It is in the cell groups that the different spiritual gifts are exercised. Cell groups take care of one another in ministry and work together to reach out to their non-Christian acquaintances.

Cell groups differ from home Bible study groups in that the emphasis is on bringing new members into the group. In fact, if the cells do not have new members after about a year, they are disbanded. It is usually the case that the cells divide into two after eight to twelve months. One benefit of the cell group method is that newcomers are quickly incorporated into the life of the church. They do not have to break into long standing groups or cast about until they find a place of service, but are quickly embraced into a small group.

The Hope of God Church in Bangkok is rapidly dispelling the notion that all Thai are resistant to the gospel. The majority of the church are made up of those below the age of thirty. The largest grouping in the church represents those in the high school and college ages. Church statistics reveal that 85% of the members are converts, rather than coming to the church as transfers from other congregations.

The Hope of God Church in Bangkok does have a

weekly worship service, but they are quick to say that the heart of their church life occurs within the hundreds of cell groups that meet throughout the city.

Conclusion

Norman and Swee Keng Chan are a new breed of missionary. No, they do not come from America, but are Singaporean. They worked in rural church planting in northern Thailand, but believed God was calling them to minister in Bangkok.

When they entered language study to brush up on their Thai following mission studies in Singapore, their idea was to plant a church among the lower middle class. The approach they were envisioning was the Bible study approach, where they would move into an unchurched part of the city and evangelize as God gave them contacts. Their expectation was that at the end of their four year term with their mission, CMF International, they would have planted one church.

But while in language study, they came to believe that God was guiding them in a different direction. "Why should we plant just one church during our term?" they asked themselves. "Is there not a better way? Can we not try to plant several churches during the same period?"

As they pondered these questions, and as they became more oriented to Bangkok, they determined to try a different approach, but one that would still result in churches being started in Bangkok. Instead of moving into an unchurched area of the city, they would stay in the city center where their language school was located, for this was also the business center of town, and their new strategy was to be based on reaching business people.

Like any other modern city, Bangkok has a business district. Many of the businessmen are from other countries and English is the language they speak. Yet

Norman and Swee Keng learned that many of these business people, even though Christian, were not attending a local church. They decided to target these business people by launching a weekly service in a hotel lobby. They would attract people to the service through advertising for an Asian Christian fellowship meeting, with services in English.

Their dream is to encourage these business people to bring their colleagues and to recommit themselves to the Lord. As they do so, they will be encouraged to give towards the planting of churches first in Bangkok, but later in Thailand and then through Southeast Asia. Those who plant the churches in Thailand will be trained Thai preachers. Thailand has several preacher training institutions. Unfortunately there are not enough congregations to employ all those who have been trained, so many of the preachers must resort to working two jobs to support their families.

The effort will be directed to Asians and will be sponsored by Asians. As such it should be more user-friendly to this audience than one that is led by an American missionary.

This is the sort of creativity that is required in reaching the unreached of our world. We must join together with others of like faith. We must realize that the missionary of today and the missionary of tomorrow are no longer primarily sent from North America and Europe as has been the case for the last two hundred years. Our strategies must fit the context where we live rather than being slavishly copied from our home countries. Since the center of gravity of the world's Christian movement no longer is the northern hemisphere but the south, we must be prepared to listen to and heed our new brothers and sisters in Christ. Unless revival comes to America and Europe, the twenty-first century belongs to Asians, Africans and Latin Americans.

9
Evangelism and Church Planting

Edgar J. Elliston

Introduction

This chapter introduces and briefly evaluates a range of strategies for evangelism and church planting. The issues raised in this chapter apply across a wide range of cultural contexts.

An assumption undergirding this whole text is that without a clear faith commitment to Jesus Christ that is demonstrated in one's lifestyle, one has no hope for eternal life. Only one way to eternal life exists and that is through Jesus Christ. Without faith in him no one has any hope beyond eternal punishment.

A clear expectation of believers is to be a part of a community of believers. Individuals may be assured of their everlasting hope through Christ, but obedience and growth take place in community.

While many strategies for evangelism have proven to be effective, the effective ones work in and through the communities of believers. The formation of new communities of believers or churches then is certainly linked to every effective evangelistic strategy.

Practical Issues

Evangelism is primarily the process of delivery of the good news about what God has done in Jesus Christ.

A simple analogy from the postal service will illustrate the process. The U.S. Postal Service has as a primary function the delivery of the mail entrusted to it. Much effort goes into the printing and sale of postage, the staffing of post offices, the maintenance of buildings and equipment, and the training of postal workers. However, if a letter entrusted to the postal service is not received by the person to whom it was addressed in a timely way, the postal service would be described as a failure in that instance. Yes, the handling of the mail is important, but the safe, timely and reliable receiving of the mail is the issue. Even the delivery to a mailbox or a postal box does not complete the postal service's responsibility. Receiving is the clear goal.

Similarly, evangelism is the delivery—and receiving of the good news of God's message of hope through Jesus Christ. The transmission of the message—as critical as that is—is not adequate or completed until it has been accepted and the person has come to apply that message to his/her life in the context of a believing, nurturing, reproducing community.

Other processes of maturing the believer follow the acceptance of the gospel. The nurture and maturation process continues for a lifetime. However, the process of evangelism is not complete until there is an acceptance. The delivery of a tract, sermon, videotape, the "Four Spiritual Laws," the whole Bible or a personal testimony to a person may be a part of the process of evangelism. However, evangelism is not complete until the message has been received.

A very good example, in fact, of the most effective single evangelistic means in history is the "Jesus" film produced by Campus Crusade. The daily decision rate as of January, 1995 exceeds 30,000.[1] Of these 30,000

---

1. Personal interview with Paul Eshelman, the international director of the Jesus Project for Campus Crusade, January 17, 1995.

many become mature reproducing members of churches. This evangelistic strategy has in fact been so successful that Campus Crusade, in some countries where the incorporation into local churches was slow, has been "forced" into forming a church planting strategy.[2] This film has been viewed by many times more people than any film in history. Currently, it is being distributed in 143 languages. It has also been reproduced for audio presentation via radio and audiotape.

To change metaphors but to focus on the same issue—an evangelist may be compared to a midwife in the delivery of a child. The midwife can take no credit for the child, but for the completion of the birth process. An experienced midwife can describe the stages of the delivery process and may help the expectant mother prepare. The work is not done, however, until the new infant is safely delivered to its mother's arms.

Why?

Answering the question of "Why?" would take more space than this book allows. The answer may be found in Peter's statement, "God is not willing for any to perish, but for all to come to repentance." God's desire for people as revealed in both the Old and New Testaments is clearly for a close relationship with himself. From the gracious promise to Eve and the merciful act of driving Adam and Eve from the garden to the death and resurrection of Jesus, his actions demonstrate a consistent reconciling drive. The good news of the gospel is that now God has again taken the initiative for us. God wants the best for us. The declaration

---

2. See Roy Rosedale's D.Miss. dissertation, *Evaluation of Campus Crusade for Christ's Strategy for Planting Churches in Rural Thailand* (Fuller Theological Seminary, 1992), which documents more than 3000 of these churches in Thailand alone.

and acceptance of this good news was the consistent message that the Old Testament prophets, Jesus and the apostles proclaimed.

A second response to the question, "Why?" relates to human need and the result of one's response to the gospel. On the one side, every person is condemned without Christ, and on the other side an acceptance of Christ and obedience to him brings the best of hope both for the present and the unending future.

Even Christians find it easy to "pass the buck" and not take responsibility for evangelism. It is certainly true that not every person is especially gifted or "called" to be an evangelist. However, both from prescription and from New Testament precedent every believer is expected to be a witness to his/her faith. Interestingly, the word, witness, is translated from the word which also means "martyr." One is expected to give the witness of one's life. The clear statement to the disciples, "You are to be my witnesses (martyrs) . . ." (Acts 1:8) applies to us as well.

If the gospel is in fact received as good news, it will be shared. People share the good news of births, weddings, anniversaries, promotions, and accomplishments. Whether in the early church or in contemporary society, when one has good news, the family, friends, neighbors and other associates cannot but hear about it.

Yes, the "evangelist" may receive a special measure of spiritual power to influence others to accept the gospel, but the clear command, "as you go make disciples. . . ." applies to the rest of us as well.

As I was growing up as a member of a church in a small midwestern town, I thought evangelism was something that was to be done twice a year. The church had a fall evangelistic emphasis and then another in the spring just before Easter. I wonder if that church and the others in that small town had worked more "continuously," perhaps others might have accepted Christ as Lord.

When?

The question of "When" might be answered another way. Paul wrote to the church in Galatia that "when the time was right God sent his Son born of a virgin born under the law to redeem those under the law" (Gal. 4:4). As we observe the proclamation of the good news of the kingdom in the gospels and Acts, we can see that the good news was given at opportune times, whether alongside a healing or an inquiry about the kingdom. It was given as and when the Spirit was preparing people to hear, such as the woman at the well (John 4) or the Ethiopian in his chariot (Acts 8).

The right time for an individual and for the community follows God's preparation of a receptive listener. The Holy Spirit's work of preparation in Jerusalem was seen in the response to the preaching on the day of Pentecost. Jesus' encounter with the Samaritan woman was certainly part of the preparation for the widespread awakening reported in Acts 8. Preparatory prayer and discernment then are needed for identifying the right time for an individual or a community.

While discernment of the "right time" is important, one must be ready to provide a "defense" of the gospel at any time (note Peter's instruction in 1 Peter 3:15). The "sowing" of the seed or the idea of the gospel is often done even in the midst of active hostile opposition to the gospel.

My friend, Wagiono Sumarto, from Indonesia tells that when he was the president of the Muslim Student Union in the University of Djakarta, a group built a church building in his hometown. He went home during a vacation time and burned the building. The pastor and elders, knowing who had torched their new building, came to him, forgave him, told him they would pray for him, gave him a Gospel of John and then left. That brief testimony led to his conversion, the conversion of his Muslim family, and through him to the conversion of several thousand Indonesian Muslims. He also led in the establishment of churches in both Indonesia and the United States.

The right time for Wagiono Sumarto was just after he had burned the church building and after the pastor and elders had prayed for him. Certainly, God had worked with him in the socio-political turmoil in Indonesia through the '60's to prepare him for change. The bold testimony and prayer of that pastor and those elders, however, were critically important.

The answer to the question, "When?" might be interpreted as "whenever," but the "whenever" should follow prayer, preparation, and discernment.

How?

The question of "How" to bring them in then leads one to look at how people respond in communities or through networks of relationship. The focus for strategy planning shifts from just the individual to families and communities. The way to deliver the good news of the gospel in a way it will be received by an extended family or a whole community will differ from "sport fishing" for the occasional individual. (See the chapter on social structures and the gospel.)

Secular businesses have developed communications strategies for marketing which selectively differentiate the population for selling their products. One can, for example, take any communication medium (newspaper, radio, television, billboards, tracts/fliers, direct mail, etc.) and see the focusing of messages to fit in terms of the respondents. Issues of timing, language, message formation, and nature of appeal all vary with the potential respondents. Advertising is highly "receptor oriented." As I drive from my house, billboards in English address broad middle class interests. As I travel to the next community the billboard language changes to a bilingual, bicultural English/ Spanish format.

The "How" of evangelism takes the "receptor" community into account and how that community perceives the gospel. Whether presented through flyers, drama, on billboards in English or Mandarin, in contemporary African-American rap music, or traditional preaching the aim is the same—commitment to Jesus Christ.

The business community has learned another important lesson that effective communication strategies normally require a wide and diverse range of converging communication strategies to influence a community. Radio, television, newspapers, telemarketing, and personal referrals are all combined to address people at the various stages of the process of decision-making to build awareness, to inform, to compare, to show simplicity, to show relative advantage, to share the results of acceptance and to "seal the deal."

A "full service church" will likely be involved in a range of community activities and needs. A church may focus on a particular "niche" or segment of the community and then address its activities accordingly. For example, one church I know has its focus on middle class "Baby Boomers" (i.e., people born between 1945 and 1964). Worship styles, meeting times, communion services, dress styles, and language styles fit this age group. Predictably, the congregation has few retirees. The church community attitudes are typical of "Baby Boomers."

The specific "hows" of effective evangelism and church planting will not only bring specific focus of communication strategies but will also engage strategic intercession as well. While the "technologies" or specific methods of evangelism and church planting may be improved to greatly improve effectiveness, the issue of strategic intercession is obviously much more significant. Theologically and practically it is the Holy Spirit that convicts of sin, righteousness and judgment. It is the Lord who "builds" and "adds to" the church. It is not through our wisdom, power or technologies.

As a person coming from a western worldview, my tendency is to look for the visible cause of an event. After discerning what appears to be causal in effective evangelism, my first inclination is often to develop a parallel "human" strategy to lead people to Christ. However, my worldview often blinds me to the reality of the spiritual struggle occurring in and around me. Like the Pharisees I find it difficult to process experience that can best be explained in terms of demonstrations of spiritual power. In the past the result was that I was largely unable to draw on the spiritual resources available through the Holy Spirit or to recognize the source or impact of the satanic influence against the ministries where I was involved. My first real attempt to rely on God's power in evangelism came as I served as an interim minister in a church in Los Angeles. The preacher who had just left was an outstanding teacher, preacher and visionary. However, the church was in steady decline with no new growth—conversion, biological or transfer. In the interim role I had virtually no right to influence anyone. I was only charged to do maintenance. However, feeling frustrated with my own weakness, I began to pray and God began to answer. Beginning from the time of prayer, the Lord led multiple families every week during my whole interim to conversion and commitment.

In Ethiopia the elders of the churches where we served came one day to complain about the limited growth rate. We had only had about 600 baptisms that year. I responded that I was too busy to add any more preaching or teaching into my schedule. I suggested that we each identify at least five people who need to be converted or renewed and then we pray daily until the decision was made. People began to pray. That year the Lord added more than 1200 to the church in that place. We began to see scattered occasions of people being delivered from demonization. Then the numbers of those delivered grew by the hundreds. As people were delivered the credibility of the church grew. As the church grew the number of people demonized decreased to where it was rare except in areas where the church was being planted.

The sick were prayed for and raised up and I continued to have my faith stretched—amazed at what the Lord was doing. It didn't fit my "systematic theology," but it was like what was described in the gospels and Acts.

One elderly woman's family called me and a doctor friend late one night to make a house call. The family already was preparing for the burial in the morning. She had typhus and was in a coma. No medical facilities were available. My doctor friend said that death was imminent—within minutes or an hour. We prayed. The family asked if an injection might help. My friend said it was too late but he would give her a shot of antibiotics. Again, we prayed. We left with the smell of death in the air. She rallied and fully recovered. The word spread and the church grew.

The causal element behind the evangelism was not carefully crafted technique or strategy. It was not as if we did not seek to do our best. The power behind the scenes was spiritual power released and directed through the prayer of many.

How should one do evangelism? The first and most important response is to pray—intercede for the ones who need the Lord. The "how" is not magic nor is it just technique. It is a recognition of whose task evangelism is and a drawing on His resources to accomplish His purpose.

Planting Reproducing Churches

The goal of evangelism must go beyond western individualism to a focus on communities. Our vision must be reproducing communities, not just individuals. While individuals are important, multi-generational reproduction requires relationships in community.

When Jesus invited the professional fishermen to become "fishers of men," the picture they would have had would certainly have been different from my youthful picture of fishing. When I have gone fishing, it has nearly always been with a fishing pole with a line and one or two hooks. They fished with nets. They looked for schools of fish. They were not fishing for sport. Similarly, the seeking of disciples should go beyond the occasional sport fishing for a limited quota to serious fishing that aims to "bring them in."

The planting of reproducing churches requires an appropriate theological perspective, a committed leadership, dependence on the Holy Spirit, an appropriate approach, a receptive community, and an avoidance of common pitfalls. These variables are obviously related, but some individual attention is needed.

Theological Perspective

Several foundational theological affirmations serve to define a perspective that goes with the successful planting of reproducing churches. Each of these affirmations reflects a strong biblical base. 1) The person who does not have faith in Christ will be lost while the person who does trust in Jesus Christ will be granted eternal life. 2) While individual conversion is essential, the planting of churches has strong biblical precedent. Early church leaders were obviously committed to the forming of groups of believers into learning, worshipping and serving communities. 3) While the functions of individuals differ, every person is expected to contribute to the life and functioning of the community. And 4) God's desire is for the church to grow in service, spirituality, numbers and as an organism/body. Other theological affirmations could be cited to expand these foundations.

A Committed Leadership

"Where there is no vision, people perish" (Prov. 29:18, KJV). A committed and visionary leadership provides an essential key to planting reproducing congregations. The senior minister typically serves as the most influential person in leading a church to plant new congregations. If the senior leader does not actively demonstrate a high level of commitment to church planting, the whole congregational energy level will drift into lethargy. Where no vision drives people to plant churches, they will simply not emerge. Passivity, apathy, disunity, scattered commitments, or an absence of a clear vision result from a lack of leadership. As in the movie "Field of Dreams," if the leader builds from a clear vision, "they will come."

Without a leadership that aims at planting reproducing churches, congregations are unlikely to reproduce. However, when a whole congregation is committed to reproduction, it may be expected to regularly reproduce. The means of reproducing new churches varies. Some common strategies include starting cell groups, "hiving," or sending a church planting team to an area. When the people are enthusiastically committed to their faith the contagion spreads as the Lord blesses.

The leader who demonstrates and teaches how to depend on God and his power can expect to see God's power at work in evangelism and church planting. While carefully thought about methods help, the work of the Holy Spirit makes it happen.

The development of leaders continues as one of the most serious practical issues. Churches need to multiply at least three kinds of leaders in a local situation: 1) lay leaders of small groups who interact with others in a face-to-face ministry, 2) lay leaders of multiple small groups who give some supervision to other small group leaders such as elders in a local congregation or department heads, and 3) leaders who lead small congregations. This last kind of leader will likely have some specific training focused on church leadership such as a Bible Institute, Bible College or seminary. Typically, this third kind of leader will be at least bi-vocational. He/she may serve a church on a full time basis. While leaders of multiple staff congregations and denominations are needed for strategic planning and vision, the other three kinds of leaders are critically important for evangelism and church planting. Again, it should be noted that it is the Spirit who calls, gifts, empowers, guides, protects and vindicates. We participate as his agents, but cannot claim credit for producing "spiritual leaders."

Dependence on the Holy Spirit

In the 1970's many effective evangelical Christian leaders began to believe that if the right methods or technologies of church growth were employed, churches would grow and multiply. Some of the focus of the Church Growth Movement on "technologies" was indeed directed as a corrective toward inappropriate evangelistic strategies both within a culture and across cultural boundaries. Many churches have seen significant improvement in both their growth and reproductive roles.

However, a singular focus on methods or strategies of church growth as if the result simply depends on what the people do is both theologically unacceptable and practically unworkable. The cultural and social complexities can never be predicted with the precision of a machine to fine tune evangelism and church planting. This kind of assumption also neglects the fact of our spiritual nature. It denies both the satanic resistance we face and the power and work of the Holy Spirit to witness to Christ.

Recent church growth literature has brought the work of the Holy Spirit back into focus with a recognition that as Christians we do not "wrestle with flesh and blood, but with principalities and powers." Renewed emphasis on spiritual warfare has reminded the church that the mission is God's mission. He is still actually at work to accomplish His purpose. The primary power to be exercised is spiritual power. The primary bases for influence do not emerge from the social structure (e.g., homogeneous units) or from personal power (e.g., leadership of small groups) but from the work of the Spirit directly and through these influential means.

The planting of reproducing churches then is more a function of the work of the Holy Spirit than human strategizing. While strategy planning and implementation is very important, it should be seen only under the clear guidance of the Holy Spirit.

An Appropriate Approach

Paul warned the church at Thessalonica not to "quench the Spirit" (1 Thess. 5:19). As he was in the areas of Phrygia and Galatia he planned to go to Bithynia, but was prevented by the Holy Spirit (Acts 19: 6, 7). Instead, he crossed the Aegean to Philippi to initiate an evangelistic church planting effort there. Clearly, the apostle Paul planned/strategized where to go and how to accomplish the mission God had given him. His methods clearly focused on going to urban centers and beginning with what would have been the most receptive group (the actively religious Jews in their synagogues). One can learn even today from his methods, especially of their appropriateness.

An inappropriate method or strategy will stifle or "quench" the impact of the Holy Spirit. The most common inappropriate method found in churches seems to be a focus on maintenance. When the focus is inward, predictable decline precedes the evaporation of any desire for church planting.

One could point to a litany of inappropriate methods which fail to take basic communicational concerns into account. Ethnocentric methods focus on transmission rather than a receptor orientation. One could also point to widespread cultural insensitivities.

Effective evangelism presents the initiatives God has taken for our good in terms that will be understood as good news in the community. Sometimes the actions that accompany the presentation of the "gospel" are interpreted as locally offensive or inappropriate. Some believers, for example, insist on mature Christian behavior from a person who would become a believer thus making the good news into bad news.

To be optimally effective, appropriate methods are essential. The appropriate method in one location and among a given community will take the community, the message and the communicator into account. The local method, if appropriate, probably will not fit well in another context or it may not fit another communicator well. If the communicator or receptor audience changes, the methods will have to re-tuned.

A Receptive Community

People may be described as receptive when after hearing the gospel in terms they can understand, they commit themselves to Jesus as Lord. Receptive people having accepted the gospel participate in the spreading of the good news. Receptivity is often difficult to "prove" in advance. Receptivity, however, may be reasonably predicted on the basics of demonstrated worldview change.

New Testament precedents and teaching amply support a focus on both individuals and communities who could be described as "receptive." While others were not neglected, the more receptive often were clearly addressed first. Jesus taught the poor even while the religious leaders were not neglected. Paul generally went first to the Jewish synagogues and to the non-Jews who had expressed interest in and around the Jewish synagogues. He began in the cities.

Many factors contribute to the development of individual, family, community and a "people's" receptivity. The primary actor, however, is the Holy Spirit. Clearly, his work of convicting of sin, righteousness and judgment is the foundational activity. Receptivity "enhancers" include "presence" and "proclamation" types of evangelism. "Presence" evangelism or "lifestyle" evangelism allows individuals in a community to observe the advantages of following Christ. It also provides a means by which the compatibility of the new way of life fits in with the old. By observing "presence" or "lifestyle" evangelism, the credibility or trustworthiness of both the message and messenger is established.

"Proclamation" evangelism further enhances receptivity by providing the essential message of good news in terms that the people can understand. Proclamation builds awareness and informs both decision-making and continued nurturing incorporation into the church.

Receptivity may be depicted along the affective taxonomy described by David Drawthwol. Degrees of receptivity may be described along the following sequence: 1) Receiving, 2) Responding, 3) Valuing, 4) Organizing, and 5) Characterization by value complex or worldview change.[3]

To enhance receptivity then requires three primary ingredients: 1) Intercessory prayer, 2) a situationally appropriate communications strategy, and 3) a trustworthy, credible witness. We must pray recognizing that the whole process depends on the work of the Holy Spirit. We must also act wisely and strategically depending on the guidance of the Spirit recognizing that God's people provide his only means of evangelism. If people are to hear and respond to the gospel, they will hear and respond only as we take the good news to them in credible understandable ways.

Common Pitfalls to Avoid

With a "way" that is more than 2000 years old, the number of possible potholes is beyond counting. However, some common current pitfalls continue to threaten evangelistic and church planting progress. These potential problems arise both within a local culture and across cultural lines. They may differ, but are not limited by educational or socio-economic levels.

- A focus on "transfer" or "biological" growth
- Formation of "comfortable" non-reproducing small groups
- Lack of vision for growth and multiplication
- Professionalization of the ministry
- "Foreign" polity or leadership patterns

3. See David Drawthwol, Benjamin S. Bloom, and Bertram B. Masia's *Taxonomy of Educational Objectives: Handbook II: Affective Domain* (New York: David McKay Company, Inc., 1974).

- Dependence on "foreign" or "outside" resources
- Inappropriate response to the selection of a place to meet
- Failure to move from small group to congregation

Conclusion

Church planting as part of God's evangelistic leading has continued to be a crucial part of His redemptive plan since the first century. God's clear desire is for all to come to accept His Son Jesus as the single guiding allegiance and for every person to receive the eternal hope He offers. Clearly, no other way of salvation is open to any person except through Jesus Christ.

10
Development and the Gospel

Edgar J. Elliston

Introduction

In the last half of the '90s the need for relief and development continues to overwhelm the resources. Political changes in former communist countries has opened new opportunities to meet needs. War and regional conflicts in Bosnia and Burundi are only two of many leading to death, destruction and population displacement. Natural disasters continue to threaten the marginalized worldwide in both rural and urban areas. The major shifts in the world economy following the end of the "Cold War" have led to new pressures on the poor. Innocuous euphemisms like "downsizing" and "outplacing" belie their impact on the poor and homelessness in modern urbanized societies.

Some of the political pressure for governments to do development has declined with the end of the Cold War. Internal economic pressures have also raised questions about the level of aid given to other countries through government sources.

The opportunities and need for the church to engage in caring for the hungry, the poor, the refugee and the prisoner continues to grow. Pressure on NGOs (non-governmental organizations) to take up the reins of development and benevolent care is mounting from governments.

From the perspective of evangelical churches the old debate about evangelism versus development, word versus deed, or evangelistic mandate versus the cultural mandate has been largely recognized as unnecessarily divisive. The western worldview pattern of polarizing disputes into simplistic slogans or polemics blurred the issues of integrating development as a part of the mission of God. These "fundamentalist/liberal" disputes of the early part of this century are giving way to a contextualized wholism with both western and Two-thirds World leadership in development. Evangelicals as a result are much more willing to lead in developmental activities. While the approaches to development differ somewhat, agencies like World Vision, Food for the Hungry, and Compassion International continue to lead the way among evangelical churches.

Beginning with the Berlin Congress on World Evangelization in 1963 and continuing through the countless meetings of the Lausanne Movement and A.D. 2000 Movement as well as the current research by Asian, African and Latin American development leaders, the focus is much more on a contextualized balance. Evangelicals no longer must choose between "evangelism" or "development," but rather now they look for ways these issues can be appropriately balanced in the local situation.

Many pictures serve to underscore the aim toward balance over the past decade. "Symbiosis" is Yamamori's favorite term to depict two different, but complementary activities.[1] The Lausanne documents' picture of "two wings of the same bird" or the "two halves of a pair of scissors" again showed how these two issues complement each other. Theologically, the two issues

---

1. Tetsunao Yamamori, *God's New Envoys: A Bold Strategy for Penetrating "Closed Countries"* (Portland, OR: Multnomah Press, 1987).

both fit into the actions and intentions of the Kingdom of God as seen in the great commandment and the great commission. A careful interpretation of each one leads to the other.

To answer which comes first one must look at the context. Jesus' ministry was characterized by both. The early church as described in Acts showed a concern for both. Obviously, the issue of eternal significance is one's relationship to God through Jesus Christ. However, a person's relationship to God is in part seen in the relationships he/she has with his/her neighbor and the environment in which they live. And, one is in part judged on the basis of how he/she has treated others in need (cf. Matt. 25). In addition to being an expression of who one is, development often contributes to the development of a receptivity to the gospel. While the loving of one's neighbor should not be conditional or used as a means for manipulation, it is often the way through which a credible witness to the gospel occurs. Likewise, while development can not be described as evangelism, it is through the provision of hope in the good news about Jesus Christ that new initiatives for social transformation predictably occur with believers.

Evangelism and the resulting conversion provide the bases for sustained development in the social, political, economic, and spiritual arenas. Conversion brings hope, truth/integrity and compassion/respect which form the bases for social transformation. For example, Christians cared for the burial of the dead in ancient Alexandria. The end of the gladiatorial games in Rome which contributed to the deaths of countless thousands of Christians was ultimately stopped by Christian influence. Christians led in the abolition of the slave trade across Africa, the end of the practice of widow burning in India and the cessation of cannibalism in the South Pacific region. Development that only treats the economic and political while neglecting or denying the spiritual dimension can be expected to degenerate into oppression. The communist and Nazi experiments of this century are but two examples. When the elements of hope, truth and respect are missing, dysfunctional aberrations may also be expected as with the crusades and conflicts in Burundi and Bosnia.

Defining Development

Defining development has posed a confusing array of possible answers to thoughtful Christians. Depending on one's fundamental assumptions or worldview, the definitions differ widely. The resulting development paradigms consequently move toward significantly different goals—even in the broader Christian community. Government-based development and even some secular foundation-based development typically aims at political and/or economic goals. Church based development ranges from compassionate concern to a manipulation of people to accept the gospel.

To come to a Christian definition of development several foundational issues of focus require clarification. Depending on one's perspective the focus may center on political outcomes, social justice, equity, community organization, economic prosperity, or conversion. One perspective from which to view development is as freedom from constraints (economic, political, spiritual) to become all that God would have for the individual person or people.

Definitions are sometimes aided by a contrast with what the concept is not. What is meant by the terms, "underdevelopment," and "overdevelopment," may be instructive. "Underdevelopment" could be characterized by several negative terms such as: powerlessness, poor, lacking essential goods and services, oppressed, depressed, spiritually deceived, uninformed, unhealthy, and so on. "Overdevelopment" might be characterized by a surplus of goods and services, waste, consumerism, oppressiveness, apathy toward the poor, and spiritual pride.

Evangelical Christians may look at development in terms of establishing or reestablishing a set of fundamental relationships: with God, with other people and with the environment. These relationships take into account both the issues of economics and politics as well the issues of spirituality, spiritual power, sin, and righteousness.

Development is often defined in terms of social transformation. Social transformation, however, may not take environmental or spiritual issues into account. Without considering these issues, development will remain shallow and will unlikely last over a multi-generational span.

Development should be distinguished from "social action" which aims primarily at political change or the changing of social structures. These changes are often addressed through community organizing and supported by some liberation theologies. While development and social action differ, they should not be seen as incompatible. They often complement each other.

A tentative definition for development then which will serve as a basis for this chapter is as follows:

Development is the process by which—

1) Men and women are brought into a committed relationship with the living God through faith in Jesus Christ;

2) People are brought into just and equitable relationships in all of their social relationships; and,

3) People are brought into a responsible stewarding relationship of their environment in a way that adequately provides their physical (food, clothing and shelter) needs.

Outcomes of Development

On the positive side of the picture, developmental activities have opened the way for significant worldview change which leads to further development and a receptivity to the gospel. This openness has on occasion been met by the heralding of the good news of the gospel. Paul wrote, "when the time was right, God sent his Son (Gal 4:4). The Greeks and the Romans had been engaged in the largest broad scale "development" or social transformation process the Mediterranean basin had seen. It was in the midst of that ferment and development of roads, language, political institutions, and economic institutions that Jesus came and the gospel spread. Similar patterns can be seen today in such diverse places as Pune, India and Turkana, Kenya. Pune is a strongly traditional Hindu, densely populated urban area. Turkana is a sparsely populated traditional pastoral setting.

While Pune has been the center of much of the fundamentalist Hindu reactionary movements across India since Indian independence, the urbanizing process which has brought urban development has opened the way for a growing receptivity to the gospel. Pune still has a minuscule percentage of the population as Christians, but now the processes of development have helped in opening space for the gospel.

Among the Turkana of northwest Kenya several development agencies and missions have been quietly introducing change. New roads have brought increased access to and from the outside. New food products, new clothing options, new medical treatments and new educational opportunities challenge the stability of the traditional Turkana worldview. While the Turkana have not been beating down the church doors, dozens of new congregations have emerged in this scorching desert. The first impression of several missionaries was that nothing would grow there except for scorpions, puff adders and hunting spiders. Development workers often despaired of progress. Now both are moving ahead at a steady pace.

The Need for Development

Whether one thinks of the improvement of local living conditions, the per capita income, self-support, freedom/democracy, food, shelter, health, peace or the redistribution of wealth, world conditions are worsening. While many peoples are receptive to the gospel, the number of areas closed the gospel is increasing among the most unreached populations of the world. In this decade one may choose any one of the major indicators of need and find conditions deteriorating.

While great strides have been made in every arena, such as education, health and food production, enormous and growing crises are arising in these areas. AIDS, chloroquine resistant malaria, and antibiotic resistant staphylococcal infections continue to threaten populations. While technology exists to eradicate hunger, famines continue to ravage peoples. While cities boast of their power, wealth and architecture, more than half of the people living in cities go to bed hungry every night. Many live in fear. The number of the homeless continues to swell. The working poor are increasingly at risk. They are often no more than one or two paychecks from being homeless.

The numbers used to calculate the debts of nations are beyond the imaginations of all but an elite few. Yet in the midst of the poverty and powerlessness are the privileged few—those with health insurance, credit cards and free frequent flyer airline tickets. While western airlines are crowded, people still ride jeepneys in Manila and matatus in Nairobi as their only means of commuting to low paying jobs. My wife in her role in the corporate office of a large bank handles the personal checks for investments of senior officers. These personal checks are regularly in the scores of thousands of dollars. However, in the same bank, the policies have been changed to employ tellers for only nineteen hours or less so they may be kept as "part time" employees on a minimal wage with no medical or retirement benefits.

In the post-cold war era "reengineering" or "downsizing" means many people are out of work in post-industrial societies. The pressure is even more acute in the great urban centers of the Two-Third's World where every year more than 100 cities reach the population mark of one million. Basic services—water, fuel, transportation, infrastructure are more frequently than not strained to or beyond the limit now. Rural-urban migration continues. Birth rates have continued in many places to hover at about 4%.

If needs are defined as "gaps" to be filled, the gaps are broadening daily. If needs are defined as conditions to be set aright, the conditions (spiritual, economic, political) continue to challenge the most powerful. If needs are defined in terms of life processes to be shared, then the politically correct concerns of our affirming multiculturalism and diversity only hint at the depth of need both on individual and global scales.

Need as suffering is splashed across the airwaves on radio and television continually. Need for food, shelter, and medical care fuels the continuing debate about government entitlements not only in the west but the rest of the world as well. Seeing the widespread and seemingly endless pain on television daily serves to inoculate many against taking action to alleviate it.

The causes of the need are explained from many perspectives—economics, politics, worldview, laziness or religion. The truth encompasses elements of all of these contributing issues.

Some Theological Foundations

The gospel cuts through the confusion and presents an answer. The good news is that a relationship with Jesus Christ works to bring transformation in all of the key relationships related to one's life now and into the future. These relationships include: one's relationship with God, others and the environment.

On the surface it appears that the gospel is simplistic, but its effectiveness in bringing transformation now has a 2000 year track record. Jesus said, "Seek first his kingdom and all of these things will be given to you."

In his Sermon on the Mount Jesus offered some straightforward instruction that applies to development, particularly in Matt. 6:25-34. Some of the developmental implications that emerge from this text include:

1. God knows the condition of people.
2. God is able to address that condition.
3. God values the small, the powerless, and the seemingly insignificant.
4. In this prescription personal commitment is required, thus avoiding a debilitating dependency.
5. Hope is a central feature of this perspective.
6. In this promise surplus and excess are not projected.
7. In this prescription a disciplined priority of activity is required.
8. In this prescription human corruption is avoided.
9. The basis for development is relational and spiritual rather than economic.
10. Values, ethics, justice, and commitment form the basis of this relationship.

When Jesus began his ministry, he cited a quotation

from Isaiah 61:1-2 to define his ministry (Luke 4:18-19).

> The Spirit of the Lord is on me, because he has anointed me to preach good news to the poor. He has sent me to proclaim freedom for the prisoners and recovery of sight for the blind, to release the oppressed, to proclaim the year of the Lord's favor.

This statement contains several clear implications for social transformation. The context is set in the ancient "Year of Jubilee." The Year of Jubilee connoted a redistribution of wealth and the reestablishment of the land tenure system. Jesus' concern for the poor and justice clearly emerges from this statement.

Western Christians working in development face a significant risk of being secularized both in their methods, goals and outcomes. For example, Christians may well see the need for community organization, technical aid and the provision of food, water and/or shelter or income generation. However, if the focus neglects spiritual power issues, these distinctives of Christian development will be lost.

Some people would consider evangelism as a "spiritual" task while "development" is a "secular" task. Both have spiritual issues to be addressed as causes of "lostness" or "underdevelopment," as processes to be addressed and as outcomes to be sought. What the apostle Paul wrote in Eph. 6:12 is no less true for Christian development than it is for evangelism.

> For our struggle is not against flesh and blood, but against the rulers, against the authorities, against the powers of this dark world and against the spiritual forces of evil in the heavenly realms.

The task facing the Christian in development is no less a spiritual struggle than that of evangelism. The causes for underdevelopment can be traced to sinful behavior. Spirituality as it relates both to an individual and to the community must be considered.

Conversion and the establishment of a right relationship with God, with one's neighbor and with the environment is as important for effective development as it is for effective church membership.

Because of the limited space this chapter cannot detail all of the implications of the following theological issues for development. However, the sample of theological themes on the next four pages suggests the breadth of theological concern involved in all three sets of key relationships. They are listed alphabetically, not in priority.

Conclusion

Theologically, strategically and practically Christians are pressed to love their neighbors. This love will work itself out in social, environmental and spiritual ways. Relationships with God, one's neighbor and the environment all demand both the sharing of the good news about Jesus Christ and working with people to bring healing, wholeness and justice.

Theological Theme	Major Development Implications	Related Scriptures
Adoption	Relations with God and among people.	Rom. 8:15,23; 9:4; Gal. 4:6
Creation	God's establishment of the key relationships. The ideal relationship between God and humans was established. Humankind was given responsibility for caring for the creation. The "nature" of humankind was defined.	Genesis 1-2
Good Works	Good works are a consequence and confirming part of the testimony of every Christian of God's grace. They are to lead toward an honoring of God or the right relationship of others with God.	Matt. 5:16; 10:42; 25:31-46; Mark 9:41; Rom. 4:2,6; Gal. 2:16; 13:3,12; Eph. 4:11; 2:10; Titus 2:7; Heb. 10:24; Jas. 2:14-26; Rev. 3:8
Incarnation	God's demonstrated way to reestablish relationships by "living among," "serving," "not grasping," "obeying," and demonstrating humility.	John 1:1-14; Rom. 8:3; Eph. 2:15; Col. 1:22; Phil. 2:5-11
Jubilee	God's revealed plan for establishing justice in the economic realm, and land tenure. It was a time of "doing justice," "showing mercy," and proclaiming liberty.	Leviticus 25:9-55

Justice	Justice places us on an equal plain before God where we are expected to act in our relationships as He would. Justice seeks for all people to have equitable access to resources, goods, services, and God's power in ways that will facilitate a full/abundant life. Justice and righteousness are closely related.	Deut. 1:17; Prov. 17:23; 21:3; Micah 6:8; Isa. 42:1-4; Amos 5:24; Hosea 6:6; Matt. 12:7
Kingdom of God	The realm in which God reigns both now and in the future in relation to us, the present earth and the new earth. The rule of God requires obedience of all in/under his domain in all of our relationships. The kingdom theme is a dominant theme through the Gospels.	Matthew 6:33
Love	Love is a willful relational decision and commitment that does not consider the personal cost, but rather the other's ultimate benefit. Love is a characteristic of God in his relationship with creation and humankind. Love is commanded both toward God and our neighbor.	John 3:16; Rom. 5:8; John 14:34-35

Neighbor	One's neighbor is the person God provides to demonstrate our love to Him in concrete and costly ways. One's neighbor is the one in need. Jesus' concept of neighbor does not speak to the question of physical proximity, but to cross-cultural helping.	Lev. 19:18; Exod. 20:16-17; Lev. 19:13; Prov. 14:21; 16:29-30; Luke 10:25-37; Rom. 13:9-10; 15:2
Oppression	Oppression is a major cause of poverty and underdevelopment. It is an expression of injustice and greed.	Exod. 23:9; Psa. 12:5; 72:14; Isa. 3:5; Hosea 8:10; Amos 3:9
Poor	The poor are people whose relationships are characterized by powerlessness, oppression and hopelessness. God especially cares for them.	Exod. 23:6; Deut. 15:7-8; 24:14; Psa. 72:13; 132:15; Prov. 14:31; Amos 2:6; 4:1; Luke 4:18; 6:20; Jas. 2:2-4
Reconciliation	Reconciliation addresses the mending of relationships between humankind and God and among people.	Rom. 5:8,11; 11:15; Heb. 10:27
Redemption	Redemption is God's initiative to restore us and the environment to an undefiled state in relationship with himself.	Lev. 25:24; Eph. 1:7,14; 4:30; Col. 1:14; Heb. 9:12
Shalom	*Shalom* is the Hebrew concept of peace, well-being, soundness, wholeness and right relationships.	

Sin	Broken relationships between people and God, broken relations among people, cursed environment.	Gen. 3:16-19; Psa. 119:160; Matt. 5:22; Rom. 1:32; 3:23; 1 John 3:4
Stewardship	Stewardship is an expression of our accountability in the use and care for the environment and the relationships we have with both God and other people. The opposite is covetous consumerism and individualistic pride.	Genesis 1:28-30

11
Mission and Culture

Doug Priest Jr.

Introduction

One morning a Maasai man from the village up the hill stopped by our home. He was obviously upset. He told us his daughter was bleeding, and wanted us to look at her. We were missionaries in Kenya and had lived in the Loita Hills area for just over a year. Though we were not trained medically, we had on occasion driven sick people two hours away to a hospital. We had also worked with the local government clinic in providing medicine for children's vaccinations.

The girl arrived supported by her mother. We noticed blood on her skirt. She rested on our floor, and when she stood up, there was a sizable puddle of blood. We got some cloth and told the girl to use it as a compress. Then we quickly loaded the group into our car and drove to the nearby clinic.

A few hours later the clinic nurse stopped by our house to give us a report. The girl had complained of itching in her private parts, and so her parents had taken a razor and cut her there "to let the worm out." The nurse told us that while this was not common, it was not an unheard of practice for the Maasai. This home remedy should not be confused with female circumcision. That operation would take place in the future for the girl. The nurse had treated her with an anti-coagulant, cleansed her wound, and prescribed some antibiotics to ward off infection. She expected that the girl would soon recover, which she did. But the nurse said it had been a very good thing we brought her to the clinic when we did.

We were shocked. There simply had not been time to get the full explanation from the man about the problem the girl was having, nor the remedy which had been used. To us, slitting the labia for an itch was incomprehensible, dangerous and revolting. We had come face-to-face with values and understandings that were totally foreign to our way of thinking.

Missionaries living in another culture often face unusual circumstances. How are they to make sense of what they see and hear? How are they to understand the customs of another group of people? How do they know what to do when they are asked for help?

Understanding the Notion of Culture

Missions is a multifaceted enterprise. Looked at from an academic point of view, missiology is described as an interdisciplinary approach to studying missions. Missiologists practice their craft by borrowing at will ideas from fields as diverse as theology, linguistics, history, sociology, anthropology, psychology, current trends and management theory.

Our focus in this chapter is to discuss missions and the concept of culture. Charles Taber, missions professor from Emmanuel School of Religion, has written a thought-provoking book on the subject of culture entitled, *The World Is Too Much With Us: "Culture" in Modern Protestant Missions*. He traces the development of the word "culture" from its first use in the German and English languages in the 1840s up to the present day. As the concept developed through the nineteenth century and into the twentieth, it gave rise to an entire academic discipline—anthropology.

By broad definition, anthropology is the study of humankind. It is the discipline whose entire focus is human beings—what they say, do and think. Anthropology not only studies living peoples, but also peoples of the past. Thus, an anthropologist can specialize in *archaeology* (looking at past civilizations), *genetics* (looking at the biological differences between past and present groups of peoples), *linguistics* (looking at languages), *psychology* (looking at the individual in different settings), or any other field whose focus is humankind.

Missiologists have made much use of the discipline of anthropology, primarily cultural anthropology or social anthropology. A focus of these branches of anthropology is the study of living groups of people. The anthropological theory that has been most often used by missiologists is that of culture.

Defining Culture

The wide acceptance of the notion of culture would seem to indicate that we need not even define the concept; everybody knows what "culture" means. Not so. As a concept, culture has been notoriously difficult to define so that all can agree to a common understanding. In fact, a book was once written that was nothing more than a collection of definitions of the term—some 200 of them!

To many, the idea of culture is linked with a respect for or participation in "Classical" activities. A "cultured" person is one who listens to classical music as opposed to rock music, one who appreciates the art of Michelangelo, or one who reads Virgil instead of Barbara Cartland or Louis L'Amour. There is a definite element of snobbery in such a view, which arose from an evolutionary understanding of peoples that unfortunately still exists to this day. Groups of people were classified as falling into three categories: barbarians or savages—usually groups of people from earlier periods of history but still to be found on remote islands or in the middle of the jungle—were placed at the bottom end of the scale. These peoples were understood as "having no culture." A step up the scale were the primitive peoples, the "uncultured" sorts to be found in the lower-class sections of the cities or those from the colonies. And finally, at the apex naturally, were civilized peoples. Who were the civilized peoples? The ones who came up with the categories in the first place. They were the "cultured" ones, and "cultured" society was the society that was to be found among the upper class in Europe in the last century. The rest of the world, with few exceptions, were made up of the primitive peoples or barbarians.

We totally reject this view.

Current thought does not limit culture to something which is possessed by only certain people, but something which all peoples have. Every people has a culture and every person is a member of a culture. Culture is what people say, do and think.

We will take our precise definition of the term from missionary-anthropologist Paul Hiebert, who sees culture as,

> The key dimensions of culture are *ideas* (the cognitive element), *feelings* (the affective element), and *values* (the evaluative element). These three dimensions working together will generally determine who a people is, what a people does, and what a people thinks.[1]

The implication of this understanding of what

---

1. Paul Hiebert, *Anthropological Insights For Missionaries* (Grand Rapids: Baker, 1985), p. 30.

constitutes a culture is obvious for missionaries. Missionaries need to understand the culture from which they come and the culture to which they go. They must understand their culture in order to differentiate between the dictates of that culture and the dictates of the Kingdom of God. Our Christianity by definition is a mixture of Western values together with biblical values. In another setting, the Western values may be irrelevant.

Missionaries need to know how to study the foreign culture before they go, and they need to devote a large part of their time upon arrival to study of the culture. The very success of their gospel communication is related to this understanding. Failure to understand results in failure to communicate. The onus is on the communicator, because inadequate understanding of culture means inadequate communication of the gospel. Missionaries who do not take the time to study the culture where they work not only shortchange themselves and the people there, but also do a disservice to their churches, and worse yet, the Lord.

Confession is said to be good for the soul, so let me confess one of my failures at this point. After spending the night in a Maasai village in Kenya I was sitting on the grass visiting with the men. One man called over his daughter to me and asked me to look at her hand. She had fallen into the fire and her little hand was now permanently in the shape of a fist. She could not open her hand because the tendons had shrunk and the skin from palm to fingers had grown together. I was moved by the girl and her lot for the future with such a hand, and wondered if a trip to a surgeon in Nairobi might result in at least partial use of her hand.

I suggested this idea to the man, who thought it was a good one. He asked, "When can you take her?" Then I made my mistake. I requested the man to give me a goat to help pay for my gas to and from Nairobi, five hours by car each way. The goat would not cover the cost of the gas, but I thought it would be a culturally appropriate way for the man to help. He preferred that I would take his daughter without discussing payment. He refused to give me a goat to help with the gas costs, so I did not make the trip.

I thought to myself, "Well, that just shows how concerned he really is for his daughter, to not even provide a single goat from his large herd."

To this day, over ten years later, I feel guilty about not taking that little girl to Nairobi. Perhaps nothing could have been done for her, perhaps something. Even though I tried to ask in what I thought to be a culturally appropriate manner for his participation, I did not make the trip because that help was not forthcoming as I insisted it should be.

I now believe that if the trip had been made to Nairobi, even if nothing could have been done for the girl, at least my concern would have been evident. Very likely, if something had been done for the girl and she was able to use her hand, the man then would have presented me with not only a goat, but a cow, for that is the Maasai way of doing things. Because I insisted on payment prior to the trip rather than allowing for eventual payment in proper Maasai fashion, an opportunity was lost. As an outsider, I should have been more diligent in inquiring into Maasai customs of payment and showing appreciation.

Taber's breakdown of culture is helpful for acquiring the kind of understanding I needed. He encourages examination of a culture from three points of view:

> *material culture*, which is concerned with the interaction of human groups with their physical habitat, including the use of its resources to make tools, implements, clothing and housing; *social culture*, which deals with how they organize their groups; and

216

ideational culture, which includes worldview, language and other symbols systems, and religion.[2]

The three points of view provide a way in which cultures can be studied in terms of what a people does, thinks and says. They help us gain understanding of a people whose ways are not our own.

Culture as Maps and Cars

One of the ways to understand culture is as a map. Members of a culture have a mental map of their culture. This map works as a guide for the individual. Members of a culture share similar mental maps, though each map is individually unique. These maps are adaptive and can be revised to incorporate new ideas and new features as the culture changes.

Culture is something that is taught and learned. Babies are not born with a culture; they are brought into a culture and are taught appropriate ways of thinking and behaving. As they learn, they fill in their maps so that the unchartered territories become known. The maps of Maasai in Tanzania allow for the daily consumption of milk in various forms, while the maps of adults in America allow for the drinking of milk only if it is desired. One's culture selects from available options for food that are available which should be eaten and which should not. In Singapore where I live, chicken and fish are food options for locals; among the Maasai neither of these are considered as options even though they can be purchased nearby and their neighbors eat these foods.

Road maps serve to show how to get from one place to another. They show the available routes.

---

2. Charles Taber, *The World Is Too Much With Us* (Macon, GA: Mercer University Press, 1991), p. 4.

Conversely, if one disregards the map, one can get lost. Like the map, culture is normative in that it both rewards appropriate behavior while punishing deviance. An individual who blazes his or her own trail by departing from the accepted cultural norms is often considered strange and may even be ostracized.

Maps are periodically updated to allow for new information. When the revisions occur, the map-makers do not begin with a blank piece of paper, but build upon what they already know. They add their data to that which previously existed. So too with culture. Each generation builds upon the accumulated knowledge of the last.

You have probably seen reproductions of old maps from several centuries ago. Often at the boundaries of those maps, the cartographers drew snakes or dragons. Or they drew land masses that were actually not there. Perhaps the map just ended because the people felt they would drop off the edge of the world if they went too far. These map-makers were communicating their understanding of what lies beyond the borders of their knowledge. They were giving their explanations or views of the world at that time.

In the same vein, map-makers often put their own country as the center of their world maps. It is always fun to look at maps around the world. American maps picture the USA as the center of the world; Asian maps have Asia as the center of the world just as European maps feature Europe. These maps are representations of the way their makers see the world.

Cultures provide for their members a way of seeing the world. They provide explanations for how the world came into being, why the peoples of the world differ from one another, how the plants and animals are to be classified, and the relation of the heavenly bodies. Most cultures see themselves as the center of the world, describing the world as made up of either "us," (members of the culture), or "them," (everybody else).

As I studied Maasai culture in East Africa I learned that the people held a totally different understanding about bushes and trees than I did. To the Maasai, trees and bushes are either holy or unholy. Holy bushes and trees were those that had large leaves so that the sun would be blocked and shade provided. Unholy trees and bushes did not provide shade, an important commodity in a hot environment. Because of their leaves, these sorts provide shelter from the rain as well. Holy bushes and trees are those that do not have thorns. I can testify to personal experience with lots of different kinds of thorns, from the spikes of the acacia bushes to the bedeviling small curved thorns that rip right through your clothes into your skin and then break off. The Maasai classification scheme makes perfect sense when you experience life as they do.

Anthropologists have been quick to point out that cultures can be seen as systems. The seemingly disparate parts, when under observation, actually work together. At this point, an analogy of culture to a vehicle is more appropriate than culture as a map. A car is made up of different systems that all work together—a hydraulic system, an exhaust system, a cooling system, a system for starting, going and stopping. Each of these systems has its own purpose, and each system is made up of subsystems, which are in turn made up of parts. When the parts are broken down to their individual pieces, it can be seen that a car is actually a combination of hundreds of thousands of bits and pieces of metal, plastic and rubber. Though a car can function with many broken parts, it functions best when everything is working together.

Cultures are made up of interrelated systems as well. These systems—economic, kinship, political, technological, religious, aesthetic—all work together in an integrated manner. Each system may be broken down into subsystems, and each subsystem may be further broken down into cultural traits. A culture is made of hundreds of thousands of individual cultural traits. When the traits all work together, the culture functions at its best.

The major car companies of the world have their own individual makes of cars. These particular makes of cars are changed from year to year. A 1994 Mercedes Benz looks very little like a 1974 Mercedes Benz. Some makes of cars have interchangeable parts with other makes. The world is made up of many cultures. Cultures from one area, such as East Africa, have many elements in common with one another, but each is individual. The purpose of all motor vehicles is to go. So cultures, no matter where they are found in the world, have some similarities with one another. But just as there is a tremendous variety of motor vehicles on the road, there is a variety of cultures throughout the world.

People purchase different types of cars for different purposes. Some like speed, some like safety, some like economy, some like diesel, and some like design. While it is possible to compare Porsches with Volkswagens, the comparison really does not do a whole lot of good except in the most general sense. That is because Porsches are best judged by how well they perform as Porsches, and Volkswagens are best judged by the criteria they are supposed to meet.

While cultures can be compared with one another, it is not helpful to judge cultures based on the standards of other cultures. It is too easy to come up with an odious schema of something like barbarian, primitive and civilized. Each culture has its own ways of forming its own laws and solving its own problems, and should be judged on how well it obeys its laws and solves its problems.

One of the first things that strikes a Westerner on

entering a Maasai home is the darkness. It is almost impossible to see inside of a Maasai home because there are no windows or lights. In addition, the pathway from the door into the house goes around corners so that light from the outside does not come into the central living area. The only light in a Maasai home comes from a fire (if kindled), or holes in the walls and ceiling (if not plugged with cloth as they normally are).

Westerners like their homes to be lighted so that they can see what they are doing—reading, cooking, sewing. They also like others to see and appreciate their possessions. Does this mean that the darkened Maasai homes are inferior to Western ones?

There are several good reasons that Maasai homes are dark. In most Maasai villages there is no electricity, and most choose not to use their cash for lanterns. A dark home is a cool home, whereas light transmits heat. In the West we shade our windows in summer to keep out the heat. A lighted house means that the insects will be awake and scurry about. In the daytime the insects are attracted to the light, and so go outside. The Maasai herds attract flies, and if a home was lighted, the flies would be a nuisance. For these reasons, even if I lived in a Maasai home, I too would keep it dark.

Despite the usefulness of picturing culture as a map or a car, we must not press the analogies too far. They are too mechanistic and simplistic to represent real people. People are individuals with minds of their own, not inanimate pieces of metal, plastic and rubber. By using such analogies we can also miss the changes that are always occurring within a culture.

Current Missions Practice and Culture Theory

One limitation of the culture idea is that the definition of one's culture is so elastic. Nashipai Nchoshoi is a graduate student at Nairobi University. To what culture does she belong? She is an African, so if there is such a thing as African culture, she belongs to it. She is a Kenyan citizen, so she is a member of that national culture. Being college-educated she is of that elite sub-culture who identify so readily with one another. Since her parents are Maasai and that is her own mother tongue, she can be considered a member of the Maasai culture. But her husband is a Kalenjin, and by that culture's definition, she has been adopted into the Kalenjin culture. Just what exactly is Nashipai?

Twenty years ago when I was taking my anthropology degree at the University of Oregon we had to read many of the Holt, Rinehart and Winston series of ethnographies from various cultures. Some of my acquaintances were Nigerians, so I knowingly asked one of my friends: "Tell me, are you Yoruba, Ibo, Hausa, or what?" To my chagrin and embarrassment, he became quite huffy and replied, "I am a Nigerian. Period."

A tendency we have had as missionaries is to be too quick to see and set supposed boundaries of a culture. The boundaries we set have been overly determined by such outward signs as language, dress, religion, food choice, art styles and physical ornamentation. Since we have tended to see each culture pragmatically as an integrated system that meets the needs of its members, we have not fully appreciated the extent of interaction between different groups. An anthropologist who studies Asia notes that,

> a major reservation that must be made about the use of a general concept of culture is that it can assume firm boundaries where they are in fact fuzzy or fluid, and it may divert analytic attention away from important relationships which can cut across cultural boundaries.[3]

---

3. Grant Evans, ed., *Asia's Cultural Mosaic: An Anthropological Introduction* (New York: Prentice Hall, 1993), p. 22.

Cultures are not isolated, but depend upon one another. Their boundaries are more artificial than we have realized. Taber rightfully points out that, "It is no more feasible to draw a sharp boundary around 'a culture' than around a definite area of the ocean."[4]

Early in the development of anthropology, field-workers focused their attention on "primitive" peoples—those who lived on islands, in the forests and jungles, or who were primarily rural and agricultural. Peoples who lived in cities and had more interaction with one another were left to be studied by sociologists.

This early "tribal and peasant" bias of anthropologists has been seized upon by missionaries, the most obvious manifestation being the current interest in "people groups." The boundaries of the people groups that we have set are much more important to us for our own agendas than they are to the people they supposedly describe. The pursuit of "unreached people groups" with the concomitant ideas of adopting a specific group and determining a unique strategy for each group has gone far beyond what the actual situation merits.

One day a BBC film crew came to the area of Kenya where I lived to do a film on the Maasai. On this specific day there was a government sponsored men's meeting that had been scheduled for some time. As a member of the community, I was told of the meeting and asked to participate. The film crew came and began shooting. At one point they politely asked me to step back from the group so I would not be in view of the camera. They wanted to convey the impression to their television audience that the Maasai were a "pure" culture with little interaction from outsiders—a misrepresentation of that society, but one that met

---

4. Taber, *The World Is Too Much With Us*, p. 162.

with their own purposes and (mis)understandings. If we make similar mistakes with our mission strategies, we are in danger of helping to establish congregations that do not accurately reflect the society in which they are found or the biblical notions of brotherhood and the breaking down of barriers in Christ.

Christian Attitudes Toward Culture

A profoundly important theological question facing Christians concerns their attitude toward culture. The Apostle Paul wrote, "Do not conform any longer to the pattern of this world" (Rom. 12:2). In seeming opposition to this, the Apostle John wrote that God loved the world and "did not send His Son into the world to condemn the world" (John 3:17). These two verses serve as convenient markers for how we are to view the world and its many cultures.

How we choose to view the world is influenced by our opinions regarding the creation of humankind. Is humankind inherently good or inherently bad? In Genesis we read that humankind is created in the image of God (Gen. 1:26). To believe that humans are created in the image of God means that some of what humans say, do and think reflects that Godly image. Therefore, all cultures reflect to some extent the Creator and His goodness. Cultures are thus good in at least some of their manifestations and potentially good in others.

On the other hand, we also read in Genesis that humankind explicitly rejected the command of God and thus sin entered the world. From that point onward, humankind lost something of its initial relationship with God, including the ability to live forever by escaping death (Gen. 3:22). Since cultures are made up of people, and all people are tainted by sin, then all cultures are sinful.

How are we as Christians to view cultures, both our own and others, in relation to this goodness and sinfulness? Is culture good, bad, or neutral? Our answer to this question will determine our acceptance of customs that are different from our own. It will also determine the advisability of using culture as a vehicle to communicate the truths of the gospel.

God has always chosen to interact with His people in terms of their own culture. He used the Greek and Hebrew languages to communicate His truths. His chosen prophets and apostles were members of a specific culture. Yet when some of them tried to make Gentile converts adapt to Hebrew customs, they were overruled.

Most missionaries fall into one of two camps (and here we will exaggerate to make our point). Those missionaries who choose to see humankind as sinful enter a culture and are quick to identify the sinful elements of society. Theirs is a constant battle to change the culture and its customs to be more like what they suppose Christian culture is like. They are highly critical of other religions and often label them as Satanic, having no redeeming value. Converts are told to leave their culture with its evil ways behind.

Another group of missionaries sees only the positive elements of cultures while ignoring its less desirable attributes. Because of the ills of their own society, they do not feel qualified to judge others. They tend to view other cultures romantically, as made up of those "whom they love" or "who are good." Converts are encouraged to remain full members of their culture. These missionaries are quick to point to the positive values of other religions.

We choose to see culture as having both good and sinful elements. But for the most part, culture is neither good nor bad, but neutral. God's truth must be communicated in ways in which the hearers can comprehend it, that is, in forms inherent in the culture. At the same time, sinful customs and social evils must come under God's condemnation and be changed. There is no such thing as a Christian culture just as there is no such thing as a demonic culture. Only aspects of culture, or better yet, people, are to be seen as either Christian or non-Christian.

The Gospel in Other Cultures

As missionaries work in other cultures their task is to help establish the Kingdom of God there. The methods used in this pursuit vary. The gospel is proclaimed leading to the establishing of congregations. Benevolent projects are carried out; biblical truth is taught. Where needed, a prophetic stance is taken. While missionaries know how to undertake these tasks in their own culture, they quickly realize that doing them in other cultural contexts presents unique challenges.

No matter what ministries are performed in other cultures, they must be appropriately carried out within those contexts. It is imperative to first listen to a culture before trying to speak to it, though sadly this is contrary to much of current missions practice.

Missiologists have coined the term "contextualization" to describe the dynamic and ongoing process of the gospel being planted, taking root and flourishing within another culture. Contextualization is "the process by which the gospel not only takes on the forms and idiosyncrasies of different cultures but also maintains a critical stance and seeks to transform them."[5]

Contextualized evangelism uses evangelistic approaches which are appropriate within the cultural

---

5. F. Ross Kinsler, "Mission and Context: The Current Debate about Contextualization," in *Evangelical Missions Quarterly*, 1978, 14:1:23-29.

context rather than borrowing methods of evangelism from one culture and foisting them upon another with the naive belief that they will work equally well in both. Evangelistic tracts may help in one context, but hinder in another. Missionaries in the Middle East run the risk of being thrown out of the country if they overtly share evangelistic tracts with Muslims there.

As a church is planted and begins to grow in another culture, the church will strive to understand, relate and apply the Bible within its unique cultural context. This process is called "theologizing," and the result is a *contextualized theology*. To accomplish this task, the church needs to involve itself in several types of exegesis. One is an exegesis of the Scriptures. Another is an exegesis of the cultural context, for that is where theology grows and flourishes. It is in the arena of daily life that God chooses to interact with humankind. If missionaries are involved in the process, they must be careful to understand the interrelation of their own culture and their theology lest they confuse the two in the new cultural setting.

Finally, an exegesis or study of traditional church doctrine must be undertaken which provides the new church with a yardstick for measuring the validity of her theology.

The three bases of a local or contextualized theology are gospel, culture and church. The beginning point is not so crucial as the end result. We can start with the Bible and then apply it to culture, as is done in expository preaching. Or we can start with the culture and the relate biblical truth to that culture, as is done in topical preaching. Biblical teaching that follows a common syllabus regardless of the cultural context is teaching that is done in a vacuum and will have limited use or relevance. But teaching that addresses needs within a culture—be they poverty, racism, gender bias, materialism, oppression, injustice, sorcery—will be lasting. In the final analysis, the results of all formal theological endeavor must be judged by the Bible.

Conclusion

A common criticism leveled against missionaries is that they go into a culture and change it, and that this is wrong. Let us first put this criticism to test, and then finally let us put it to rest. To criticize missionaries for entering and changing a culture, with the assumption that this is wrong, is to misunderstand culture and culture change. All cultures change. There is no culture that does not change. Unless a culture changes and adapts, it will not live. It will cease to exist. So it is simply naive to think that without missionary presence, a culture will not change.

Cultures are beset with outside influences to change. Cultures are not isolated pockets of individuals with no connections to the outside world. There are tremendous forces for change acting on all cultures. To list just a few: political pressure, economic pressure, the push towards modernization, and religious pressure. Why is it that Christian missionaries are criticized, but the same criticisms are not leveled at politicians, the executives of multinational companies, the promoters of Western media, or even the missionaries from the other religions who are also working hard to bring their version of the Truth and secure converts? To criticize Christian missionaries alone for "causing culture change" is simply inconsistent with the facts.

A view that is much more accurate is that missionaries have stood alongside of peoples from other cultures and helped to insure that their rights were not trampled by outsiders who wished to exploit them. Politically oriented missionaries have more often helped oppressed minorities rather than standing idly by while minority cultures have been trampled by others.

Any outsider who ventures into another culture brings new ideas which can be accepted or rejected by the members of the culture. But it is the members of a culture who determine to accept or reject these changes. This fact is well known by those who study innovation across cultures. A well-known proverb says the same thing: "You can lead a horse to water, but you cannot force it to drink." The view that blames missionaries for foisting change upon a group insults the self-determination and evaluative abilities of that group.

Finally, to think that it is wrong to change cultures arises from a romantic view of culture that suggests "primitive" cultures are better than modern cultures. It is assumed that such cultures are made up of simple, pure and happy people. This is the myth of the "noble savage" propounded over a hundred years ago by Jean Jacques Rousseau. It is also the myth that was almost as quickly abandoned by anthropologists and philosophers when they realized from firsthand experience that all cultures, whether "primitive" or modern, have elements of both good and bad in them. Do missionaries have a right to present new ideas to cultures? As much right as anybody else. Not only a right, but a mandate from the One who created all cultures, died for all cultures, and will one day be worshiped by those "from every tribe, and language and people and nation" (Rev. 5:9).

12
Belonging and Identity

Robert Douglas

God is "a people person"! Beginning from Genesis 1 the Bible shows he has been committed to people. That commitment prompted him to reach out to Adam and Eve, the crown of his creation, from the first moment in the Garden. God has always met people where they are. The alternative is for God to expect us to meet him where he is—a most unlikely venture given our limitations. And where are people? In the midst of cultures which they have created as expressions of their God-given abilities and responsibilities.

God's determination to be with humans where they are is seen repeatedly in the Old Testament and the New Testament. The ultimate expression of God's people orientation took place in the Incarnation. There God not only met people where they are, but also became flesh, "the man Christ Jesus" (1 Tim. 2:5), "made like his brothers in every way" (Heb. 2:17). The marvel of the Incarnation saves women and men from the necessity and tragedy of being isolated and insulated away from their Greatest Friend. Without the Incarnation God would be remote at best, little more than the deists' watchmaker. In and through the Incarnation, rich communication with God is made possible, the Almighty becomes real to us, and grace and love take on specific concrete expression. I know I am loved—and how I am loved! In the language of communication theory God takes the role of a receptor oriented being; in anthropological terms, God identifies with his creation through participation; in psychological idiom, God seeks to bond with people.

Incarnation: A Costly Process

Incarnation is a costly process for God (Jesus). For both God and Christ it meant the sacrifice of incredible things—sacrifices undertaken for our benefit. The New Testament alludes to those sacrifices on several occasions. Jesus voluntary forsakes being "rich" to become "poor," for only one reason—"for your sakes" (2 Cor. 8:5). It is next to impossible for us to grasp what is summed up in these few simple words "rich" and "poor."

Other passages tell us more. For example, though "Jesus was in the very nature God" and enjoyed "equality with God" he did not hang on to that privilege but he made himself "nothing," "a servant," "in human likeness," "a man." And if that was not enough "he humbled himself" enduring "death" and specifically "death on a cross" (Phil. 2:6-8). In the dramatic act of Incarnation, Jesus laid aside status, privilege, independence of will and immunity from the world's ills. He risked reputation, embraced vulnerability and looked the worst Satan and humans could do in the face.

Incarnation/Identification: A Multifaceted Approach

Through Incarnation, Jesus identified with those God loved, you and me. That Incarnation/identification expressed itself in a multitude of ways. Jesus interacted with people socially, personally and religiously, participating in the ritual acts of everyday living, establishing friendships, and giving himself away in service to those drawn to him. He ate, celebrated, worshiped, wept and laughed with people. From the beginning of his ministry, Jesus was typecast in various ways by Jewish society. His behavior impacted different segments of society in different ways. Some saw him in a positive light, though their reaction to him was sometimes fickle, sometimes confused. For others his actions were unacceptable because they did not match their preconceived ideas about "rabbis," Jesus' chosen role.

Jesus' Identification: Multilevel

Jesus' identification took place on several levels at once. First, he was Jesus "the man," knowing all the limitations and temptations of life as a person, fully experiencing all the dynamics common to the human situation. At the same time, he identified with a specific people in a specific land at a particular time in their history and cultural development. He was a Jew, not a Roman; a Palestinian, not a Hellenist; a "rabbi," not a temple guard or sandal-maker; a first century person, not a third century individual. Each of these details was basic to the unfolding of God's purpose and served to define the details of how God would communicate salvation to the world.

In his identification Jesus conformed to many Palestinian Jewish cultural norms, while also shattering others. He seems not to have been concerned to make his behavior match the religious establishment's view of a "good man" or a "rabbi." He also does not seem to have been particularly concerned about this "failure." The common people who were not greatly appreciated by the religious elite were enthralled by him—and sometimes confused too. They were attracted by Jesus' non-traditional stance, but often failed to grasp the implications of his teachings. Jesus' patience and persistence in being one with them point to his commitment to them and to their spiritual development.

Jesus' Incarnation: A Model For Us

Jesus' Incarnation is more than a vehicle for revelation. It also is a model with tremendous implications for Christians concerned to relate to others in cross-cultural ministry. Jesus reminds us that he sends us as the Father sent him (John 20:21). Following Jesus' example, cross-cultural workers are called to the high standard of incarnational identification. The basic issues in achieving this goal are the same for us as they were for him. There is a price to be paid, privilege to be laid aside and risks to be taken. The specifics of another culture must be approached seriously. We, like Jesus, must enter another world, learn a specific language, become "belongers," and find roles that allow for clear communication of the good news. It all starts with a commitment to identification.

Identification: The Heart of Cross-Cultural Work

Identification with the host culture is at the heart of good cross-cultural work. The ultimate impact of the gospel rests with the Holy Spirit who will "convict the world of guilt in regard to sin and righteousness and judgment" (John 15:8). However, the Spirit partners with people. Where those partners remain aloof from identification the progress of the gospel usually slows to a crawl. Identification must not remain a theory; it needs to be owned as a goal and implemented with deliberately planned effort. To translate the goal of identification from the abstract to the concrete it is necessary to consider several things which are part of redemptive incarnation. Three fundamental areas are knowledge of the target culture, lifestyle and attitudes toward that culture. In other words, identification engages thought, action, and feelings. Jesus' life as a Jew reflected all of these. The absence of any one of these will rob identification of core ingredients.

Identification in Knowledge

The knowledge required is specific in nature. It involves knowing a people's worldview, beliefs, values, and behaviors, all of which come to focus in their language. There is always interplay between language, worldview, beliefs, and values. It is possible to learn the spoken aspect of a language without ever comprehending a people's "silent language" which is as important as words and grammar.

Identification Includes Participation

Participation in a people's lifestyle includes sharing their food, clothing, customs, celebrations, rituals, and more—always in ways appropriate to the gospel. Often workers face the temptation to avoid participation in another culture because of ideological considerations. For example, it is easy to equate the unfamiliar with the bad and thus to judge incorrectly what is before us. A negative evaluation is readily sensed by nationals. Participation at more than a superficial level can challenge missionary outlooks at deep emotional levels, especially in areas such as concepts of private property and the right of privacy. But remember Jesus. So many things associated with "just living" have profound symbolic connotations. How these are handled builds bridges or barriers with people.

Identification and Attitudes

Attitudes stand to the heart of identification precisely because they are heart issues. Here one ultimately succeeds or fails in identification. Jesus, though critical of a number of ideas and practices of his adopted society, was seen by the common people as one who cared for them and empathized with their situations. In the midst of diverse opinions about him some who should have been his enemies could argue, "No one ever spoke the way this man does" (John 7:46). On another occasion as Jesus wept over Lazarus, the Jews commented, "See how he loved him!" (John 11:36). Through thoughtful identification we can hope likewise to meet with similar appreciation. To know and to participate while our hearts are loveless, resentful, or hypercritical is largely wasted effort.

Attitudes touch the very nerves of life, both ours and those of our host people. Just as other people have well known traditional ways of communicating "hello" and "good-bye" so the fabric of their culture provides avenues for clearly expressing emotions. To make these channels our own and to infuse them with feelings appropriate to specific occasions is a challenging but accomplishable task. Empathy is a one word summary of what is needed—seeing and feeling ourselves one in true love and mutual reciprocity with those to whom we wish to minister God's grace.

Limits of Identification

Identification has limits. Even Jesus did not identify totally with first century Palestinian Jewish culture. For example, he did not conform to the mores that governed the elite in their interaction with the common people. They tended to treat ordinary people with contempt, talking down to them and about them. The masses were "this mob that knows nothing of the law—there is a curse on them" (John 7:49)—hardly sentiment that encourages positive relationships. Evidently, the Sanhedrin's sense of class superiority was basic to how they viewed society and even God's ordering of life.

Historical Reactions to Identification

The history of missions points to a variety of reactions to the idea of identification. Some who set out to be cross-cultural workers fell victim to an attitude of total avoidance of identification! "Identification? Never!", was the message they lived. When this approach prevails, people isolate themselves from the local culture. Little attempt is made to acquire the local language. A safe secure insulated life is lived. The resultant lifestyle may express itself in "compound" living. Literal compounds with walls, gates and guards are not unknown. A variation without literal walls involves limiting oneself to only to expatriate friends, foods, and fellowship. Nationals are reduced to "scenery" or "machinery"; they are not treated like real people. Withdrawal of this kind is ineffective if the goal of missions is to establish a biblically and culturally viable church which can reproduce itself with maximum impact. Mainstream nationals do not want to become North Americans; the compound mentality is not inclined to allow them to "join up." Jesus' example stands in stark contrast to this model.

The other extreme regarding identification involves attempting to become so totally one with the host culture it is labeled "going native." "Going native" implies a total rejection of one's birth culture, and is accompanied by an overly negative disposition toward everything associated with it. Those who go native have lost perspective. They tend to emphasize the externals of identification while forgetting that they will always remain outsiders to some degree. An Anglo-American will never be mistaken for an African, however much he may identify. Christians who fall into this behavior ignore biblical insights which teach that all cultures are under God's standard of judgment. They are greatly handicapped in speaking a whole gospel with its call for repentance and change.

Christian psychologists suggest that those who go native reflect less than normal emotional stability.

Ideal Identification

The ultimate aim of identification is to become a genuine belonger, a bicultural individual who is as much at home in her adopted culture as in her original culture. Again, Jesus is the model. He became flesh and was "the man," yet he remained Jesus the Son in whom the fullness of deity dwelt bodily, who related unhindered to the realm from which he came.

Ultimately then incarnational identification is that process by which missionaries surrender certain of their own cultural distinctions while adopting others from the host culture. This is a process. Behind it and fundamental to it is another process—spiritual formation. Spiritual formation is the process by which people consent to be transformed by the Holy Spirit into the image of Christ. Deficiencies in this arena undercut one's capacity to identify incarnationally. Identification is not just an issue of strategy nor one with mental health implications. At heart it involves discipleship issues and relates to spiritual maturity.

Identification and Role Selection

Crucial to identification is suitable role selection. As Christian workers move across cultures to carry on Jesus' work, they are faced with the prospect of being typecast in predetermined ways by their hosts. Jesus was. A role will be attributed to them almost automatically. "Role" has to do with who others say we are, not who we say we are. "Role" has to do with behavior. Different roles inherently carry different behavior expectations. Societies have clear ideas about how nurses, taxi drivers, policemen and garbage collectors look, talk, and act. The odds are we will not be seen in ways we wish to be known without intentional and persistent efforts on our part to conform to a specific role. But effort in and of itself does not insure a productive outcome. A vital question is, "What roles are available to us and which would be useful to kingdom causes among my chosen people?" How does one decide? And having decided what can a worker do to insure nationals see him in his adopted role?

Ministry Context and Role Definition

The context of ministry will determine the perimeters of workable roles in identification. The range of believable, helpful options is apt to be larger in urban areas than rural, tribal, or nomadic settings. A major consideration in role identification in any region of the world is basic cultural values. Roles that are perceived as a threat to people, social structures, economic interest or long held religious beliefs and practices are counterproductive. In some societies great stress is placed on avoidances of direct encounter or confrontation. Certain roles seem to have built-in predispositions to confrontation: lawyer, seller, teacher. On the other hand, roles like learner, trader and story teller may be quite helpful for kingdom purposes.

Culture and Role Expectations

Role expectations differ across cultures as do foods, dress and language. At least four aspects of a role have been identified: the degree of personalness expected; the degree of formality or informality required; the degree of hierarchy associated with a role; and the amount of deviation from the "ideal" allowed role behaviors. Each of these influences role suitability.

The degree of personalness expected has to do with whether one is seen as a total person, or only as a representative of a specific vocation. Degree of formality can be illustrated by different expectations in teacher-student relations. In the West, it is not uncommon for teachers and students to use first names in addressing each other. In Japan such would never occur due to greater formality. Some roles may carry such a degree of formality in the host culture as to present a significant barrier to communicating the love and grace of God. The impact of hierarchy is evident in the military in the rigid separation between officers and enlisted men. Degree of acceptable deviation from a role is seen in Jesus as rabbi. In the eyes of the people, he was a rabbi though his behavior was somewhat un-rabbi-like in associating with sinners.

Shaping Valid Roles

Valid roles for kingdom purposes will have to integrate principles of righteousness and legitimate responses to felt needs, which in turn are shaped by cultural contexts. No role in and of itself automatically brings these necessities together—some because they contradict kingdom concerns, others because of cultural definition associated with a role, still others because of perceived specific needs.

Exploitation and Role Selection

Any hint of exploitation must be avoided in one's role selection. To be a businessman in a given country may be a constructive role, but it also may not be helpful to the kingdom. In part, it depends on the perceptions of people regarding business enterprises and especially foreign business people. Businesses seen as taking unfair advantage of resources, people, law or property sooner or later will be resented, no matter how pure the heart of the entrepreneur. Business ventures which aim to serve, assist in development or improve living conditions also can be misunderstood. What is and is not perceived as "exploitive" is conditioned by cultural, economic and political factors. Unfortunately, in today's world nationalistic sentiments are easily aroused by accusations of new colonization directed against foreign institutions.

Carefully chosen roles are absolutely essential for the advancement of the gospel in a new culture. Viability of role helps the Christian worker be held in great affection; however, it does not instantly or automatically insure it. Person-to-person relationships in a new culture also are foundational if the missionary is to learn his host culture and its language. Relationships also are the vehicle by which nationals learn to develop trust in the missionary. They allow him to be seen up close and as a human. Cultural isolation is fatal to the person-to-person connections on which the gospel thrives. Timing is critical in achieving these goals. The worker who puts off building close associations with nationals is missing a *kairos* moment in his own adjustment and development. Mission strategists have long stressed the importance of immediate "bonding" as a basis for launching culture and language learning, relationship building and initiating ministry which is authentic.

Bonding and Role Development

Bonding aims at the creation of relationships which in the initial stages of one's cross-cultural time will facilitate constructive entry into a new world. Due to the limitations of time and energy, one person can only develop so many relationships. Since the missionary's concern is kingdom work, the laborer must think clearly about the "who" of relationships. All people are of equal worth before God. However, different individuals have different potential for the gospel when it comes to serving as bridges into the widest segment of a target people. Learning one's host culture requires having access to participation in the dominant institutions of that culture, there to relearn roles through a process of imitation, instruction and influence. Bonding gets this process started.

The most effective way to bond is upon arrival to find a national family with whom to live, preferably a family that does not speak the missionary's language. Immediate cultural immersion is the result. In this setting, a foreigner has the greatest possible exposure to the nitty-gritty of how people go about the daily tasks of living.

Bonding prevents a merely surface contact with the host culture. It introduces one into networks inherent in the target culture. These networks provide a measure of support to the newcomer and can become avenues along which the good news of Christ can flow. Human nature is such that any major change in life involves a sense of loss and accompanying grief. This phenomenon, an aspect of culture shock, is part of the cross-cultural worker's journey and needs to be dealt with healthily. Through bonding a worker is able to offset some of the grief experienced due to his loss of his place in his own culture.

The process of bonding however does not eliminate another type of trauma, that is, culture shock rising out of value conflict. In fact, bonding intensifies this stress. In the long run this is positive because communication of the gospel essentially involves ministering a message which embodies values conflict. Culture shock can occur at cognitive and behavioral levels as well as at the affective level. It seems to be most acute "among those who will later be the most effective—i.e., those who have a high orientation to relationships, and who are aware of the limitations of their knowledge."

Goal of Cultural Sensitivity

Identification, choice of role, and bonding are not just niceties of cultural sensitivity. The goal is not politeness but the proclamation of the redeeming work of Christ, the saving of people and the transformation of societies. Communication in all of its multifaceted dimensions is basic to kingdom goals. Identification, role and bonding play major parts in this venture for God. They do not take place in isolation but within wider social structures. All people live in communities which provide structures allowing them to relate to others in orderly ways. Social order which has been determined over time makes human interaction possible. Social systems are never static, but constantly undergo modification. The complexity of human societies is reflected in the different levels at which people interact—personal networks, groups, whether kinship or geographical, and within complex systems such as cities.

Contextual Communication

Communication always takes place in a context. That context is made up of a host of variables each of which impacts the flow of information. Included are basic elements such as a people's worldview, language and ways of thinking. To these, social structure must be added. Different societies have different social structures which in turn give rise to different communication patterns. Who talks to whom, how and with what affect? Understanding these dynamics is vital to the progress of the gospel.

Social Structure Impacts Communication

Sociological structure defines and reflects who functions in the role of "gatekeepers," or "bridges," that is, who are people of influence who in turn impact the widest group. These people can be crucial to the gospel's spread. Christian workers need to give careful and prayerful consideration to how and where they want the gospel to flow. God's desire is that all people be saved. Finding and drawing near to God's bridges must be a high priority. Care is needed to avoid creating a Christian subculture (though Christianity always has counterculture qualities to it)—an enclave cut off from meaningful interaction with the larger body of people.

Face-To-Face Societies

Students of how people live have identified different basic social structures. These are often divided into two categories: "face-to-face" societies and urban societies. "Face-to-face" societies have been further subdivided into bands and tribal and peasant societies. Given the rich diversity within humankind, these categories are very general and serve only to assist in the broadest kind of classification of societies. Tribal and peasant societies each lay a great deal of stress on kinship and group orientation. At the heart of "tribe" is a mono-ethnic group sharing one language and culture and identified with a given territory. Tribal peoples live by hunting and gathering, by practicing simple agriculture or as nomads (pastoralism). Bands and tribal societies usually have little hierarchial social structure. Tribal groups generally look to elders for information and direction. Significant communication flows vertically from elders, top to bottom. Within the wider society of the tribe information travels easily horizontally from person to person for there are few socially erected barriers. Major decisions are made by tribal leaders, kinship groups and families.

Peasant societies consist of multi-ethnic groups and classes with a relative degree of economic self-sufficiency, often based on agriculture. Within peasant societies hierarchy exists between groups more than between individuals. Communication again takes place with ease within groups. Between groups communication typically moves from top down, that is vertically. People with greater ascribed status influence those who are "beneath" them; the reverse generally does not occur. In the village decisions are made by families but go no farther than ethnic or class grouping.

Incarnational identification and bonding in the early stages of ministry is vital for missionary well-being. Both, however, must be done with social structure clearly in view. Those who would identify must determine which people in their host society are in a position to pass on the message as widely as possible and with as great an impact as can be had. Communication with positive impact requires enduring personal friendships to allow for the diffusion of the gospel within a society. A message challenging people to change their belief needs to be modeled in practical ways. "Practical" modeling will differ depending on whether one is relating to a tribal or peasant setting. It is essential that the message is addressed initially to those capable of making valid decisions who can also influence others positively.

Urban Societies

The world is becoming more urban. Urban areas, defined politically, are made up of many ethnic groups, with complex systems of commerce, communication, government and religion. Cities differ widely from one location to another in the world. They reflect new complex systems which impact life at all levels. They are magnets attracting wealth and expertise. "City" is almost synonymous with "diversity." In the public realm hierarchy reigns giving shape to institutional interaction while preserving dominant group status.

Not all cities are urban in outlook. A bewildering diversity of social structures exists. Many are conglomerates of tribal peasant enclaves. However, rapid change is at work in urban settings; more traditional enclaves within the city do not escape this influence. In enclave based neighborhoods, group decisions prevail. Outside such neighborhoods more non-traditional approaches come to the fore. Where urban influence prevails great value is placed on individualism and with it, personal decision making. People find reference groups or networks in voluntary associations connected with vocation, location, or interests. Organization by kinship and hierarchy tends to be less important in shaping life. Upper class people are more individualistic, looking to networks of friends and trusted opinion leaders as well as drawing on their own feelings and thought processes.

Urban settings likewise call for identification and bonding as part of proclaiming the good news. But with which segment of society? Prayer and care are in order in seeking answers. Answers are available and in today's urbanizing world are all the more critical. In each specific setting lessons from Jesus' Incarnation need to be explored and applied.

Kingdom work is of such a nature as to call for only the very best. God set the standard by sending his Son. Jesus was content with nothing less than Incarnation. Through it he identified with us to such an extent that we cannot miss the wonder of divine love. Jesus embodied the importance of relationships for therein he nurtured and shaped his disciples. The Master was understandable and appreciated by his followers within a chosen framework. He was "master," "rabbi" and in time he was seen by them as so much more.

Jesus sets the standard. He modeled the essence of

good cross-cultural witness. As he was sent so he sends us—to identify, live incarnationally, carefully choose among roles, bond, pay attention to society's structure—all for the sake of King and kingdom.

13
Keys to Communication

Doug Priest Jr.

Introduction

The Bible is preeminently a book about communication. In the miracle of Creation, God created man and woman in His own image, and He talked with them. From the dawn of history we see that the nature of God was to communicate. Why else would those created in His image be able to talk? Our God is a God of communication, both communicating with us and desiring communication from us.

The patriarchs all communicated with God and He with them. Whether the vehicle was a burning bush, a cloud in the sky, an altar, a vision or a dream, God was in the business of communicating with all of His created beings throughout the entire world.

Through the mystery of the Trinity, God is never far from us. By His Spirit, He continuously leads and guides us into a deeper knowledge of Himself. With the Advent, His Word became enfleshed and He dwelt among us for a season. God speaks to us through the written Word.

The coming of Christ to earth must be understood as God's continuing desire to communicate with His world. To leave His home in glory, to humble Himself by taking on the form of a servant, to learn human language, and to be comfortable in diverse cultures such as were found in Palestine in the first century shows how much God desired to communicate with humankind. The strategy God employed through the Incarnation in missionary terminology is called "cross-cultural communication."

Understanding Cross-Cultural Communication

Simply put, communication is the transfer of understanding between two or more people. Cross-cultural communication is the transfer of meaning across cultures. An easy way of visualizing the process of communication is through the diagram below. There are three components: a sender, a message, and a receptor. The sender sends a message to the receptor, the one who receives the message.

SENDER ▶━━▶ MESSAGE ▶━━▶ RECEPTOR

As we examine our own communication practices we can see which of the three components we emphasize the most. With our Western love of the printed word, in our churches, Bible colleges and seminaries we spend literally years studying the message. It is fairly obvious that we value the message component of the communication process very highly. Such is as it ought to be. Those who do not take the time to do solid and regular Bible study cannot be good communicators of the Word.

In these same Bible colleges and seminaries we are also taught verbal communication and homiletical skills. We are taught the art of preaching. In these skills the emphasis is primarily on the sender, emphasizing his or her ability to get the message across.

If the communication is between people who share the same culture, then the transfer of understanding between sender and receptor is fairly straightforward.

The reason for this is because people from the same culture share a common frame of reference. They speak the same language, obey the same laws, eat the same sorts of food, duplicate clothing styles, follow fads together, shop in common locations, and know similar things.

But in cross-cultural communication, the hearer and the receptor do not share a common culture. Their frames of reference are different. Meaning is not so easily transferred as in communication between members of the same culture. The success of communication is in direct proportion to the amount of overlap between the frame of references of the speaker and hearer.

As meaning is attempted to be shared back and forth between sender and receptor in cross-cultural communication, three possible outcomes can occur. First of all, and unfortunately happening very often, there can be a loss of meaning. How many times have I gotten directions in a new city, followed the directions as best I understood them, and ended up totally lost! Somewhere in the communication process there was a loss of meaning.

Secondly, in cross-cultural communication, meaning can be shared. After landing in the Jakarta, Indonesia airport, I was able to get a lift across this huge city to the bus terminal. There, I caught a bus that actually ended up in the distant city of Bandung, my destination. In this case, thankfully, meaning was shared.

A third possibility in cross-cultural communication results in the addition of unintended meaning. On another occasion I told a cabby in central Java that I wanted to go to the town of Boyolali. Since few foreigners go to that town, he assumed that I wanted to go to a factory near to that town where some foreigners worked. It was only after much effort that I was able to convince the driver that he was on the wrong road.

We must realize that it is not the hearer's responsibility to enter the frame of reference of the speaker. Contrary to much common missionary practice, communication does not begin with being understood by one's audience. It begins first with understanding the audience. It is crucial that missionaries learn both the culture and the language of the people they are trying to serve. People who travel to a new culture will not be able to communicate effectively unless they stay long enough to get into the minds and worldviews of their listeners.

Missionaries who do not know the language or the culture of the people where they work manifest a failure to communicate effectively. They are often misunderstood. Their communication is not two-way. In fact, it is often not even one-way because they are not able to transfer meaning. The receptor does not get the message that the sender wishes to send. The most crucial missionary shortcoming is not an inadequate study of the message or text. After all, we have spent years studying the Bible. It is a failure to study the context adequately where the text is to be proclaimed.

Many is the missionary who can attest to the cultural blunders made by visitors who try to communicate in another setting without first taking the time to learn something of the language and culture. I was once told in Indonesia of a visiting preacher from America who chose to use an illustration on the importance of love between husbands and wives, surely an important message coming straight from the Bible. Unfortunately, his illustration of the principle was a little too graphic for his audience. Though his illustration would have been totally appropriate in America, in Indonesia it was totally inappropriate.

Such situations happen often in these days of

instant missions. We can only be thankful for the graciousness of our hosts, whose customs and language we so often trample in our desire to quickly preach the Word so that we can catch the next plane home!

Lest I paint too bleak a picture, let me be quick to state that cross-cultural communication is indeed possible, and at times takes place even though little homework has been done by the sender. All people share the same Creator and have common needs and desires. Everybody comprehends the need for food, water, warmth and shelter. Through the influence of worldwide media such as radio and television, people from diverse cultures have much in common. Within seconds, citizens from all over the entire world knew that Brazil had won the World Cup! Yet again, through the use of interpreters, some communication between cultures can take place, albeit in a limited form.

However, the communication of events or outward behavior is much more readily understood than the communication of ideas or thoughts. Ideas and values come from the very core of our being, and to espouse the changing of such values, as we do when we preach Christ, calls for a disciplined learning of the frame of reference of the receptor.

Following Christ's Example

Earlier we alluded to God's intense desire for communication with His creation as made manifest by the sending of His Son to earth. The coming of Jesus is a lesson in cross-cultural communication. Not only did Jesus leave His home in Heaven to come to a new culture, He adjusted to that culture so well that most of the people did not even recognize His divinity. When He spoke, it was in the various literary styles of His hearers—using parables, proverbs and riddles. His illustrations were taken from the surrounding culture—fishing, farming, and fasting. Nor must we forget that Jesus spent some thirty years in preparation before commencing His ministry of communication.

While we could learn much from a full study of the cross-cultural communication techniques used by Jesus, we will focus on just one incident from His early life. Luke relays the episode in his gospel:

> Every year his parents went to Jerusalem for the Feast of the Passover. When he was twelve years old, they went up to the Feast, according to the custom. After the Feast was over, while his parents were returning home, the boy Jesus stayed behind in Jerusalem, but they were unaware of it. Thinking he was in their company, they traveled on for a day. Then they began looking for him among their relatives and friends. When they did not find him, they went back to Jerusalem to look for him. After three days they found him in the temple courts, *sitting* among the teachers, *listening* to them and *asking* them questions. Everyone who heard him was amazed at his understanding and his *answers* (Luke 2:41-47, *emphasis mine*).

Jesus was separated from his parents for a total of four days, during which time he was in the temple courts. What he did during these four days are instructive for us, particularly in the precise order that Luke records the event. We can glean four communication lessons from this passage.

Sitting

The first principle of communication to note is that Jesus sat with the teachers. We are not told how much of the time Jesus spent sitting, but we can infer that being a youngster in the presence of religious leaders, Jesus was probably content to sit and observe for some time. How often we neglect the importance of being there with people from another culture and just sitting with them. In our hustle and bustle lives where we set our schedules according to watches and day-timers, we take little time for just sitting. If we have to sit and be still for any length of time, most of us will begin to squirm in our seats. We become nervous and even feel guilty because we are not doing anything.

Not so with Jesus, and not so with much of the rest of humankind. There are many places in the world where simply sitting with people communicates volumes. Recently, a missionary friend and I sat in the home of a Javanese man. The man we were visiting was seriously ill and death was close at hand. During our several visits to his home we chatted with the family, drank tea, talked with the man, prayed, and served the Lord's Supper. But mostly we just sat, for our being there in the time of need was what counted. In tight-knit communities such as Javanese villages, non-participation in community events is tantamount to disrespect and disregard for harmonious relationships. The good cross-cultural communicator will be aware of the need for sitting with people.

Listening

Luke next records that in addition to sitting, Jesus listened. Those who study communication have noted that people divide their time in communication skills according to the following percentages: reading 12%; speaking 16%, writing 14%, and listening 58%. They have also noted that there are five different types of listening:

1. *Ignoring* what the other person is saying and making no attempt to understand.
2. *Pretending* to listen, often making verbal noises to convince the other person that we are listening.

3. *Selective* listening where we hear only parts of a conversation.

4. *Attentive* listening, or paying attention to what is being said.

5. *Empathetic* listening occurs when we try to interact with the feelings of the one who is talking to us. The goal of empathetic listening is to fully understand.

Attentive listeners try to understand the message. They realize that listening requires discipline and effort. Listening is hard work. One of the reasons language teachers suggest quickly moving beyond the use of language interpreters is that when we depend on interpreters, we begin to filter out the sounds of the foreign language much like we have learned to filter out the sounds of the freeway or a ticking clock when we are sleeping.[1] When we must depend on interpreters, we simply do not listen to the language or the one speaking the language.

Is it any surprise that Jesus spent time listening? He made an arduous attempt to enter the worldview of the religious teachers in the temple courtyards. That he was successful in later being heard by them, I believe, was because he had spent time initially sitting and listening before He began to speak. Though "listen before speaking" is a lesson that we were taught at our mother's knee, we so often forget.

Asking

The third communication principle that Jesus followed, and that naturally followed upon the foundation of sitting and listening, was that He asked questions. He sought clarity from the religious teachers. I can just see the grudging admiration growing in these

---

1. Elizabeth Brewster, personal conversation with author, 1994.

religious teachers for the young lad of a mere twelve years who had sat with them for several days, listening, and then asking questions. Most boys would have been too busy or too bored. But not Jesus.

There are many reasons for asking questions. One goal might be to achieve understanding. Another might be to analyze a situation, while yet another might be for evaluation. To ask questions is to acknowledge and show interest in the other party. All successful physicians and counselors have learned that diagnosis and cure can be aided through the asking of questions. Questions are even asked with the purpose of getting others to change their behavior.

Answering

Finally, the fourth cross-communication principle followed by Jesus was that He answered the questions that were put to Him. After first being in their presence for several days, then Jesus was free to engage in two-way conversation. When He did, He amazed His teachers with His answers. In other words, Jesus understood His message and He was able to communicate it with his receptors so that they understood Him.

If we want to be successful in cross-cultural communication, we would do well to follow the example set for us by Jesus. He manifested what Charles Kraft calls "receptor-oriented communication."[2] Jesus spoke in the thought forms of His hearers. He communicated in their language and He was understood because He entered their frame of reference. We must go and do likewise. Cross-cultural communications specialist Viggo Søgaard sums up this attitude when he writes,

2. Charles Kraft, *Communication Theory for Christian Witness* (Nashville: Abingdon, 1983), p. 23.

The incarnation must be the ideal we strive for. Incarnation begins with a concern for making the message clearly understood in each specific context. For such communication to happen we must take the cultural context seriously, and the audience in particular. Listening to their needs and their cries is the starting point of true and effective communication.[3]

How Do We Do It?

If cross-cultural communication is to be receptor-oriented, then missionaries must make every effort to use the communication forms that are inherent in the culture they are trying to reach. We can illustrate how this has been attempted in Indonesia.

The thousands of islands comprising the nation of Indonesia are home to many different cultures. Indonesia is the world's fourth most populous nation and is home to the world's largest Muslim population. The island of Java has over one hundred million people, with the largest group being the Javanese speakers. While traditionally most Javanese have been rural farmers, today there is a rapidly growing movement towards urbanization and industrialization on the island.

Upwards of 95% of the Javanese are Muslim, though of course their adherence to Islam ranges from superficial belief to strict orthodoxy. Many of the Javanese are folk Muslims, with their Islamic faith being a veneer over animistic practices. As Clifford Geertz states,

> The village religious system commonly consists of a balanced integration of animistic, Hinduistic, and Islamic elements, a basic Javanese syncretism which is

---

3. Viggo Søgaard, "Dimensions of Approach to Contextual Communication," in Gilliland, *The Word Among Us*, pp. 160-161.

the island's true folk tradition, the basic substructure of its civilization.[4]

Communicating with Rural Farmers

Missionaries from the Christian Churches and Churches of Christ began to work in central Java in the 1960s and 1970s. With few exceptions their work has been with the rural Javanese. Thirty churches have been started. Some of these missionaries have become fluent in both the national language of Indonesia (Bahasa Indonesia) as well as the mother tongue of the Javanese people (Bahasa Jawa). Their work has complemented the efforts of the local Indonesian Christians.

When the missionaries first arrived in central Java they began their study of the Javanese culture. They did so because they wanted their gospel communication to be receptor-oriented, taking place in the frame of reference of their hearers. They learned that for the Javanese a supreme goal in life is the attainment of well-being, *slamet*. The achievement of well-being depends upon both the observance of religious practices as well as the gaining of esoteric knowledge about the controlling forces of life. Concerning the gaining of this knowledge, one missionary wrote,

> Not everyone can see the deeper truths. Many truths, in fact, have been "wrapped up" or disguised intentionally. The Javanese ancestors who possessed deep knowledge are considered to have been very sparing in imparting it to others. They sometimes wrapped up their knowledge in what I call "historical folk tales" in such a way that only the truly informed could understand them.[5]

---

4. Clifford Geertz, *The Religion of Java* (London: The Free Press of Glencoe, 1960), p. 5.

5. W. Michael Smith, "An Eye Opener for the Rural Javanese," in *Unto the Uttermost*, ed. by Doug Priest Jr. (Pasadena, CA: William Carey Library, 1984), pp. 218-219.

In a fascinating account, W. Michael Smith tells how Christians in Java have used one of these historical folk tales as a vehicle for sharing the truth of the gospel.[6] Because the tale was thoroughly Javanese, containing elements of history, myth, treachery, bravery, and cleverness, many responded to its "hidden" message about Christ. The story is about a young man named Aji Saka who is reputed to have lived in the first century A.D. and is credited with developing the Javanese alphabet and calendar. We will closely follow Smith's development and explanation of the tale:

> Long ago the kingdom of Medangkamulan was ruled by a murderous king, named Dewatacengkar. Everyday he demanded the flesh of one of his subjects for his food. Of course, none of his subjects could live in peace. Fear and anxiety dominated their lives.

> But God took pity on the citizens of that oppressed kingdom and sent a young man from a far country to help them. This young man named Aji Saka obeyed his calling from God and formed a plan. Aji Saka offered to become the meal of the wicked king. As a final petition he requested on behalf of his poor foster parents a piece of land the size of the cloth he used for his turban. The king mockingly granted the request but as he unfolded Aji Saka's turban, he was startled to see it expand further and further until he found himself backed up to the sea. At that point, the clever Aji Saka snatched back his turban cloth with such power that the king was thrown headlong into the sea where he was changed into a white crocodile.

> There was great rejoicing that day, and Aji Saka was made king. All the citizens who wanted deliverance from the oppression of the king had to be willing to be covered by Aji Saka's turban cloth. As a commemoration of these events, Aji Saka developed the Javanese alphabet.

6. Ibid., pp. 216-228.

There is more to this story than meets the eye. As it was passed down from generation to generation, most have forgotten its meaning. It has become just another story. But some of those early ancestors knew the truth it contains.

Smith then goes on to unlock the hidden meaning of this story. The word Medangkamulan can be translated as "blanketed by the sword," and the ruler's name in English means "without understanding of God." The wicked ruler lived by the sword and knew not God. Only one from outside the kingdom, Aji Saka, could help. His name means "pillar," and he was sent by God. Anybody who wanted to be saved had to be ritually covered by Aji Saka. By the very translation of these names, the story of Christ can be told.

The Javanese alphabet that Aji Saka developed also has a hidden meaning. When the letters of the alphabet are said orally and in their proper order, they form the following sentences (when translated into English): "There was a messenger, the same in power and might, not hesitant, to become a dead body." The explanation of these sentences is linked to the coming of Christ to the world, His willing death and resurrection so that people might be saved.

The use of a traditional folk tale to convey the gospel is an attempt to communicate with relevance to an audience of Javanese villagers. Sitting upon woven mats on the floor with kerosene lantern overhead, sipping sweet tea, and explaining hidden meanings communicates something of God's love for the Javanese people.

Communicating with Urban Dwellers

Not everybody on the island of Java lives in villages or harvests crops for a living. Over the past fifteen years the country of Indonesia has been going through a dramatic change. There has been a tremendous push towards urbanization, and the economy of the country is rapidly becoming industrialized. Indonesia's cities are where population growth is occurring. When students complete their education they do not want to move back to their farming villages. They are attracted by the opportunities of the city, and they want to live there. It is in the urban areas where the jobs are to be found.

Indonesia's economic growth rate is one which makes many Western nations envious. Most of this growth is in industry, not in agriculture. Fewer and fewer people till the soil each year. Indonesians say that today, only the very old or the very young still live in villages.

Cities are linked with modernization trends. In the cities are malls, fast food chains, theaters showing the most recent movies, and even video arcades. It is the urban areas which are the centers of influence in today's Indonesia.

With its look backward into Javanese history rather than forward into the future, we would not expect that the Aji Saka story would receive the results in the city that it achieved in the rural villages. For one thing, the story is told in Javanese, but the primary language of the cities in Java is not Javanese but Bahasa Indonesia.

Some missionaries who have observed these trends in Indonesia are now beginning to focus their efforts on the cities. They wish to augment their previous rural ministry with an urban ministry. Village Christians flocking to the cities will be able to find fellowship as urban churches are begun.

One common characteristic of most city dwellers is their desire for modernization. They wish to expand their horizons and so pursue education, both formally and informally. There are new schools and special courses being offered everywhere. Most city people read the daily newspapers in an attempt to keep current. For some in the city, modernization is equated with Western culture, so they watch Western movies, read Western books, and listen to Western music. Hand and hand with a desire for modernization is a desire to speak the English language.

Christians are tapping into the frame of reference of the city dwellers. Churches cater to this desire for modernization by having contemporary worship services, many of the songs being sung to Western tunes. Courses and seminars on various subjects are continually being offered by the churches. Christian business people join together for prayer before going to the office. English courses are taught by Christians.

The communication media being used by the Christians in reaching city dwellers are not foreign media to the city. The printed page, cassettes, microphones, amplifiers, and classroom instruction are all to be found in the city and hence are not foreign media added by Christians.

Conclusion

Anybody who engages in missionary endeavor at any level desires to be a good communicator. We know that as emissaries of the most high God, this is the goal for which we must strive. But those of us who come from the West have been enamored with the notion of *immediacy*. When we want something, we want it NOW! We have come to expect fast service in all that we do as a way of life, as typified by fast food restaurants, turning a spigot and getting hot water, pushing a button and seeing a television show, pumping our own gas so we do not have to wait in line, microwave ovens zapping TV dinners in ninety seconds, and instant access to the world through telecommunication. Our culture in so many ways conditions us to assume that results can be achieved immediately.

It is a hard lesson for us to realize that truly meaningful cross-cultural communication cannot be achieved immediately. We only deceive ourselves when we think that it can.

Long ago the Apostle Paul wrote to the people in the region of Galatia that a fruit of the Spirit is patience (Gal 5:22). Can we Christians rediscover this fruit in the latter days of the twentieth century? As missionaries and followers of Christ, our role demands that we do.

14
Societies and the Gospel

Edgar J. Elliston

The social context of a people constrains the how, when, why, to what extent, and who will become disciples of Christ in that context. Social structures may serve as receptive growth arenas for the planting and growth of churches or they may erect hostile and resistant barriers to evangelism and to the nurture of believers. People respond to the gospel largely on the basis of how they perceive the gospel. This perception is always socially conditioned. Missional effectiveness then requires an understanding of the social context.

Every group of people establishes patterns of shared learned behaviors. These patterns soon become assumptions and form a largely unconsciously held worldview. The shared learned behaviors or cultural forms relate to every dimension of a people's life, including language, social organization, and the way their material world is organized and used. Disciplines such as anthropology, sociology, political science, psychology, and economics all provide tools to help understand these patterns. When people commonly believe these established patterns to be functioning well, they often hesitate to change. Depending on the local circumstances these patterns may move toward stronger reactions such as receptivity or resistance to the gospel.

Worldview Influence

One can hardly over estimate the influence that a people's worldview has in their society and the way it functions. It is like the operating system of a computer. The operating system serves as a "platform" for everything done in a given computer whether it is a Macintosh, UNIX, DOS or some other platform. All of the programs depend on it to run. An operating system may be changed, but a change requires a "deep level" involvement in the machine. If the operating system changes, programs may also have to be changed because they are tailor-made to fit with the operating system. An "update" in the operating system requires attention to assure compatibility. Similarly, the worldview of a people may be changed, but it requires a deep level transformation. If it changes, one may expect unexpected effects in every arena of behavior. As a computer operating system may serve to drive many different kinds of programs that interact or relate to each other, people sharing the same worldview may employ many different paradigms or perspectives for different kinds of status and roles. They may communicate with understanding because they share the same worldview. Typically, as one seeks to use a computer program, one cannot use it with a different operating system without translation/adaptation. Until now the translation across different "platforms" is often difficult and results in unexpected changes. As one moves from one worldview to another one cannot assume that anything will work in the one as it did in the other. Changes can be expected in every domain based on the worldview. The differences emerge from fundamental discrepancies in assumptions. For example, I can use a future tense in the English language to indicate an intent for the future. However, when I go into several African languages where the assumption that time is cyclical, I will not find a future tense in the language. To discuss the concept of "long-range planning" is very difficult. A translation is possible, but to generate the similar meaning requires significant effort.

When the gospel is proclaimed among a people with a different worldview, it will always be interpreted through the operating system/worldview of the people who are listening. If they do not have similar categories for interpreting, significant distortion or meaningless gibberish will result. To effectively communicate the gospel among a people with a different worldview requires several steps. Again, to use the computer analogy—one must learn the operating system and then translate or adapt the code to fit the new system. The message of the gospel must be expressed in terms that the people can understand.

This adaptation or translation process is sometimes described as "contextualization."

Worldview differences may also be experienced in subcultures. For example, my children interpret information differently from me. Generational differences may be seen in most modern urbanized societies. Even "minor" worldview differences may result in major misunderstandings as many parents of teenagers may attest. Differences in socio-economic standing also lead to worldview differences. My wife works in a large bank. The worldview differences among the employees of the bank range widely because of socio-economic influences. The officers of the bank who work on the 72nd floor interpret everything including the good news of the gospel very differently from the janitors who clean their offices. They may all speak English, but the dialects will differ and the deep level assumptions about life differ.

A person's worldview provides a perceptual framework for understanding all of the events, relationships and processes one might experience. When an experience occurs which cannot be interpreted using one's worldview or deep level assumptions, dissonance occurs. In computer terms the system may "hang up" or "crash." For a person who is used to working in a "Windows" environment, the term is an "unrecoverable application error." The Pharisees' worldview prevented their "seeing" or "understanding" Jesus' miracles. Many people whose worldview has been influenced by the "Enlightenment" or modern secularism find it very difficult to understand issues of spiritual power. To effectively communicate the gospel, then, requires a deep level understanding of the worldview of the hearer and how it may differ from that of the communicator. An understanding of how worldview changes can also provide a great help to the communicator of the gospel.

Social Structures and Communication

A society (a people who share the same broad based worldview) provides the context/matrix in which the gospel will be communicated. Social structures with a society facilitate or inhibit communication both within a culture and across cultural boundaries. Three primary sets of social structures serve as modes to explain social organization: traditional/tribal, peasant and modern urban. Within each of these broad kinds of social systems one will find subsystems which account for or express family structures, economics, politics, education/socialization, ideology/religion. Each of these structures is interlinked through a shared worldview within the society. For example, one's ideology/religious beliefs will influence how she relates in her family or how she spends her money. Similarly, how a school system is organized will reflect the local political system as it is justified by the leader's ideology.

As with a computer, these social structures are like

compatible programs running on the same computer using the same operating system. They seem to act independently, but they may share data as they all share common assumptions. Typically, if one can operate in one program, the language of moving to another in the same operating system is not difficult. However, when a new program is introduced, compatibility becomes a critical word. A lack of compatibility may cause a systemic failure. While compatibility is not the only criterion in a social system for the acceptance of a new idea such as the gospel, it certainly is one of the major concerns. As new elements are introduced in a social system, incompatibility can produce significant breakdowns or failures.[1] An inappropriate substitution can have similar devastating effects in a society.[2]

The three different basic social systems mentioned above operate very differently in every domain. While one may examine economics, interpersonal relations, religious behavior or family structures in any one of these three social systems, the resulting descriptions would vary greatly. Variability also occurs within social systems of the same type, i.e., traditional/tribal, peasant or modern urban.

---

1. An example: When steel axes were introduced among the Yir Yiront, the people experienced a near total collapse of the authority system of their leaders and a serious strain in their trade relations. The authority structure had depended on the lending of stone axes which belonged to the older men. The lending practices served to maintain the authority patterns. When steel axes were simply provided to the younger men, the whole system was disrupted including the trade relations by which the stone for the axes was secured.

2. An example: When church leaders introduced western marriage ceremonies to the Turkana people of northwestern Kenya in lieu of their practice of "spearing the ox," the result was family degeneration, child abandonment and discipline problems. The introduction of a wedding cake did not carry the same meaning as the spearing of an ox and sharing in the eating of that ox.

Since the acceptance of the gospel typically follows social networks, it is imperative to know how the receptor culture is structured. In a traditional culture and in peasant cultures the extended family is a critically important structure for the communication of the gospel. In these kinds of societies family structures tend to be located in an area and interlink across a community. However, in a modern urban society extended families are much more difficult to maintain in part because people tend to be much more mobile. Other kinds of relationships may provide primary sources for personal influence. For example, the people in a person's car pool, small group in a church, or work group may have much more contact and a deeper level of influence. Influence follows communication and relationships. If communicational networks are non-existent and relationships are weak, influence cannot be expected. However, one may find that work, recreational, or other group relationships provide the bases for effective communication. While the "homogenous principle" should not be seen as prescriptive, it still remains true that people tend to communicate best with people like themselves and to congregate with people like themselves. As a strategic perspective, however, it remains valid.

To effectively and efficiently communicate the gospel the wise Christian leader will take time to learn the social structures and design the communication of the gospel to work through these structures. The Christian leader will also take note of how these social structures are organized in order to influence the polity of local churches and missional agencies.

Cultural Values and the Acceptance of the Gospel

Cultural values influence the rate at which the gospel is accepted. Whether one is a member of a tribal, peasant or modern industrial/urban society, the values of that culture profoundly impact the ways and rate the good news of the Kingdom are accepted. For our purpose in this chapter three broad types of cultures will be noted to illustrate the different ways that the gospel may be accepted.

Traditional/Tribal Peoples

The social structures of traditional tribal peoples serve as powerful multilinked networks to communicate the gospel. Tribal peoples typically remain in contact with their communities through countless kinship, affinal, economic, religious and geographic relationships. These relationships are typically life-long. The possibilities of a "people movement," i.e., a widespread multi-individual decision is great in a tribal group because of the multiple overlapping networks influencing every individual. Often tribal peoples are less individualistically oriented. For example, in some African tribal settings a person would never be known or addressed by his or her own personal name. One would always be addressed in terms of his or her key relationships, e.g., an adult woman would be known as "the mother of . . . ." An adult man might be known as "the father of . . . ."

The economic systems of tribal peoples tend to focus on subsistence activities. For example, the Turkana until recently depended almost entirely on camel milk, goat meat and some millet. Their focus was on subsistence in their economy. Their social structures focused on subsistence. Their patterns of "begging" served to distribute wealth and guarantee the subsistence of everyone. The idea of one person rising significantly above others in the society in terms of wealth was difficult to imagine.

To communicate anything new in such a traditional social structure requires the building of credibility within the community. Such relationship requires time and effort to know the local situation and to become known. To gain an opportunity to speak a person has to earn the right by being an advocate for the local people. Language and culture learning precede lasting influence. Short-term missional approaches typically have minimal effect.

Often to be effective in a traditional kinship based tribal society a person or a whole family will be adopted into the society. New local names may be given. Some missionaries have even participated in initiation ceremonies. The establishment of permanent relationships is expected in part because that is the only kind of relationship the local people have known.

Peasant Societies

Typically, in a peasant society role differentiation is more clear than in a tribal setting. The economy is based around markets rather than subsistence. The status of the gospel advocate here is an important issue. Often one's status and accompanying role(s) in a peasant society will either open or block the way for communication. A peasant society is often stratified with little effective communication between the hierarchical levels. A communicator of the gospel then needs to enter the appropriate status and role sets to communicate effectively. This task may be difficult because in some settings an appropriate status may be difficult to enter. No "missionary" status may exist. The accompanying role expectations of the missionary's status may not be acceptable. For example, a missionary family moved into one situation I know. There the people "knew" that "missionaries" "always" establish schools and clinics. When this expectation was not met immediately, dissonance occurred in the community. The people did not know how to relate.

Typically, in peasant societies relationships tend to be more specialized, but they are still long-term. People typically know the extended families of all of their friends and families.

The economy of peasant societies typically focuses around a market system. The Oromo of western Ethiopia, for example, have a system of weekly markets. These markets provide not only the place where they buy and sell their locally made goods and some external goods; it is the place where much of the communication occurs. That is the place where the news is shared, plans are made and relationships are maintained.

One should not assume that the social structures in either the traditional tribal or peasant societies are simple. The complexities simply differ from the modern urban industrial society. One illustration may serve to show this complexity.

The Samburu people in north central Kenya could be described as a traditional kinship based society. Theirs until recently was a tribal society. They are now in transition toward a peasant y. Previously, and still to a large extent they have a stock based economy. Stock ownership, however, is a very complex phenomenon. For example, a man may give a bull calf to a friend. He then expects a heifer will be returned at some later unspecified time. If the recipient delays, the heifer's calves might also be expected. Any given cow then might have several claims to ownership—which may remain unclaimed. If, however, a disaster or other need occurs, the multiple claims across a wide area serve as a kind of insurance for the individual. He may restore his herd by simply exercising his claims. However, all of this economy is closely regulated in the living memories of the elders. The details of who has which claims are maintained through the discussions of the elders. Stock ownership and exchange serves as a means of social control for the community. With stock serving as the primary component of the bride price, the complexities go well beyond the imagination of most westerners. Westerners might expect endless conflict because our values and worldview perspectives about ownership are very different. However, conflict has not been the rule. Rather a sense of equality and justice traditionally prevailed. An interesting paradox emerged. Over time the more generous person would have more to give. The more one would give, the more security and potential would emerge to give. The communication of the gospel in this context requires a different set of assumptions related not only to economy, but social organization as well.

Urban Contexts

Urban contexts differentially influence the acceptance of the gospel. Now more than half of the world's population lives in cities. Both the traditional and peasant societies are being increasingly influenced by urban society. The mass media—newspaper, radio, television and movies—are influencing even the most remote peoples. One cannot escape the radio. People may not read or have electricity for a television, but radios are available to virtually every person on earth. Not everyone has a radio, but few people do not have regular access to a radio. Modern urban societies are influencing widely through the mass media. These media reach not only locally, but regionally and internationally. International short wave radio services, for example, can be heard around the clock in all of the world's major languages and in hundreds of local languages. Recently, while I was in the city of Jos in northern Nigeria I watched US news on CNN as it was being broadcast in the US. As I was in a small town on the eastern coast of Taiwan, I saw an American movie that had been dubbed in Mandarin and had Chinese subtitles.

The social structures of modern industrial urbanized societies differ in every social function from the traditional and peasant societies. Within urban society complex social networks emerge, but they are typically not based on geography or kinship. Kinship patterns differ across cities. Often the focus becomes much more on the nuclear family than the extended family. Single parent families have become a common phenomenon in many cities. With the change in family structures lasting relationships are often built around a person's work or profession. The modern corporation provides another kind of complex social structure. It emerged in the city with its own individual subculture and legal status.

Whereas communication occurs in tribal or peasant societies through long-term relationships in face-to-face encounters, often such is not the case for the modern urban dweller. Short-term "function oriented" relationships prevail. One is no longer dependent on the market to gain information. Information or "news" of the community comes through newspapers, radio or television. Business communications are increasingly dependent on impersonal voice mail, facsimile and e-mail. Extended face-to-face times to communicate within one's extended family are becoming rare.

The economic structures of modern industrial societies are typically complex commercial concerns. The complexities are multiplied by overlapping local, state and national legal systems. International trade agreements often further complicate the local business. In the "peasant" culture where I was reared it was unusual to go to any business in the market town near where I lived and meet anyone whom I did not know. It was just as strange to find anyone who did not know my family and me. In the city where I now live only rarely do I meet anyone I know in any business I frequent.

Given the diversity around every conceivable issue and an awareness of the diversity in cities, and the reduced initiatives for long-term relationship building, alienation is common. A key descriptive word may be "isolation." Hostility that would have been rare in a tribal or peasant society becomes commonplace.

The disparity between the rich and the poor grows in the city. Whether in Manila, New York, or Johannesburg, the range between the rich and the poor is growing wider. As more luxurious high-rise office and apartment buildings emerge, the conditions in the slums grow worse.

Cities are the centers of power. Economic, political, information, and religious power grows in the cities and reaches out to the neighboring regions. Larger cities disproportionally influence their nations. In some cases cities influence neighboring countries such as Hong Kong and Singapore.

The challenge of new ideas emerging from the cities of the world reminds a person of the ancient debates on Mars Hill in the Areopagus where the daily entertainment was to listen to and debate new ideas. This flood of new ideas threatens to overwhelm the individual and often conditions a person to resist any significant commitment. People commonly expect something better will come soon and leave the present as obsolete.

Summary

One should not think that these three different social structures are entirely distinct or that an essentially evolutionary structure leads from one to another. Even in tribal societies trade commonly provides an important set of relationships to other groups. In peasant societies diversified subsistence economic activities are common. In complex commercial enterprises transactions occasionally move to non-commercial exchanges of goods and services. Modern industrial societies obscure the subsistence and simpler market subsystems that often continue within them.

While a great many tribal and peasant peoples have become Christian over the past two centuries, the current frontier or challenge for the church in mission is the city. In spite of difficulties in the city noted above unparalleled opportunities abound for the communication of the gospel. Whether through mass media, small groups and cell churches, megachurches, specialized or focused ministries opportunities for the communication of the gospel have never been seen as they are presently. Now, for example, for the first time in human history it is possible to communicate (via radio) with virtually every person on earth.

Cultural Change/Interference

Star Trek's "prime directive" illustrates a dominant contemporary American cultural view of intercultural interactions. The moralistic base for this popular television program prohibits interference in another culture to change it. This absolutizing of cultural relativism is diametrically opposed to the *missio dei* as seen in through the Old and New Testaments and stated in the Great Commission. This perspective cannot be accepted by Christians who would accept the authority of the Great Commission and the Great Commandment.

This perspective seems to undergird the thinking of people who criticize the Christian for entering into a culture with a view to leading people to convert to a commitment to Jesus Christ. Critics often ask, "What right do you have to change people and their culture?"

In spite of what Christians do or do not do cultures are changing. The idea of a culture remaining untouched and unchanging is woefully naive. John Donne's statement, "No man is an island," has never been more true. People everywhere are being increasingly influenced by others.

The aim of the gospel—the good news of the kingdom—is to build and reconcile relationships beginning with one's relationship with God. Relationships with others then follow. The outcomes of these relationships in human terms are affirmed by human law; e.g., love, joy, peace, patience, kindness, gentleness, goodness, and self-control (Gal 5:22-23). The acceptance of the good news of Jesus Christ rather than threatening culture serves to build a society with integrity and an enduring hope based on what God has done.

The forces that commonly seek to influence cultures seldom aim at the ultimate good of the receptor people. Most often they seek to serve their own needs—either politically or economically. A government may offer food aid for the hungry or build roads into a remote region. Benefits for the local people, however, if no political or economic gain is anticipated for the contributing government, the aid will be very slow in coming or quickly discontinued.

However, the kingdom mandate is to love one's neighbors and to serve them. While some missions in the past took advantage of their status with colonizing governments and their political power and ambitions, such is not the biblical mandate or example. Nor is this kind of political alliance the rule. The goal of evangelism is committed obedient disciples, not improved economic resources or a broadened power base. Ironically, however, an almost inevitable outcome of even a converted minority is an improved economic situation and improved living conditions for all.

Participation in the daily life of a people with the

goal of influencing them to accept the gospel can be expected to bring social changes. The loving, responsible evangelist will continue to work within the society to help bring adjustments to these changes. This kind of participation leads to development as described in another chapter in this book. As change comes through conversion or other means, one can expect a growing receptivity to the gospel.

Social Conditions And Receptivity

People may be described as "receptive" when they are presented with the gospel in terms that they can understand will accept it and become obedient disciples of Jesus Christ. Receptivity can only be "proven" after people have become Christian. However, receptivity may be projected by looking at the social and religious conditions of a people or community. Several conditions positively correlate with receptivity.

When people are experiencing dissatisfaction with the status quo in their social functions or social institutions, an opportunity exists for receptivity to increase. If worldview change is underway then one can expect receptivity to the gospel to be relatively higher. This change may be assumed with social changes in other arenas are evident, e.g., when political, economic or religious change is underway. When one's key relationships are undergoing change, one may expect a higher level of receptivity, e.g., at the time of marriage, relocation or job change.

How the society perceives the gospel greatly influences the way not only individuals, but the whole society will respond to the gospel. Some characteristics of social attitudes toward the gospel will positively influence receptivity.[3] Some of these characteristics include

---

3. See Everett Rogers, *Diffusion of Innovations* (New York: Free Press, 1983) for a more complete discussion of perceived attributes of innovations.

the following: 1) Relative advantage. When people see that adopting the proposed innovation is to their advantage, they will be more receptive. 2) When the new idea is believed to be compatible with their existing values, people are more disposed to accept it. 3) When the new idea is easily understood and not perceived as too complex, receptivity is enhanced. 4) When the results of accepting the new idea can be observed or tried in a real life situation, people are more likely to receive it.

When the advocate is perceived as credible or trustworthy, the new idea will be more likely to be positively considered. The advocate for the new way should be seen as one who respects the local people and customs. The advocate should be seen as competent, comprehensible, respectful and an "empathetic insider" to the extent that is possible. When the advocate can be seen as a defender or spokesperson for the local people, the potential for local influence is likely to increase, or receptivity is likely to increase.

Conclusion

A recognition of dominant current social structures is important to communicate the gospel. Distinguishing the local culture from the three archetypical cultural types is only a beginning point of understanding. Whether the society is kinship/traditional/rural/tribal based in face-to-face, lifelong relations with closely knit groups, or a peasant or urban society an understanding of local social structures is essential. Each of these different kinds of societies requires very differing communicational approaches because the people's perceptions of the gospel and its advocates differ so widely.

The gospel advocate/missionary is an agent of social/cultural change and should be seen as one who will bring change to bring truth and hope. This change will bring reconciliation in key relationships (God, neighbor and environment). Since change is inevitable, we (as Christians) should not only be obedient to God, but help our neighbor at the same time.

The idea of the "noble savage" or "pristine primitiveness" is an untrue, useless, and unsustainable myth. People without Jesus Christ in fact do not have hope. They live in fear with alienation, anger and cursing. The good news of Jesus Christ brings hope, joy and peace. We can more effectively bring that hope to people if we work within their social structures, system and worldview.

15
Teamwork to Finish the Task

Paul McAlister

One of the very encouraging realities frequently mentioned in mission circles today pertains to the ratio of believing congregations to the number of remaining unreached peoples. Some put this figure at near 600 to one. Think about that—six hundred congregations to every one unreached people group. These numbers can and have been challenged. Even if those numbers are reduced substantially, there is still a vital sense that the task of reaching every people group is indeed, possible. We could, and should, recognize that the God of Scripture is persistent and faithful to His purpose. The task of reaching every people group seems to be overwhelming. However, we serve a living God who is at work in the world and who has called all His people to the task. This task is not peripheral to the work of the church, it is central!

What will it take to faithfully carry out God's mandate? We could list many resources, technologies, and numbers of workers, but the central need is for teamwork! This essay will address some of the areas in which the church must commit to a new, or vitalized teamwork. We shall comment regarding the individual congregation's recognition of teamwork in mission, as well as the need for partnering with many other groups to fulfill the task.

Many estimates of the number of unreached people

groups in the world today are somewhere near 11,000. We shall examine first the implications for the local church, then we shall move beyond to those implications relating to strategies, and networking with other Christians from around the world. Before we describe the possibilities for networking, or teaming, we need to ask if such is desirable. The Bible presents a consistent view of people being involved in teamwork. As has often been pointed out, many of the great leaders of the Bible were, in fact, team members. Joshua and Caleb, David and Jonathan, Paul and Barnabas, are all examples of teamwork. The Apostle Paul constantly greeted, affirmed, and gave thanks to those with whom he labored. Whether Aquila and Priscilla, or Phoebe, Romans 16 directs our attention to those who have given of themselves to ministry, and personally to Paul himself. The biblical concepts of ministry, such as Mark 10, all suggest that Jesus' model was "Servanthood." I would argue that servanthood, by nature, is more concerned with the task than with turf. The task ahead of the church in our day, in order to reach the unreached, and to address the enormous complications of ethnic controversy, limited access, and runaway urbanization will demand that we take servanthood and teamwork as primary models.

Teamwork and the Congregation

There have been major "paradigm shifts" in world evangelism. Bruce Camp highlights some of these shifts in a helpful way. He describes, first of all, the paradigm of "supporting." This supporting model has centered in financial commitments. The church members are generally uninvolved in the lives of the missionaries, and even less aware of the people whom the missionaries seek to reach. The focus is on the missionary we support. All responsibilities for mission rests upon people from outside the congregation.

Changes in this dominant paradigm began to be seen in the early eighties. Missionaries spent most of their time in the country trying to secure support. Churches, on the other hand, gave less money to more missionaries. This undercuts congregational ownership in the specific mission of anyone and makes missions someone else's responsibility. The next major shift of paradigm could be labeled "the sending church" model. The focus is more on people than money, as in the previous model. This model has allowed the church to see herself as a significant part of mission. The church takes more responsibility for her own mission strategy and program. There is greater identity with the missionary and the people to whom that missionary goes. There is more ownership of the mission and it becomes identified as "my" mission. The last paradigm, offered by Camp, is the "synergistic model." This model sees the missionary and church as partners in mission. Sender and sent become meshed in common prayer, planning and participation. Mission becomes the task of everyone in the church. Clearly, this paradigm looks beyond the local church to partnerships with other Christians and agencies, as well as the use of all resources, both in people and technologies. All of this to get the task done! These paradigms are worthy of careful consideration and reflection. They can be like looking in a mirror, or, they can be the catalyst for careful, prayerful planning. Teamwork to finish the task must become our priority! Every Christian in mission is the need of the day. This model helps the North American church recognize the need for global partnering with other Christians to finish the task.[1]

---

1. Bruce Camp, "Paradigm Shifts in World Evangelization" in *International Journal of Frontier Missions*, El Paso, July/August 1994, pp. 132-138.

Teamwork Possibilities

There are many potential opportunities to look creatively toward finishing the task. Here, we will suggest just a few of the areas in which we can find teamwork opportunities.

Many peoples within our world are beyond easy access. Some of these countries, or peoples, are within "limited access" areas—areas where one could not enter as a missionary, or, at least the numbers of missionaries are severely limited. "Tentmaking" has become a well-known option. Tentmakers derive their support from vocational skills, such as teaching English, or from some technical expertise. These workers can be prepared through education in the Word, the culture they are entering, and an awareness of cross-cultural communication skills. This approach provides access and expands the mission force[2] or, consider the more recent call for God's special envoys.[3] These tentmakers can become part, even the leading edge, of a mission strategy. They need recruitment, support and partnership.

The tentmakers are very much a part of the centrifugal dimension of mission. Yet another approach presents concern for often the same peoples, but the effort may begin in the States, though the same idea is being carried out by Christians in other countries also. This "Teamwork" possibility relates to the ministry to "International Students."[4] International students demand much attention. These students often come to the US and remain anony-

---

2. See J. Christy Wilson, *Today's Tentmakers* (Wheaton: Tyndale House, 1989).

3. See Tetsunao Yamamori, *Penetrating Mission's Final Frontiers* (Downers Grove: InterVarsity. Press, 1993).

4. See Lawson Lau, *The World at Your Doorstep* (Downers Grove: InterVarsity Press, 1984).

mous. These students represent a centripetal move-ment, the world coming to us. Not only do these students need ministry, but they also represent bridges to their peoples back home. Mission agencies working with campus ministries can form dynamic teams.

As we speak about Teamwork, we cannot but focus upon the primary assumption of our Lord. It is the church which is held responsible for reaching the world, not the "American Church"! The task demands that we take a long and hard look at the church throughout the world as partners in mission. Our "colonial" attitudes will weaken the power of the church worldwide. Christians in other people groups often find easier access to certain groups than Americans are able to find. This is simply a cultural reality. We must learn that we are not the only Christians in the world, and that by working together we can reach great numbers of unreached people. We need to become more prayerfully and strategically aware of the great number of international Christians and agencies at work.[5] This will allow us to see others at work, to learn from them, and to work with them. Some real areas of growth are needed in attitudes allowing us not to be identified as competitors, but colleagues in these tasks. We can surely see opportuni-ties to be involved in the efforts of others to reach the world. This may take some soul searching. There is a disproportionate amount of financial resource in the U.S. Are we able to see our way clear to focus on people groups in need and not on who reaches them? There is great growth among Restoration Movement churches throughout the world. These Christians too, must be encouraged to share in the mission of the church, and we need to trust them to be the church. So, whether international agencies or the existing

---

5. See Larry Pate, *From Every People* (Monrovia, CA: MARC, 1989).

Christian community in the world we must partner to complete the task.

This growing sense of partnership will demand a new perception of missionary education, the internationalizing of education.[6]

Teamwork, as we have been discussing, will demand some deep commitment and deep understanding. To partner may mean that we, at times, must be willing to share our resources without demanding total "control" of national churches. There is much we can, and need to learn from out Christian brethren around the world. To carry out our Lord's mandate, we need to create bridges, not barriers. Our Lord is at work in the world. He is the Living God, the God of all peoples. From the beginning of God's covenant with Abraham, He has been revealing His missionary nature to reach all peoples. This mandate demands that we recognize at least two primary assumptions. God is persistent! Even though His people often fail to see the vision, God is faithful to His own missionary nature. We are a part of His victorious will! At the same time, taking seriously the magnitude of the remaining task, we must commit ourselves to the church worldwide to carry out the task.

A major issue facing the church in the present and the future is the incredible reality of "Urbanization." Cities dominate the landscape of the future. Cities are by their nature complex and multifaceted. Everything from political dynamics, economic devastation, ethnic diversity, and violence complicate the city. Throughout Scripture God had addressed His word again and again to the city. The image of Jesus praying over Jerusalem is a haunting reminder of His passion. The city represents often the crucial influence system of a people. Not only will most peoples live in the city; the

---

6. See William David Taylor, *Internationalising Missionary Training* (Grand Rapids: Baker, 1991).

city is also the nervous system of the entire people within the country.

The complexity and strategic importance of the city demands teamwork if we are to make impact. The city will be key to reaching the majority of the world. Christians need to recapture Paul's heart and mind regarding the city.[7] To demonstrate the multidimensional character and need of the city is to admit that this task is enormous. It will take careful strategies, great resources and, clearly, great teamwork if the city is to be reached.[8]

Conclusion

Our Lord left the church with a mandate for all peoples. The church world wide is commissioned by the Lord to be partners in evangelization. The task is enormous. Our God is the God of all nations and He is able to accomplish through His people His mission. We are part of the victorious God's will! We must approach the future with confidence and surrender. If the task is to be carried out we must first acknowledge God's will and power, then we must commit ourselves to work together that all people may know of His victory. The task is one which belongs to the whole church. Congregations, colleges, agencies—all must accept that God has intended them to be part of His mission in the world. Mission is not an afterthought on God's part; it is not a benevolent idea dreamed up by a "blessed" America. Often churches, colleges and others have failed to recognize that mission is the very heart of the church's life. If we are Christian, we are involved in mission. Earlier we spoke of paradigm shifts; speaking of such is not simply an intellectual

7. Wayne A. Meeks, *The First Urban Christians: The Social World of the Apostle Paul* (New Haven, CT: Yale University Press, 1983).

8. Roger Greenway and Timothy Monsma, *Cities: Mission's New Frontier* (Grand Rapids: Baker, 1989).

discussion. The church must see herself through new eyes, the eyes of God's mission. We can do great things only as we allow God's mission to define and structure our church program and academic curricula! We must be driven by teamwork. Mission is the task of the entire church, here and around the earth.

Here is where we need a special note focused on the "Restoration Movement." Our plea has been that we are "Christians Only"! The task ahead, the enormity of reaching around 11,000 unreached people groups, challenges us and provides us with one of the most important opportunities in our history. The task ahead will allow us to show the world that we have a powerful commitment and powerful purpose. We believe that the world needs the word. We must show that we are more concerned with the task than with turf! Sometimes our very successful, direct support mission system has led some into competition with others. For the sake of the Kingdom and our Lord's purpose (Matt. 24:14), we must exhibit, perhaps more than others, that we are a team and we seek synergistic partnership for the purpose of reaching the world Christ died for. We must be open to working with each other, to share with all those who seek to get the word to the world. Churches, colleges, and agencies must become strongly committed to the task and to each other. If we wish to be a part of God's global and eternal purpose, we must be defined by mission and partners with all who share the vision.

The days are exciting! Our victorious God is moving in great ways. The task is still formidable, but partnership with all God's people in keeping with the priorities of God will enable us to finish the task. Mission is about the whole church, reaching the whole world in anticipation of His return. The task is urgent as thousands die daily without hearing. Let's let the world hear before it is too late for more people! The task awaits—Come join the Team!!

Contributors

Stephen E. Burris is the Director of Distance Learning at the Fuller School of World Mission in Pasadena, California. He is also an Instructor in Intercultural Studies at Pacific Christian College in Fullerton, California. He holds the Master of Arts degree in Missiology from Lincoln Christian Seminary and is currently pursuing the Doctor of Philosophy in Intercultural Studies from the Fuller School of World Mission.

Robert Douglas is the Professor of World Missions and Church Growth at Lincoln Christian Seminary in Lincoln, Illinois. He holds the Doctor of Philosophy degree from the University of Southern California.

Edgar J. Elliston is the Associate Dean for Academic Programs and Associate Professor of Leadership at the Fuller School of World Mission. He holds the Doctor of Philosophy degree from Michigan State University. He serves on the executive board of Christian Missionary Fellowship.

Robert Kurka is an Associate Professor of Bible and Theology at Lincoln Christian College. He holds the Doctor of Ministry degree from Trinity Evangelical Divinity School.

Paul McAlister is the Professor of Theology, Missions, and Social Ethics at Minnesota Bible College and Lecturer in Medical Ethics at the Mayo Clinic in Rochester, Minnesota. He also serves on the board of Pioneer Bible Translators. He Holds the Doctor of Ministry degree from Bethel Theological Seminary.

Doug Priest Jr. is the Asia Coordinator for Christian Missionary Fellowship. He holds the Doctor of Philosophy degree from the Fuller School of World Mission.

Rondal Smith is the President of Pioneer Bible Translators in Duncanville, Texas. He holds the Doctor of Philosophy degree from Indiana University.

Resources for Further Study

Abraham, William. *The Logic of Evangelism*. Grand Rapids: Eerdmans, 1988.

Arias, Mortiner. *Announcing the Reign of God and the Subversive Rule*. Nashville: Abingdon Press, 1984.

Allen, Roland. *Missionary Methods: St. Paul's or Ours?* Grand Rapids: Eerdmans, 1962.

Barna, George. *User Friendly Churches*. Ventura, CA: Regal Books, 1991.

Bevans, Stephen B. *Models of Contextual Theology*. Maryknoll, NY: Orbis Books, 1992.

Borgmann, Albert. *Crossing the Post-Modern Divide*. Chicago: University of Chicago Press, 1992.

Bosch, David. *Transforming Mission: Paradigm Shifts in Theology of Mission*. Maryknoll, NY: Orbis Books, 1991.

Braaten, Carl E. *The Flaming Center: A Theology of the Christian Mission*. Philadelphia: Fortress, 1977.

Brewster, E. Thomas and Elizabeth S. Brewster. *Bonding and the Missionary Task: Establishing A Sense of Belonging*. Pasadena: Lingua House, 1982.

Burris, Stephen E. "A Biblical Basis for the Homogeneous Unit Principle." M.A. Thesis, Lincoln, IL: Lincoln Christian Seminary, 1980.

_____. "The Academic Dilemma of the Frontier Mission Educator." *International Journal of Frontier Missions*, Vol. 9:2, April 1992.

_____. "Building the Missing Bridge: Education for People on the Run." *Mission Frontiers Bulletin*, Vol. 14, Number 9-12, 1993.

Burris, Stephen E. (ed.). *Declare His Glory Among the Nations.* Joplin, MO: College Press, 1994.

_____. *Getting In Step With the God of the Nations.* Joplin, MO: College Press, 1995.

Camp, Bruce. "Paradigm Shifts in World Evangelization." *International Journal of Frontier Missions*, July/August 1994.

Chaney, Charles L. *Church Planting at the End of the Twentieth Century.* Wheaton, IL: Tyndale House, 1992.

Conn, Harvie M. *Theological Perspectives on Church Growth.* Presbyterian and Reformed, 1976.

_____. *Eternal Word and Changing Worlds, Theology, Anthropology and Mission in Trialogue.* Grand Rapids: Zondervan, 1984.

_____. *A Clarified Vision for Urban Mission.* Grand Rapids: Ministry Resources Library, Zondervan, 1987.

Cottrell, Jack, and Stephen E. Burris. "The Fate of the Unreached: Implications for Frontier Missions." *International Journal of Frontier Missions*, Vol. 10:2, April 1993.

Crockett, William V. and James G. Sigountos, (eds.) *Through No Fault of Their Own?* Grand Rapids: Baker, 1991.

DuBose, Francis M. *How Churches Grow in an Urban World.* Nashville: Broadman, 1978.

Dyrness, William. *How Does America Hear the Gospel?* Grand Rapids: Eerdmans, 1989.

Elliston, Edgar J. "An Ethnohistory of Ethiopia: A Study of Factors that relate to the Planting and Growth of the Church." M.A. Thesis, Fuller Theological Seminary, 1968.

_____. *Home Grown Leaders*. Pasadena: William Carey Library, 1992.

Elliston, Edgar J. (ed.). *Christian Relief and Development*. Dallas: Word Publishing, 1989.

Elliston, Edgar J. and J. Timothy Kauffman. *Developing Leaders for Urban Ministry*. New York: Peter Lang Publishers, 1993.

Elliott, Ralph H. *Church Growth that Counts*. Valley Forge: Judson Press, 1982.

Engel, James F. *Contemporary Christian Communications: Its Theory and Practice*. Nashville: Nelson, 1979.

Evans, Grant (ed.). *Asia's Cultural Mosaic: An Anthropological Introduction*. New York: Prentice Hall, 1993.

Filbeck, David. *Social Context and Proclamation*. Pasadena: William Carey Library, 1985.

_____. *Yes, God of The Gentiles, Too*. Wheaton, IL: The Billy Graham Center, 1994.

Foster, John. *Beginning From Jerusalem*. New York: Association Press, 1956.

_____. *To All Nations: Christian Expansion From 1700 to Today*. New York: Association Press, 1960.

_____. *Church History I: AD29-500: The First Advance*. London: SPCK, 1972.

_____. *Church History II: AD500-1500: Setback and Recovery*. London: SPCK, 1974.

Geertz, Clifford. *The Religion of Java*. London: The Free Press of Glencoe, 1960.

George, Carl. *Prepare Your Church for the Future.* New York: Revell, 1991.

Gibbs, Eddie. *I Believe in Church Growth.* Hodder and Stoughton, 1990.

Gilliland, Dean S. (ed.). *The Word Among Us.* Dallas: Word Publishing, 1989.

Green, Michael. *Evangelism in the Early Church.* Grand Rapids: Eerdmans, 1970.

Greenway, Rogers S. and Timothy M. Monsma. *Cities: Mission's New Frontiers.* Grand Rapids: Baker, 1989.

Grigg, Viv. *Companion to the Poor.* Monrovia, CA: MARC, 1990.

Hedlund, Roger E. *The Mission of the Church in the World.* Grand Rapids: Baker, 1991.

Hiebert, Paul G. *Anthopological Insights for Missionaries.* Grand Rapids: Baker, 1985.

_____. "Social Structure and Church Growth." In *Perspectives on the World Christian Movement,* Revised Edition, edited by Ralph D. Winter and Steven Hawthorne. Pasadena: William Carey Library, 1992.

Hesselgrave, David J. *Communicating Christ Cross Culturally.* Grand Rapids: Zondervan, 1991.

_____. "A Missionary Hermeneutic: Understanding Scripture in the Light of World Mission." *International Journal of Frontier Missions,* 10:17-20, 1993.

_____. *Scripture and Strategy: The Use of the Bible in Postmodern Church and Mission.* Pasadena: William Carey Library, 1994.

Hunter, George G., III. *To Spread the Power: Church Growth in the Wesleyan Spirit.* Nashville: Abingdon Press, 1987.

_____. *How to Reach Secular People.* Nashville: Abingdon Press, 1992.

Johnstone, Patrick. *Operation World* (5th edition). Grand Rapids: Zondervan, 1993.

Kaiser, Walter C., Jr. *Toward an Old Testament Theology.* Grand Rapids: Zondervan, 1978.

Kane, J. Herbert. *Christian Missions in Biblical Persepective.* Grand Rapids: Baker, 1976.

Kinsler, F. Ross. "Mission and Context: The Current Debate about Contextualization." *Evangelical Missions Quarterly,* 14:1:23-29, 1978.

Kraft, Charles A. *Communication Theory for Christian Witness.* Nashville: Abingdon Press, 1983.

_____. *Christianity With Power.* Ann Arbor: Servant Publications, 1989.

Kuhn, Thomas S. *The Structure of Scientific Revolutions.* Second Edition. Chicago: The University of Chicago Press, 1970.

Kurka, Robert. "The Doctrine of Salvation." In *Essentials of Christian Faith,* edited by Stephen E. Burris. Joplin, MO: College Press, 1992.

Larson, Harry. "Eras, Pioneers, and Transitions." In *The World Christian Movement,* edited by Jonathan Lewis. Pasadena: William Carey Library, 1994.

Latourette, Kenneth Scott. *A History of Christianity.* New York: Harper Brothers Publishers, 1953.

_____. *The First Five Centuries. A History of the Expansion of Christianity.* Contemporary Evangelical Perspectives Edition, 7 Vols., Grand Rapids: Zondervan, 1970.

_____. *The Thousand Years of Uncertainty. A History of the Expansion of Christianity.* Contemporary Evangelical Perspectives Edition, 7 Vols., Grand Rapids: Zondervan, 1970.

_____. *Three Centuries of Advance. A History of the Expansion of Christianity.* Contemporary Evangelical Perspectives Edition, 7 Vols., Grand Rapids: Zondervan, 1970.

Lau, Lawson. *The World at Your Doorstep*. Downers Grove: InterVarsity Press, 1984.

Lewis, Jonathan (ed.). *Working Your Way to the Nations: A Guide to Effective Tentmaking*. Pasadena: William Carey Library, 1993.

Lingenfelter, Sherwood. *Transforming Culture: A Challenge for Christian Mission*. Grand Rapids: Baker, 1992.

Logan, Robert E. *Beyond Church Growth*. New York: Revell, 1989.

Luzbetak, Louis. *The Church and Cultures: New Perspectives In Missiological Anthropology*, Second Edition. Maryknoll: Orbis Books, 1988.

Malphurs, Aubrey. *Planting Growing Churches*. Grand Rapids: Baker, 1992.

McGavran, Donald. *The Bridges of God*. New York: Friendship Press, 1955.

_____. *Understanding Church Growth*. Revised Edition. Grand Rapids: Eerdmans, 1990.

Neighbour, Ralph W. *Where Do We Go From Here? A Guidebook for the Cell Group Church*. Houston: Touch Publications, Inc., 1990.

Neill, Stephen. *A History of Christian Missions*. Baltimore: Penguin Books, 1964.

Parshall, Phil. *New Paths in Muslim Evangelism*. Grand Rapids: Baker, 1980.

Pannell, William E. *Evangelism from the Bottom UP*. Grand Rapids: Zondervan, 1992.

Pate, Larry D. *From Every People*. Monrovia, CA: MARC, 1989.

_____. "The Changing Balance in Global Mission." In *Perspectives on the World Christian Movement*, Revised Edition, edited by Ralph D. Winter and Steven Hawthorne. Pasadena: William Carey Library, 1992.

Peters, George W. *A Biblical Theology of Missions.* Chicago: Moody, 1972.

Pierson, Paul E. "Historical Development of the Christian Movement." Syllabus and Lecture Outlines, Fuller Theological Seminary, 1990.

Priest, Doug Jr. *Doing Theology With the Maasai.* Pasadena: William Carey Library, 1990.

_____ (ed.). *The Gospel Unhindered: Modern Missions and the Book of Acts.* Pasadena: William Carey Library, 1994.

Richardson, Don. *Peace Child.* Glendale: Regal Books, 1974.

Robb, Joh D. Focus: *The Power of People Group Thinking.* Monrovia, CA: MARC, 1989.

Rogers, Everett M. *Diffusion of Innovations.* Third Edition. New York: Free Press, 1983.

Schaller, Lyle E. *44 Questions for Church Planters.* Nashville: Abingdon Press, 1991.

Shaw, R. Daniel. *Transculturation: The Cultural Factor in Translation and Other Communication Tasks.* Pasadena: William Carey Library, 1988.

Shenk, Wilbert R. *Exploring Church Growth.* Grand Rapids: Eerdmans, 1983.

Shenk, Wilbert R. (ed.) *The Challenge of Church Growth.* Institute for Mennonite Studies, 1973.

Siemens, Ruth E. "Tentmakers Needed for World Evangelization." In *Perspectives on the World Christian Movement*, Revised Edition, edited by Ralph D. Winter and Steven Hawthorne. Pasadena: William Carey Library, 1992.

Sjogren, Robert. *Unveiled at Last.* Seattle: YWAM Press, 1992.

Smith, Donald K. *Creating Understanding: A Handbook for Christian Communication Across Cultural Landscapes.* Grand Rapids: Zondervan, 1992.

Smith, W. Michael "An Eye-Opener for the Rural Javanese." In *Unto the Uttermost*, edited by Doug Priest Jr. Pasadena: William Carey Library, 1984.

Speer, Robert E. *Christianity and the Nations*. New York: Revell, 1910.

Stearns, Bill and Amy Stearns. *Catch the Vision 2000*. Minneapolis: Bethany House Publishers, 1991.

Søgaard, Viggo "Dimensions of Approach to Contextual Communication." In *The Word Among Us: Contextualizing Theology for Mission Today*, edited by Dean S. Gilliland. Dallas: Word Publishing, 1989.

Taber, Charles R. *The World Is Too Much With Us: "Culture" in Modern Protestant Missions*. Macon, GA: Mercer University Press, 1991.

Taylor, William D. (ed.). *Internationalising Missionary Training*. Grand Rapids: Baker, 1991.

Tippett, Alan. *Church Growth and the Word of God*. Grand Rapids: Eerdmans, 1980.

Tonna, Benjamin. *Gospel for the Cities*. Maryknoll, NY: Orbis Books, 1982.

Van Engen, Charles. *God's Missionary People: Rethinking the Purpose of the Local Church*. Grand Rapids: Baker, 1991.

Van Engen, Charles, Dean S. Gilliland and Paul E. Pierson (eds.). *The Good News of the Kingdom: Mission Theology for the Third Millennium*. Maryknoll, NY: Orbis Books, 1993.

Van Engen, Charles and Jude Tiersma (eds.). *God So Loves the City*. Monrovia, CA: MARC, 1994.

Van Rheenan, Gailyn. *Communicating Christ in Animistic Contexts*. Grand Rapids: Baker, 1991.

Wagner, C. Peter. *Your Church Can Grow*. Ventura, CA: Regal Books, 1984.

_____. *Spiritual Power and Church Growth*. Altamonte Springs, FL: Strang Communications Company, 1986.

_____. *Church Planting for a Greater Harvest*. Ventura, CA: Regal Books, 1990.

_____. *Prayer Shield*. Ventura, CA: Regal Books, 1992.

_____. *Warfare Prayer*. Ventura, CA: Regal Books, 1992.

_____. *Breaking Strongholds in Your City*. Ventura, CA: Regal Books, 1993.

_____. *Churches That Pray*. Ventura, CA: Regal Books, 1993.

_____. "Those Amazing Post-Denominational Churches." *Ministries Today*, July/August 1994.

Williamson, Mable. *Have We No Right?* Chicago: Moody Press, 1957.

Wilson, J. Christy. *Today's Tentmakers*. Wheaton: Tyndale House, 1989.

Winter, Ralph D. "Four Men, Three Eras, Two Transitions: Modern Mission." In *Perspectives on the World Christian Movement*, Revised Edition, edited by Ralph D. Winter and Steven Hawthorne. Pasadena: William Carey Library, 1992.

_____. "The Two Structures of God's Redemptive Plan." In *Perspectives on the World Christian Movement*, Revised Edition, edited by Ralph D. Winter and Steven Hawthorne. Pasadena: William Carey Library, 1992.

Winter, Ralph D. and Steven Hawthorne (eds.). *Perspectives on the World Christian Movement: A Reader*. Revised Edition. Pasadena: William Carey Library, 1992.

Wright, Christopher. *An Eye for An Eye*. Downers Grove: InterVarsity Press, 1983.

Yamamori, Tetsunao "Forward." In *Working Your Way to the Nations: A Guide to Effective Tentmaking*. edited by Jonathan Lewis. Pasadena: William Carey Library, 1993.

_____. *God's New Envoys: A Bold Strategy for Penetrating "Closed 'Countries."* Portland, OR: Multnomah Press, 1987.

_____. *Penetrating Mission's Final Frontiers*. Downers Grove: InterVarsity Press, 1993.

Zunkel, C. Wayne. *Church Growth Under Fire*. Scottsdale, PA: Herald Press, 1987.

Index

Cranfield, C.F.B., 55

Creation, 25-29, 137-138, 154, 206-207, 224, 231-232, 241, 249, 253

creative access, 167

culture, 9, 12, 48, 59, 66, 69, 77, 98, 102, 120, 122-123, 126, 129-131, 138, 144, 149-150, 154, 163, 165, 169, 171, 188, 192, 211-229, 234-242, 244, 250-255, 258-259, 263, 268, 270-272, 275, 277-278, 280, 286

  change, 228

  defined, 213-217

  ideational, 217

  material, 216

  shock, 242

  social, 216

  theory, 221

  traits, 220

Dayton, Edward, 144, 147

definition, 97, 101, 122, 130, 146-147, 167, 198-199, 213-215, 221-222, 239-240

Delitzsch, 50-53

demonic, 153, 226

demons, 154

development, 7-8, 29, 42, 74, 77, 90, 93-94, 106-107, 109, 111-112, 121, 168, 172, 188, 191, 195-201, 203-206, 212, 223, 233-234, 241, 260, 279

downsizing, 195, 202

Drawthwol, David, 192

Dualism, 165

empathy, 236

ethnic strategy, 115, 120

Europe, 72-73, 81, 84-85, 88-89, 97, 101, 118-119, 126, 142, 175, 214, 218

evangelist(s), 47, 49-50, 57-58, 62, 122, 149-150, 155, 168-169, 179-180, 279

evangelization, 8, 18, 22-23, 31, 48, 75, 94-95, 97, 100, 105, 110-111, 113, 116, 121-122, 124, 132, 136-137, 139-140, 142, 144, 146-147, 150-154, 156-158, 196, 285, 289

evangelize, 23, 81, 112, 123, 129-130,

143, 147, 151, 166, 174

Evans, Grant, 222, 295

exegesis, 16, 108, 227

exploitation, 240

Filbeck, David, 16-17, 36, 45, 295

Galilee, 48, 56, 58, 65

Geertz, Clifford, 258-259, 295

genealogies, 48, 57

Gilliland, Dean, 23, 34, 66, 68, 258, 296, 300

Goerner, Cornell, 62

good works, 206

Great Commission, 11, 16-17, 23, 29-30, 33, 47, 54, 72, 116, 132, 135, 142, 146, 156, 197, 277

Greenway, Roger, 289, 296

Grigg, Viv, 172, 296

group conversion, 163

Hamilton, Donald, 169

Hedlund, Roger, 19, 22, 296

hermeneutic, 15-17, 19, 23-24, 45, 68-69

Hiebert, Paul, 61, 102, 214, 296

Hindu(ism), 118-119, 200

Holy Spirit, 13, 63, 65, 70, 72, 113, 141-142, 144, 150, 156-157, 181, 184, 186, 188-192, 234, 238

homogeneous unit(s), 99-101, 113, 189

identification, 113, 232-239, 243, 245-246

image of God, 26, 138, 224

incarnation, 57, 206, 231-232, 234, 246, 250, 258

Incarnational approach, 171

Indonesia, 119, 132, 135, 181-182, 251-252, 258-259, 261-262

information age, 159

innovation(s), 229, 279-280

internationalization, 94, 100-101

Islam (see also Muslim), 79-81, 83, 85, 118-119, 132, 258

Javanese, 255, 258-262

Jerusalem Council, 64, 141